Butterflies

How To Identify And Attract Them To Your Garden

Butterflies

HOW TO IDENTIFY AND ATTRACT THEM TO YOUR GARDEN

MARCUS SCHNECK

FOREWORD BY
RICK MIKULA

Rodale Press, Emmaus, Pennsylvania

A QUARTO BOOK

Copyright © 1990 Quarto Publishing plc

Published in 1990 in the United States of America by
Rodale Press, Inc.

If you have any questions or comments concerning this book, please write:

Rodale Press
Book Reader Service
33 East Minor Street
Emmaus, PA 18098

This book was designed and produced by
Quarto Publishing plc
The Old Brewery
6 Blundell Street
London N7

Senior Editor: Sally MacEachern
Editor: Carol Hupping
Artists: Paul Richardson, Simon Thomas
Chart composition: Elly King
Designer: Carole Perks
Art Editor: Anne Fisher

Art Directors: Moira Clinch, Nick Buzzard
Publishing Director: Janet Slingsby

Library of Congress Cataloging-in-Publication Data

Schneck, Marcus
    Butterflies, how to identify and attract them to your garden / by
Marcus Schneck : introd. by Rick Mikula.
        p.   cm.
    Includes index.
    ISBN 0–87857–917–6 hardcover
    1. Butterflies. 2. Butterflies – North America – Identification.
    3. Butterfly attracting.   I. Title.
    OL542.S36   1990   595.78'9–dc20   90–36274 CIP

Distributed in the book trade by St. Martin's Press

Typeset by Ampersand Typesetting Ltd, Bournemouth
Manufactured in Hong Kong by Regent Publishing Services, Ltd
Printed by Lee Fung Asco Printers Ltd, Hong Kong

2   4   6   8   10   9   7   5   3   1   hardcover

CONTENTS

FOREWORD 6

INTRODUCTION 7

HOW TO USE THE DIRECTORY 32

DIRECTORY OF 250 BUTTERFLIES 33

INDEX 158

ACKNOWLEDGMENTS 160

FOREWORD

MANKIND'S APPRECIATION AND fascination with butterflies transcends recorded history. From the Bronze Age frescoes of Thebes to the Greek statue of Psyche, this insect has always been depicted in art. Be it the Monarch that decorated the ceremonial headdress of Chief Sitting Bull or the exquisite jade artwork of the Chou dynasty, Lepidoptera have always played a part in human life. These loveliest of creatures evoke only the happiest of memories to all who chance their way.

This book expresses the delight so many have for these blithe, beautiful beings. Where most modern guides rely on photographs that convey only a harsh, cold, scientific view of these insects, this work uses superbly illustrated prints to enhance the text. The artists' affinity for the subject is reflected in the delicate and alluring beauty of each plate.

From egg to the emergence of an adult, the butterfly's life still holds many mysteries. Metamorphosis may never be fully understood. The pages that follow place equal importance on every stage of development in hopes of unlocking some clues to the mysteries. Many caterpillars are as beautiful as the adults and deserve equal presentation. Locating the golden ovum of a Zebra Longwing can be as exciting as witnessing the flight of a Giant Swallowtail.

Over the years, attitudes concerning butterflies and the collecting of them have changed. Lepidopterists have come a long way since the explorer A. S. Meek first collected Birdwing butterflies with the aid of the Papuan natives and their bows and arrows. Many species have become extinct, with many more added to the endangered list all the time. The destruction of habitat and the spraying of pesticides have taken their toll. However, there is hope for these fragile jewels. Butterfly consciousness has swept the world. Many conservationally minded naturalists realize that the enjoyment received from releasing a precious quarry outweighs the satisfaction of a full Riker mount. This is most evident today with the proliferation of butterfly zoos worldwide. Most lepidopterist societies have changed their focus from collecting butterflies to photographing and rearing them. And they have found that the challenge of the camera exceeds that of the net.

The reasons people become involved with Lepidoptera are often as varied as the unwitting souls who fall under their spell. It may be for scientific research, for photographic aspirations, or merely to idle away a summer afternoon. No matter what the reason, one thing is for certain: More important than the largest of nets is the smallest of books. Since before the Renaissance, early naturalists have compiled and used journals to assist them in their work. Such note taking is even more important today. With rapid land development and lightning-fast worldwide travel, butterfly populations can sometimes appear or disappear almost overnight. Harmful species can infest an area seemingly out of nowhere. Likewise, a specimen thought to be extinct may be rediscovered. This is why a good book that records the appearance, habitat, and habits of butterflies is a must. An amateur can be an excellent monitor of the natural world, but the purpose of his or her endeavor should not be to collect every species but to understand them.

No library is ever complete. Every new volume yields some novel clue to help solve the mystery. The scope of this book should accomplish just that. This manual will assist you in the identification of 250 butterflies most likely to be encountered in the continental United States. Its easy reading and informative passages are designed to enlighten the novice as well as refresh the seasoned veteran. The coverage of butterflies in every stage of development will enable readers to gain a keener insight and appreciation of these marvelous creatures.

A good field guide can become your dearest friend, presenting hours of joy and relaxation. Its pages become wings on which to soar. Recreational weekend observing is as noble as scientific research. Does the pleasure derived from watching a Fritillary alighting on its host plant to deposit an egg really need a reason? The important thing is to enjoy and understand a little about these wonderful works of art before, perhaps, they are no more.

Rick Mikula

INTRODUCTION

Left *With their bright colors and delicate appearance, butterflies have captured our imagination. This Pygmy Blue looks like an ornament on a Christmas tree.*

QUICKLY, NAME THREE spiders. Now name three butterflies.

If you're like most people, chances are excellent that the second task proved much easier than the first. Perhaps the first even proved impossible.

Spiders and butterflies occupy the extremes of the animal kingdom, at least from an entirely human viewpoint. With their kaleidoscope of colors and patterns, and their delicate flight, butterflies are often viewed differently from most other animals. They capture the imagination, offer a peaceful moment. Without the means to sting, bite, or otherwise inflict human injury, they inspire curiosity rather than caution or revulsion.

The average person probably knows more about butterflies than about most other animal life. But even

that knowledge is generally limited to a few notes on behavior and the names of a few common species, such as the Cabbage White, the Monarch, and maybe a couple of Swallowtails.

This book aims to build on that basic knowledge, keying on a select group of butterflies – the most common and widespread North American species. Of the more than 700 butterflies on the continent, I've selected the 250 that the reader is most likely to encounter.

The bulk of the book will offer detailed artwork to identify each of these species and comprehensive natural history notes to lend insight into their habits and habitats. But first we must arrive at a common understanding of butterflies in general.

BUTTERFLY EVOLUTION

OUR UNDERSTANDING OF the evolution of butterflies is sketchy at best. This should come as no surprise when their relatively delicate composition is considered.

The most revealing specimens have been those few found encased in amber, which is the fossilized resin from ancient plants. The oldest of these have been dated to the Cretaceous period, about 100-140 million years ago. Fossil evidence suggests that this was the same period that saw the first flowering plants, including magnolia, beech, and fig.

Some researchers have suggested that the well-defined nature of these plants at that time points to a much earlier beginning in their development, perhaps as early as the Jurassic period more than 200 million years ago. Because much of the evolutionary development of flowering plants and the insects that feed on their nectar, and in turn spread their pollen, has been closely linked, this could also indicate an earlier butterfly ancestor.

Tracing the ancestry still further, we would eventually arrive at a segmented animal, quite similar to today's silverfish and springtails. This was probably the ancestor of all insects.

THE ORDER LEPIDOPTERA

Modern-day butterflies are members of the insect order Lepidoptera, a word that actually describes the presence of scales on their wings. It is derived from the Greek words *lepis*, for scale, and *pteron*, for wing. The order is further divided into superfamilies, two of which constitute those species that are the focus of this book: the true butterflies (Papilionoidea) and the skippers (Hesperiordea).

The body of the true butterfly is slender, while that

Above Butterflies, together with moths, make up the order Lepidoptera. This is a Common Blue.

of the skipper is thick and bulky. True butterfly wings are large and full by comparision, while skipper wings are proportionately smaller and triangular. In flight, the true butterfly may be swift but generally is not powerful. Its wing strokes are not so fast as to appear a blur. The skipper flies swiftly, often in a darting fashion and often with wings blurred.

While a basic knowledge of the differences between the two superfamilies is important to a thorough understanding of our topic, from this point we will use the word butterfly to cover both true butterflies and skippers.

The two superfamilies are further divided into 11

Above This Orange Sulphur is a member of the family of true butterflies, Papilionoidea.

Left A Zebra Swallowtail. The ancestors of today's butterflies date back 100-140 million years.

families, the members of each family bearing many similar characteristics. The families are Papilionidae, Swallowtails; Pieridae, Whites and Sulphurs; Lycaenidae, Gossamer-winged; Riodinidae, Metalmarks; Nymphalidae, Brush-footed; Libytheidae, Snout; Danaidae, Monarchs; Satyridae, Satyrs and Wood Nymphs; Heliconiidae, Tropical Heliconians; Hesperiidae, True Skippers; and Megathymidae, Giant Skippers.

Such taxonomic divisions, continuing below the families into genus, species, and subspecies, are essential to scientific study of the animal kingdom. Linnaeus was the first to propose the current binomial, or two-name, system of subdivision in 1758 in his "Systema Naturae." Under this system each creature is identified by two Latin names, the first (beginning with a capital letter) is the genus and the second is the species. For example, the scientific name of the Comma is *Polygonia comma*.

Many changes have been made to Linnaeus' original scheme, and debate and rethinking of some classifications continues, but the binomial names of all animal life are precise and tend toward the necessary uniformity. Common names may seem more familiar and easier to use, but they can be unreliable and lead to the same butterfly being identified with several different names.

Above *In modern classification each creature has two Latin names, the first is the genus and the second the species. The taxonomic name of this Edwards' Hairstreak is* Satyrium edwardsii.

Left *The body of a true butterfly, such as this Harris' Checkerspot, is long and slender, while that of the skipper is thick and bulky by comparison.*

THE STAGES OF LIFE

EVERY BUTTERFLY HAS four stages to its life: egg, caterpillar (larva), chrysalis (pupa), and adult. The gradual passage through the four stages is known as metamorphosis.

The cycle begins as the adult female lays her eggs, each one covered by a strong membrane known as chorion. Freshly laid eggs are generally yellow-white, but their color changes and can become quite showy as the chorion dries and becomes solid.

The eggs might be laid singly like the Monarch's, in chains like the Question Mark's, in rows like the Baltimore's or in clusters like the Tawny Emperor's. There might be only a few of them, or there might be several hundred.

Egg production in some species can be inextricably linked to food availability. Many of the Sulphurs, for example, are not able to lay eggs without having ingested nectar. Females of the Checkerspot species have laid only half of their normal quota when they were not fed.

The shape and texture of butterfly eggs varies from the ribbed vase of the Queen, to the smooth sphere of the Tiger Swallowtail, to the segmented oblong of the Falcate Orangetip. Blues generally lay flat, beehive-shaped eggs, while Whites generally lay tall, thin eggs.

In a depression somewhere on the surface of each egg is the micropyle. In mating, this opening allowed the male's spermatozoa to penetrate the egg. Now it allows the tiny embryo inside the egg to breathe.

The eggs of some species will lie dormant until hatching the following spring. Others will hatch before the approaching winter has arrived. Temperature is the environmental factor that has the most influence over their development.

Most butterfly species are severely limited to one or only a few closely related plant species that can successfully serve as host plants for the caterpillars that will hatch from their eggs. Partly through the co-evolution of host plant and butterfly species, the caterpillars of some species have come to actually need certain chemical constituents that only specific plant species can provide. These specialized chemicals may have originally evolved in the plants as a repellent to most insects, while the caterpillars in turn became so adapted to coping with them that they now actually need them for proper development.

Thus, caterpillars can be monophagous, living off only one plant species; oligophagous, living off a few related plant species; or polyphagous, living off plant species from different families. In some of the

monophagous species, the specialization sometimes extends as far as only certain parts of the plant.

The most catholic of the polyphagous species appear to base their host plant selection on a determination of which plants are most succulent and abundant.

Feeding, growth, and energy storage are the only functions of this next phase, the caterpillar that hatches from the eggs. The caterpillar's body is composed of 13 segments, plus a rounded head that sports a pair of antennae. Several pairs of simple eyes, known as ocelli, are found on many species.

But it is the mouth that is the true functional equipment of this chewing machine. A pair of powerful, platelike mandibles or jaws, usually equipped

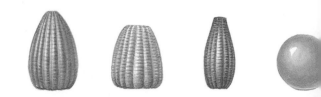

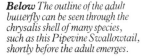

Right *The caterpillar of the Monarch butterfly feeds exclusively on milkweed plants, gaining a noxious taste which protects it from predators.*

Below *The outline of the adult butterfly can be seen through the chrysalis shell of many species, such as this Pipevine Swallowtail, shortly before the adult emerges.*

Left *The life cycle of the Silver-bordered Fritillary (clockwise from top right) egg, caterpillar, chrysalis, adult emerging from chrysalis shell, adult butterfly, mating.*

with teeth along their inner edges, protrude between the upper and lower lips.

The lower lip also is the location of the spinnerets, the outlets for the silk glands. With these mechanisms the caterpillar spins the silk or secretes the liquid to secure itself as it enters the chrysalis stage. Only the larvae are equipped with these mechanisms.

The caterpillar propels itself via three pairs of jointed legs, one pair on each of three thoracic segments, and nonjointed prolegs that generally appear in pairs on the third, fourth, fifth, sixth, and tenth segments of the abdomen. The tenth-segment pair is often modified into antennae-like ornaments, an adaptation designed to confuse potential predators.

Internally the caterpillar is quite similar to the adult

Left *The diversity of butterfly eggs is revealed by these examples from the Monarch, Silver-bordered Fritillary, Falcate Orangetip, Tiger Swallowtail, Question Mark and Baltimore.*

butterfly, although its glands are much more highly developed. In addition to the silk glands, the caterpillar carries the necessary glands to produce the hormones that regulate its molting and growth. Two antagonistic hormones are responsible for the amazing feat: the molting hormone known as ecdysone and secreted by the prothoracic gland, and the juvenile hormone secreted by the copora allata, located behind the brain.

Some species also have a gland in the thorax that produces an acidic liquid that can be secreted as a defense when necessary.

MOLTING TO GROW

As the caterpillar eats and grows, it must shed (or molt) its nonexpandable skin several times, entering and exiting several stages between molts that are known as instars. The number of molts varies from three to five, according to species, temperature, and food availability. Feeding stops during each molt, as the caterpillar rests for a day or two and replaces its cuticle covering.

There are two other occasions on which the caterpillar will cease its otherwise continuous eating/growing activity and survive on its reserves for a period. Quiescence is an immediate reaction to abrupt changes in the environment, such as drops in temperature. Activity will begin again as soon as normal conditions return. Diapause is similar to the "hibernation" of vertebrate species. Immobility comes on gradually as inhospitable conditions approach.

Most caterpillars are solitary creatures, but a few – such as those of the Baltimore – will occupy a communal web during their first season.

When the caterpillar is fully grown, the next molt results in the chrysalis – a nonfeeding, stationary, resting/transforming stage. During this period, the chrysalis nears complete immobility, with the exception of severely limited adjustment and defense motions. The anal and genital openings are sealed. Breathing is accomplished through the spiracles.

In some species, such as the Mourning Cloak, the chrysalis hangs by its tail, attached to its host plant by a silken pad known as the cremaster. In others, such as the Pipevine Swallowtail, it hangs in an upright position, held in place by a silken girdle surrounding its thorax.

Inside this shell, nearly all of the larval tissues are broken down and rebuilt into the organs of the adult butterfly. When the full transformation has taken place, the skin of the chrysalis splits open and the butterfly – in the winged form that we tend to visualize in connection with the name – crawls free.

At this point, its wings are frail, shriveled things that are barely opened. The butterfly immediately sets

Above *This newly emerged Monarch adult must pump hemolymph (insect blood) through* *the veins of its wings to spread them to their full extent and let them stiffen.*

about pumping hemolymph (insect blood) through the veins of the wings, which gradually spread to their full size. After they have stiffened, the insect is ready for flight.

There will be no further growth after this final molt, the emergence. This is the final stage of this butterfly's life. Small butterflies do not grow into large butterflies.

Old World Swallowtail caterpillar

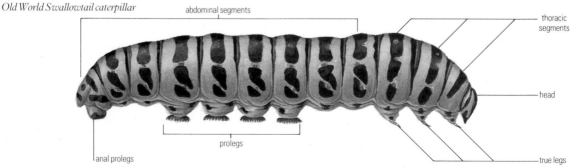

abdominal segments

thoracic segments

head

true legs

prolegs

anal prolegs

THE ADULT

THE PRIMARY TASK for the insect now is reproduction, and very shortly after it can fly the adult begins its courtship, followed by mating and laying of the eggs. Courtship can include wing stroking between partners, aerial dances, and prenuptial flights. Mating might last several hours, and this is in flight for many species. This adult stage can last from a week to eight months, varying from one species to the next, with most averaging two to three weeks.

The body of the adult butterfly has three segments: head, thorax, and abdomen. It has no inner skeleton but is supported and enveloped by a multilayered exoskeleton. This external integument is of uniform thickness but has less strengthened lines so that movement is possible.

The head features a pair of clubbed antennae, two palpi, two compound eyes, and one long, coiled proboscis. Smell, touch, and orientation are accomplished via the antennae, while the palpi also receive sensations and protect the sensitive proboscis. Each eye is made up of thousands of facets that transmit what is thought to be one integrated, color image to the butterfly's brain.

Butterflies, under experimental conditions, have been found to be able to distinguish between two points separated by only 30 microns, while the minimum possible for humans is 100 microns. A micron is equal to one-millionth of a meter. The butterfly is also able to see ultraviolet light invisible to

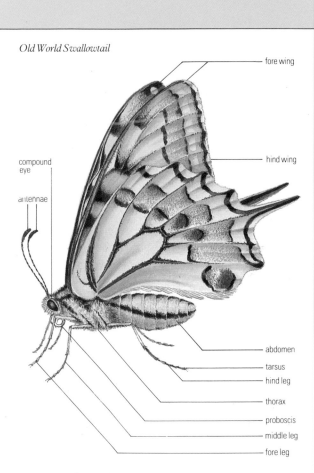

Old World Swallowtail

- fore wing
- hind wing
- compound eye
- antennae
- abdomen
- tarsus
- hind leg
- thorax
- proboscis
- middle leg
- fore leg

Left *The body of the adult butterfly has three segments: head, thorax and abdomen. This is a Black Swallowtail.*

Above When not being used for drinking the butterfly's proboscis can be folded in a spiral under its head.

humans, enabling the insect to differentiate between flowers that appear entirely alike to the human eye.

On the other hand, the butterfly eye is not nearly as well developed as that of the human in terms of seeing at a distance. It has been estimated that the insect's compound eye would need to be more than a meter in diameter to equal the resolution offered by the human eye. The differences reflect the needs of two contrasting lifestyles.

The proboscis is actually the outer lobes of the insect's upper jaws that have been modified into two tubes that extend parallel to one another and are linked to work like a pair of drinking straws. Equipped with alternating rings of membranes and muscles, it can be folded in a spiral under the head or fully extended to drink nectar.

The thorax is made up of three segments. A half dozen legs and the butterfly's four wings are attached to this section of the body.

Each leg of the insect is jointed in five sections: coxa, trochanter, femur, tibia, and tarsus. The clawed tarsi serve as feet and perform a sensing function similar to taste. Their contact with a nectar or similar liquid causes a reflexive uncoiling of the proboscis. Females also use them in scratching and sampling potential host plants for their eggs.

The forelegs of some, like the Brush-footed butterflies, have degenerated into tiny appendages no longer useful in walking.

WONDROUS WINGS

Wings are attached to the thorax by small structures at their bases, to which are connected systems of internal muscles. These muscles are used to move the wings, but they can also be moved by alterations in the thorax shape. The insertion points on the thorax are covered by mobile tegulae.

The wings are composed of double membranes crisscrossed by several tubular veins to hold their structure in place. These veins also transmit insect blood (hemolymph), function as part of the insect's respiration process, and provide ducts for the nervous system.

Hairs and flattened hairs (scales) cover the wing surface. They are held in place in their roof-tile-like arrangement by short stalks inserted into the cuticle.

The brilliant butterfly colors come to the wings either through the pigments in the scales or in the structures of their surfaces. Both the pigment and structural colors are often present at the same spot on the wings, producing a truly spectacular display.

Pigmentation is caused by chemical substances produced through various metabolic processes. For example, urea – a waste product – gives rise to the white, yellow, and orange pigments (pterins) in members of the family Pieridae, a unique trait of these species alone. Melanin, a common pigment, causes the blacks and browns. Others include erythropterin, red; chrysopterin, orange; xanthopterin, yellow; and leucopterin, white.

Right Scales, which are actually flattened hairs, cover the wing surface.

Structural color is a mechanical process, requiring no pigments to produce its generally iridescent colors. The exact process can be accomplished through ridges on the flat surface of the scale, tiny granules in a contrasting medium, or thin films. Blue is always a structural color, as are any metallic effects.

VARIATIONS ON A THEME

Coloration is one of the characteristics that can vary within a given population for both genetic and nongenetic reasons. Despite common lineage, individuals can vary due to mutations of their genetic makeup. Far from the science fiction image of the word, mutation is a totally natural and surprisingly common occurrence. Whether the mutated variation continues beyond a single generation or not depends on its interaction with the environment. Charles

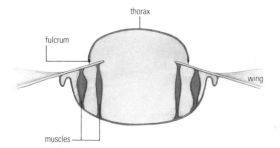

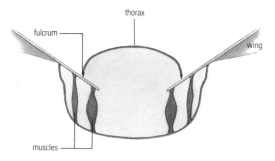

The mechanism of the fore wings: the wings are lifted as the muscles inside the fulcrum contract (top) and then the muscles outside the fulcrum contract, pulling the wing down (bottom).

Darwin, the originator of modern evolutionary thought, termed this process natural selection.

In addition, sexual dimorphism, whereby the sexes are easily identified by their differences (most notably wing pattern and color) is relatively common in butterflies. There is also a rare condition known as gynandromorphism, in which both male and female characteristics are found in different parts of the same body. This is caused when the sexual chromosomes are separated irregularly during the first divisions of the egg cell.

The same species can also vary according to geography, gradually when the population is distributed continuously without significant physical barriers, or markedly when the various populations are isolated from one another. If the isolation persists over a long period, the populations may also become reproductively isolated. They are then distinct species.

Also on the wings of some males are specialized scent scales, known as androconia. They can be arranged in groups, scattered across the surface of the wing among other scales, or concentrated in patches called stigmata.

The 11 segments of the abdomen carry the insect's sexual and digestive mechanisms, as well as a row of spiracles on each side that allow for the intake of air.

UNDER CLOSE SCRUTINY

Butterfly experts rely on the genitalia at the rear of the abdomen for exact species identification. This is because there are very limited variations in these organs within species but wide variations between species. Among some groups, notably the skippers, the genitalia are the only reliable method for identification. Such identification generally necessitates dissection and magnification.

Despite this variation, the sex organs generally follow a basic pattern. The male's two testes are connected by canals to the ejaculatory duct, which discharges through the aedeagus.

The female's two ovaries, where the eggs develop, are linked to one common oviduct, which may end in the anal duct or lead to the outside separately. In about 97 percent of all species the female has two genital openings: one for copulation and one for egg laying. Special mechanisms are connected to the female apparatus to gather spermatozoa from the male and release them gradually as the eggs are laid.

Several broods can be produced each year by some species in warmer regions, but those in the mountains or arctic regions might bring only one brood to maturity every two years. While family patterns generally are carried through, many species with more than one brood per year show radical seasonal variation. For example, spring broods in species of the family Pieridae tend to be much paler, with reduced borders and spots, than later broods.

The digestive system begins with the pharynx, equipped with strong muscles to produce the sucking action of the proboscis. The esophagus extends into the insect's body from the pharynx, ending in a crop that accepts and holds the nutritive portion of the butterfly's intake. A digestive tube leads from the terminus of the esophagus to the final outlet for waste matter through the anus.

Like most other living things, butterflies also have nervous, circulatory, and respiratory systems.

The butterfly brain is found in its head, along with another brainlike mass, known as the suprasophagael

Above A pair of Pipevine Swallowtails fulfills the primary function of the adult phase, *creating the next generation and completing their life cycle.*

ganglion, that controls the workings of the mouth. A connected series of ganglia lead from the brain through the length of the abdomen. Lateral nerves connect to this chain to serve all regions of the body.

Unlike vertebrate systems, the butterfly's circulatory system is not physically connected to the respiratory system. A dorsal vessel extends from the abdomen into the thorax, where an aorta is formed. A series of openings connect this primary organ to the rest of the body to circulate the hemolymph (insect blood) through the tissues.

Butterfly respiration is accomplished through a bodywide tracheal system connected to the external environment through stigmas (pores). The system transports oxygen directly to the butterfly's organs without utilizing the blood stream.

PREDATORS ABOUND

IN ALL THEIR life stages, butterflies fall mostly into the prey category, although a few species such as the Harvester are predators as well. The Harvester, the only North American member of a tropical family of carnivorous butterflies, feeds almost exclusively on woolly aphids and their aphid honeydew. But, for the most part, butterflies are prey to a large number of other animals, including other insects, birds, lizards, frogs, toads, and small mammals.

A few species carry a repellent, generally introduced from the host plant on which they feed, but protection usually means concealment or escape. Both of these functions are served in varying degrees by the animal's form and coloration, and almost every manner employed to this end in the animal kingdom is represented somewhere among the butterflies. There are a half dozen primary types:

• Warning coloration incorporates bright, easily seen colors and patterns, with the goal of attracting attention. Species that are inedible because of the poisonous or noxious nature of the plants they eat employ such coloring to actually advertise this fact to potential predators and to warn them. The Monarch, given its poisonous/noxious ability from the milkweed on which the caterpillar feeds, is the most famous example. Its familiar orange-brown coloring signals its presence from quite a distance, but its slow, meandering flight indicates its lack of concern over that fact.

• The Viceroy is the classic example of mimicry in coloration. Feeding on poplar and willow, the butterfly would be satisfactory food for birds. But it carries the colors and habits of the Monarch and thus gains protection from birds that have learned to avoid anything resembling a Monarch.

• Some species have coloration and shape that give them the appearance of some object that holds no interest for potential predators. The young brown and white caterpillar of the Tiger Swallowtail, for example, is a nearly exact replica of a bird dropping.

• Other species employ coloration and shape to blend into their backgrounds, such as the dull, leafy-colored adult of the Eyed Brown.

• Flash-and-confuse coloration allows species like the American Painted Lady to suddenly expose and hide bright, flashy colors in escape attempts. The butterfly shows the dull coloration of one side of its wings while

Above *Many animals, including other insects, birds, lizards, frogs,* *toads and small mammals, prey on butterflies.*

resting, then flashes gaudy colors in flight, and finally returns suddenly to the dull coloration as it drops. The predator is generally left behind.

• Disruptive coloration, such as the black bands and red-orange or yellow spots of the Eastern Black swallowtail caterpillar, breaks up the insect's outline to provide protection.

Parasites are an even greater danger than predators, and the chief threats come primarily from viruses and bacteria that remain only poorly understood. Members of two other insect orders, Diptera (flies) and Hymenoptera (wasps, bees, and the like), also do a lot of parasitic damage to some butterfly species.

In general these insects do not kill the butterfly immediately. Instead the female parasite lays her eggs on the butterfly, often in the caterpillar stage, and the developing parasitic larvae feed on their host. Often one of these parasites will emerge from a chrysalis in place of an adult butterfly.

While most parasites attack the caterpillar phase of the butterfly, no stage is completely predator-free.

Right *Protective, concealing coloration is a principal defense for* *butterflies. This member of the Sulphur group resembles a leaf.*

HUMANS AND BUTTERFLIES

UNTIL QUITE RECENTLY, involvement with butterflies automatically translated into man as yet another predator, amassing dead specimens neatly arranged in display cases. The success of the lepidopterist, academic or amateur, was in no small way measured by the size and diversity of that display.

However, we are in the midst of a growing recognition by both long-time enthusiasts and hordes of newly interested neophytes that butterflies have so much more to offer the observer than a quick snatch with the net, followed by a plunge into the killing jar. Living butterflies, in all their stages, have a myriad of habits and activities to reveal.

Collecting, killing, and mounting still occur, with merit in some instances, but a growing number of butterfly fanciers are quite content to do their fancying in the field or with captive but alive specimens.

Flight habits are among the most easily observed butterfly characteristics. Every species has its trademark flight; some are so distinctive as to make the species recognizable from as far off as it can be seen. Flight varies from the lazy drifting of the Monarch to the frenetic darting of the Comma.

A specialized aspect of flight is the flyways that several species have been noted to use consistently. On occasion such localized but repeated use of an aerial path has been confused with true migration. Often

these paths lead to sleeping assemblies and thus warrant investigation at every opportunity.

A sleeping assembly is a group of butterflies gathered together late in the afternoon to pass the night huddled with one another for warmth and protection. This practice is common among the Heliconius butterflies, including the North America species of Zebra Longwing and Crimson-patched Longwing. It has also been reported in several of the Swallowtails.

Other gathering points for large numbers of butterflies may be puddles and other damp places. Groups of several hundred have been reported. In

Above *Damp places are often gathering spots for large numbers of butterflies in a practice known as "puddling".*

Left *Butterflies reward the careful observer with a never-ending succession of interesting activities. This is a Gulf Fritillary.*

Above The Silver-spotted Skipper is one of several highly territorial butterflies that are willing to put up a determined defense of their "home ground".

some species, this "puddling" is a habit primarily of young bachelor males. Many puddle visitors are there by happenstance, but some species are consistent in the activity. Some of these species are Tiger Swallowtail, Zebra Swallowtail, Buckeye, Pearly Crescentspot, and several of the Sulphurs.

Of course territoriality is also quite common among the butterflies, including some of the same species that will "puddle" together at other times. Various theories speculate that the cause of the activity is either to drive competing males from the claimed territory or to mate with females that pass through quickly. Some notable territory defenders are the Buckeye, Pearly Crescentspot, American Copper, Silver-spotted Skipper and Mourning Cloak.

Territories are not necessarily huge expanses of ground. On just a short walk along a woodland trail, the stroller might find himself engaged by several Mourning Cloaks in defense of their territories.

WINTERING

Butterflies also have developed a wide range of behaviors for coping with winter.

Migration is both the most extreme of these behaviors and the ultimate variation in flight, and the Monarch is the most famous of the butterfly migrants. It is the only species with the birdlike North and South annual movements, on a regular continuing schedule.

Individuals that were fluttering about the northeast and midwestern regions of North America in the fall will spend their winter in the high-altitude fir forests of central Mexico's Sierra Madres. Some will have made a journey of 2,000 miles at an average speed of 12 miles per hour. Monarchs of western North America and the Sierra Nevada Mountains will winter in groves of eucalyptus, pine, and cypress in southern California.

Many of these wintering Monarchs will begin the return trip northward in spring, but it will be their offspring that complete the circuit. The old butterflies

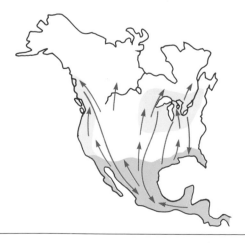

The Monarch is the only butterfly that makes birdlike migrations on a regular, continuing basis; the map (left) clearly shows its routes.

The Monarch's bright coloration (above) warns would-be predators of its noxious taste.

breed along the way as they move North, producing their successors to finish the trip.

Monarchs, however, are not the only butterfly species that make migrations. Although not in so spectacular and distant a fashion, species including the Cloudless Sulphur, Painted Lady, and Buckeye do engage in migrations of a limited nature.

Others have developed their own wintering techniques. At least some species hibernate in every one of the four life stages. Many of the Hairstreaks overwinter as eggs, while Swallowtails can lie dormant for a year in this form.

Caterpillars of species such as the White Admiral, Red-spotted Purple, and Viceroy roll willow leaves about themselves and secure the arrangement to twigs with silk. These are called hibernaculi.

Adults of the Mourning Cloak, Tortoiseshells, and Anglewings hibernate in tree hollows, rock crevices, and open buildings.

And still other species, including the Red Admiral, Buckeye, and American Painted Lady, simply die off in the northern portion of their range each fall, only to have new individuals recolonize it the following spring. The new occupants of the territory will similarly die off in the fall.

PUBLIC BUTTERFLY GARDENS

Such interesting creatures with such fascinating behaviors have naturally spurred a great deal of interest in humans, although in this respect butterflies are a relative newcomer. Indicative of this aroused interest are the increasing number of public butterfly gardens. This recent phenomenon, part of the growing popularity of butterflies, began in Europe in the early 1980s and hit the shores of North America with a vengeance in 1988.

The first of these gardens, Butterfly World in Coconut Creek, Florida, opened its doors in March 1988. It was followed in quick succession by Butterfly World at Marine World Africa U.S.A. in Vallejo, California, in May 1988 and Day Butterfly Center at Callaway Gardens in Pine Mountain, Georgia, in September 1988. Public interest has been strong, with a healthy number of repeat visitors.

Butterfly World in Florida offers two screened aviaries, one packed with native species and the other housing a tropical rain forest of butterflies. An active breeding laboratory, a large collection of preserved specimens, an outdoor milkweed pasture, and the Botanical Vine Walk through a jungle of passion flowers and pipevine are also part of the tour. The address is 3600 West Sample Road, Coconut Creek, FL 33073.

Butterfly World in California has enclosed a rainforest environment in a 5,500-square-foot glass greenhouse. All of its butterflies are purchased elsewhere and brought to the structure as chrysalises. The address is Marine World Parkway, Vallejo, CA 94589.

Day Butterfly Center features an octagonal, high-

Left Butterfly gardens, both public and backyard, are springing up across the nation as interest in butterflies increases.

ceiling, glass conservatory that is billed as the largest glass-enclosed butterfly conservatory in North America. The center also raises about two-thirds of its own butterflies, and visitors can observe this process in some of their special greenhouses.

About an acre and a half of outdoor gardens have been designed to attract the native species. Seminars are offered for home gardeners who want to plant to attract butterflies. The address is Callaway Gardens, Day Butterfly Center, Highway 27, Pine Mountain, GA 31822-2000.

The interest in butterflies has also spawned a small but growing private industry. It is estimated that more than 1,500 people in the United States and Canada now raise insects professionally. One of the top butterfly farmers in the United States places his production at about 1,500 per week for a clientele of insect zoos, universities, and aviaries.

Common species sell for $3 to $12 each, while some rare species can cost upward of $500 and some individual specimens have reportedly sold for $4,000.

Other entrepreneurs have found a market for butterflies as novelties, such as inside birthday cakes, chrysalises in Christmas tree balls that will hatch on Christmas Day, or chrysalises in necklaces.

Hobbyists are also transforming the old concepts of butterfly collection. Taking advantage of the fact that chrysalises are excellent shipping containers, given the proper precautions and care, informal exchanges of the pupal stages have developed for trading of specimens.

While some may view a few of these practices as demeaning to the animals, the fact remains that such experiences are the initial contact with the natural world for many people. If not for such opportunities, far too many individuals would continue through their workaday worlds without ever fully realizing the existence of the natural world and man's impact upon it. In addition, it is common among the entrepreneurs to preach a conservation ethic and to urge that the butterflies be released into the wild after emerging.

DEVELOPMENT AS A THREAT

In our modern world of nonstop development, with its seemingly endless appetite for converting open, wild spaces into closed, domesticated spaces, every effort toward helping people respect Nature and save as much of it as possible should be appreciated. Today's North America is vastly different from the wild,

Right A small, but growing, industry has been born from the new interest in butterflies. Chrysalises make prime shipping containers for those raising insects professionally.

unsettled land that existed prior to the arrival of the European settlers. Previously, almost every locale had achieved its own equilibrium, its own balance among all of its inhabitants and resources.

That balance, except in a few areas, is gone forever. In its place we have created a human balance. The land is developed for people's use. Beyond that point, whatever creatures can also make use of it are sometimes allowed to exist there.

Butterflies are so closely linked to their environments that such drastic changes in the ecosystem can be devastating to a localized population or species. Moreover, some populations are so dependent upon particular plants that if they try to flee from changing conditions they will starve.

As a result, we have seen dramatic declines in butterfly populations across the face of the Earth in recent decades. Much of this loss is occurring in the disappearing rain forests of warmer locales, but North America has not been without its many tragedies, too.

The namesake of the Xerces Society, the Xerces Blue, for example, was lost forever in 1943 when the expansion of a military base destroyed the coastal sand dunes near San Francisco, California, that were the only home of the final colony of the butterfly. It's an appropriate name for one of the leading butterfly and insect habitat conservation organizations in the world.

Organizations like the Xerces Society and the growing butterfly consciousness in the general population are reassuring. And, despite the noted declines, we still have an amazing diversity of butterflies left. Nearly 170,000 species have been identified to date, and most insiders see that number as a minority of the total that really exists.

YOUR OWN BUTTERFLY GARDEN

FOR THOSE WHO HAVE a mind to do their part to preserve butterfly populations, creating a butterfly garden in the backyard, on the patio, or even on the windowsill is a substantial first step.

The starting point for development of your own butterfly garden is a survey of the butterflies that are already visiting your neighborhood. With notebook in hand, spend some time watching butterflies in other gardens, parks, vacant lots, and similar open spaces. Jot down the names of flowers and plants you see butterflies visiting.

While guides, such as this book, are helpful in identifying butterfly species and describing their general ranges, nothing can compare to direct observation of what is already happening naturally. Cosmopolitan species like the Cabbage White or the Monarch may in fact be rare or altogether absent in your small corner of the world. A certain plant species may be the universal recommendation for attracting a particular butterfly species, but it may grow poorly in your locale. Your own observations, coupled with guides for exact identifications, will reveal these important details as you plan your butterfly garden.

A local natural history museum, college entomology department, or butterfly club can also help point you in the right direction.

Next, incorporate your observations of the local environment into the basic features found in every fully functioning butterfly garden: areas of sunlight, nectar sources for adult butterflies, food sources for caterpillars, puddles, shelter, and rocky areas.

Many species of butterflies are most active in sun-filled areas, so large open areas are mandatory for any butterfly garden. Low-lying ground covers, such as clover mixed with grasses, provides these areas, and they are also sources of nectar and food.

Taller nectar and food plants can be planted at the edge of the open areas to provide additional diver-

Above To begin planning your own butterfly garden, first survey your neighborhood. If you're lucky you might find some of the more colorful species, such as this Lorquin's Admiral.

sity while allowing the butterflies to remain fully in the sun.

As the Earth rotates, different areas of the garden will naturally fall into the sunlight at different times of the day. As different species of butterflies take nectar at different times as well, you will want to scatter plants to accommodate as many as possible.

The active season of your butterfly garden can be extended by incorporating plants with different but overlapping blooming seasons. Such diversity of plants is also advisable because of the highly selective nature of many butterfly species toward the plants they will use as hosts for eggs and chrysalises, food for caterpillars, and nectar sources for adults. The more diverse the offering in your butterfly garden, the more species you are likely to attract.

Use the following list as a guide to the preferences of some of the more common North American butterflies. The "food plant" listing for each plant tells which species use the plant as food in their cater-

Left Areas of sunlight, such as the edge of this swimming pool, are essential if you want to attract a healthy population of butterflies.

pillar stage. The "nectar source" listing refers to the preferences of adult butterflies.

You will soon notice that this list includes both cultivated and wild plants. The simple reason for this is that many wild plants are also excellent attractors for many butterfly species.

To help in your identification of the species you encounter, the remainder of this book displays and discusses 250 of the most common and widespread species in North America. I've compiled what I feel is the most comprehensive visual treatment available of these 250. Whether you find them in caterpillar, chrysalis, or adult form, this book will assist you in making exact identifications.

Consider some of the most hated of "weeds" – dandelion, milkweed, and nettle. A garden filled with nothing but these species would attract a quite respectable diversity of butterflies.

Of course, no one wants a garden or backyard made up of only – or even primarily – these "weed" species. In many municipalities, weed ordinances would prohibit the practice. But a distant corner of the garden left to these species will reward the gardener with a rainbow of butterfly color for minimal effort. The healthiest, most attractive gardens are blends of man's cultivated plants and those that Nature will provide if given the slightest opportunity.

So, use this list and your local observations to decide what you want to achieve and what you will be comfortable with, always remembering that wildlife – in this case butterflies – will surely reward your efforts in kind.

Above *Thistle, another despised weed, serves as a food plant and a nectar source for many species.*

Left *Ironweed is a nectar source for many species, such as this Tiger Swallowtail.*

PLANTS FOR BUTTERFLIES

COMMON NAME	LATIN NAME	FOOD PLANT	NECTAR SOURCE
Alfalfa	(*Medicago sativa*)	Marine Blue	Eastern Black Swallowtail, Orange Sulphur, Dogface Butterfly, Large Wood Nymph, Tawny-edged Skipper
Apple	(*Malus* spp.)	Spring Azure, Red-spotted Purple, Viceroy	
Aspen	(*Populus* spp.)	Western Tiger Swallowtail, Mourning Cloak, White Admiral, Red-spotted Purple, Viceroy	
Aster	(*Aster* spp.)	Pearly Crescentspot	Checkered White, Common Sulphur, Orange Sulphur, Question Mark, Milbert's Tortoiseshell, American Painted Lady, Painted Lady, Red Admiral, Buckeye, Common Checkered Skipper, Fiery Skipper
Beans	(*Phaseolus* spp.)	Gray Hairstreak, Marine Blue, Silver-spotted Skipper	
Beggar-ticks	(*Bidens* spp.)		Gulf Fritillary, Red Admiral, Viceroy, Monarch, Queen, Common Checkered Skipper, Fiery Skipper
Black-eyed Susan	(*Rudbeckia hirta*)		Great Spangled Fritillary, Pearly Crescentspot
Blueberry/ huckleberry	(*Vaccinium* spp.) (*Gaylussacia* spp.)	Brown Elfin	
Burdock	(*Arctium* spp.)	American Painted Lady, Painted Lady	
Butterfly bush	(*Buddleia* spp.)		Pipevine Swallowtail, Anise Swallowtail, Tiger Swallowtail, Western Tiger Swallowtail, Comma, Mourning Cloak, Milbert's Tortoiseshell, American Painted Lady, Painted Lady, Red Admiral
Buttonbush	(*Cephalanthus* spp.)		Tiger Swallowtail, American Painted Lady, Painted Lady, Monarch
Carrot	(*Daucus carota* var. *sativus*)	Eastern Black Swallowtail, Anise Swallowtail	
Cherry	(*Prunus* spp.)	Spring Azure, Red-spotted Purple, Viceroy	
Chicory	(*Cichorium intybus*)		Buckeye
Daisy	(*Chrysanthemum* spp.)		Cloudless Giant Sulphur, Pearly Crescentspot, Milbert's Tortoiseshell, Red Admiral, Queen, Fiery Skipper
Dandelion	(*Taraxacum* spp.)		Cabbage White, Sara Orangetip, Common Sulphur, Comma, Red Admiral
Dogbane	(*Apocynum* spp.)		Spicebush Swallowtail, Checkered White, Common Sulphur, Orange Sulphur, Gray Hairstreak, Spring Azure, Pearly Crescentspot, Mourning Cloak, American Painted Lady, Buckeye, Silver-spotted Skipper, Tawny-edged Skipper
Dogwood	(*Cornus* spp.)	Spring Azure	
Elm	(*Ulmus* spp.)	Comma, Mourning Cloak	
Everlasting	(*Anaphalis* spp., *Antennaria* spp., *Gnaphalium* spp.)	American Painted Lady, Painted Lady	
False foxglove	(*Aureolaria pedicularia*)	Buckeye	
False indigo	(*Amorpha* spp., *Baptisia* spp.)	Dogface Butterfly, Marine Blue	
Fireweed	(*Epilobium* spp.)		Red Admiral
Glasswort	(*Salicornia* spp.)	Eastern Pygmy Blue	

Goldenrod	(*Solidago* spp.)		Common Sulphur, Orange Sulphur, Gray Hairstreak, Milbert's Tortoiseshell, American Painted Lady, Red Admiral, Viceroy
Grass family members Gramineae		Large Wood Nymph, Fiery Skipper, Tawny-edged Skipper	
Hackberry	(*Celtis* spp.)	Question Mark, Mourning Cloak, Hackberry Butterfly	
Hops	(*Humulus* spp.)	Question Mark, Comma, Red Admiral	
Hollyhock	(*Alcea* spp.)	Painted Lady, Common Checkered Skipper	
Ironweed	(*Vernonia* spp.)	American Painted Lady	Tiger Swallowtail, Great Spangled Fritillary, Monarch, Fiery Skipper
Knapweed	(*Centaurea* spp.)	Painted Lady	Common Sulphur, American Painted Lady, Common Checkered Skipper, Fiery Skipper
Lantana	(*Lantana* spp.)		Anise Swallowtail, Spicebush Swallowtail, Cabbage White, Gulf Fritillary, Fiery Skipper
Lupine	(*Lupinus* spp.)	Common Blue, Silvery Blue	Common Blue
Mallow	(*Malva* spp.)	Gray Hairstreak, Painted Lady	American Painted Lady, Painted Lady, Red Admiral, Monarch
Marigold	(*Tagetes* spp.)		Milbert's Tortoiseshell, American Painted Lady
Milkweed	(*Asclepias* spp.)	Monarch, Queen	Pipevine Swallowtail, Eastern Black Swallowtail, Giant Swallowtail, Tiger Swallowtail, Western Tiger Swallowtail, Spicebush Swallowtail, Checkered White, Cabbage White, Common Sulphur, Orange Sulphur, Gray Hairstreak, Spring Azure, Common Blue, Great Spangled Fritillary, Pearly Crescentspot, Question Mark, Mourning Cloak, American Painted Lady, Painted Lady, Red Admiral, Viceroy, Monarch, Queen, Hackberry Butterfly, Fiery Skipper
Mint	(*Mentha* spp.)		Western Black Swallowtail, Anise Swallowtail, Western Tiger Swallowtail, Cabbage White, Gray Hairstreak, American Painted Lady, Painted Lady, Red Admiral, Monarch, Large Wood Nymph
Nettle	(*Urtica* spp.)	Question Mark, Comma, Satyr Anglewing, Milbert's Tortoiseshell	
Parsley	(*Petroselinum crsipum*)	Eastern Black Swallowtail, Anise Swallowtail	
Passion flower	(*Passiflora* spp.)	Gulf Fritillary	Gulf Fritillary
Penstemon	(*Penstemon* spp.)		Western Black Swallowtail
Peppermint	(*Mentha* x *piperita*)		Pearly Crescentspot
Pigweed	(*Chenopodium* spp.)	Western Pygmy Blue	Western Pygmy Blue
Pipevine	(*Aristolochia* spp.)	Pipevine Swallowtail	
Plantain	(*Plantago* spp.)	Buckeye	Buckeye
Plum	(*Prunus* spp.)	Spring Azure, Red-spotted Purple, Viceroy	

PLANTS FOR BUTTERFLIES

Poplar	(*Populus* spp.)	Western Tiger Swallowtail, Mourning Cloak, White Admiral, Red-spotted Purple, Viceroy	
Privet	(*Ligustrum* spp.)		Spring Azure, American Painted Lady, Painted Lady, Red-spotted Purple, Silver-spotted Skipper
Purple coneflower	(*Echinacea* spp.)		Silvery Blue, Great Spangled Fritillary, Tawny-edged Skipper
Queen Anne's lace	(*Daucus carota* var. *carota*)	Eastern Black Swallowtail	Eastern Black Swallowtail, Gray Hairstreak
Rabbitbrush	(*Chrysothamnus nauseosus*)		Orange Sulphur, Painted Lady
Red Clover	(*Trifolium pratense*)		Cabbage White, Great Spangled Fritillary, American Painted Lady, Painted Lady, Red Admiral, Silver-spotted Skipper, Common Checkered Skipper, Tawny-edged Skipper
Rock cress	(*Arabis* spp.)	Sara Orangetip, Falcate Orangetip, Spring Azure, Mourning Cloak, Milbert's Tortoiseshell	
Salt bush	(*Atriplex*)	Eastern Pygmy Blue	Eastern Pygmy Blue
Seaside heliotrope	(*Heliotropium curassavicum*)		Orange Sulphur, American Painted Lady
Scabiosa	(*Scabiosa* spp.)		American Painted Lady, Painted Lady
Self-heal	(*Prunella* spp.)		Cabbage White, American Painted Lady, Silver-spotted Skipper
Snapdragon	(*Antirrhinum* spp.)	Buckeye	
Spicebush	(*Lindera benzoin*)	Spicebush Swallowtail	
Stonecrop	(*Sedum* spp.)		Milbert's Tortoiseshell, Painted Lady, Red Admiral
Sweet pepperbush	(*Clethra alnifolia*)		Spicebush Swallowtail, Question Mark, American Painted Lady, Red Admiral, Red-spotted Purple
Sweet pea	(*Lathyrus odoratus*)	Gray Hairstreak, Marine Blue, Silvery Blue	Gray Hairstreak
Thistle	(*Cirsium* spp.)	Painted Lady	Pipevine Swallowtail, Tiger Swallowtail, Western Tiger Swallowtail, Spicebush Swallowtail, Dogface Butterfly, Gulf Fritillary, Pearly Crescentspot, Milbert's Tortoiseshell, American Painted Lady, Red Admiral, Viceroy, Monarch, Silver-spotted Skipper, Fiery Skipper, Tawny-edged Skipper
Tickseed	(*Coreopsis grandiflora*)		Common Sulphur, Orange Sulphur, Pearly Crescentspot, Buckeye, Monarch
Verbena	(*Verbena* spp.)	Buckeye	Great Spangled Fritillary
Vetch	(*Vicia* spp.)	Common Sulphur, Orange Sulphur, Gray Hairstreak, Silvery Blue	American Painted Lady
Violet	(*Viola* spp.)	Great Spangled Fritillary	Spring Azure
Willow	(*Salix* spp.)	Tiger Swallowtail, Western Tiger Swallowtail, Mourning Cloak, White Admiral, Red-spotted Purple, Viceroy	Brown Elfin
Winter cress	(*Barbarea* spp.)	Checkered White, Cabbage White, Falcate Orangetip, Spring Azure	Checkered White, Brown Elfin, Gray Hairstreak, Spring Azure, Pearly Crescentspot, Silver-spotted Skipper
Wood nettle	(*Laportea canadensis*)	Comma, Red Admiral	
Wormwood	(*Artemisia* spp.)	American Painted Lady	Tiger Swallowtail, Great Spangled Fritillary, Monarch, Fiery Skipper

SOME OTHER NECTAR SOURCES

Rotting fruit and tree sap are also nectar sources for many species, including the Question Mark, Comma, Satyr Anglewing, Mourning Cloak, Milbert's Tortoiseshell, Red Admiral, White Admiral, Red-spotted Purple, Viceroy, Hackberry Butterfly, and Large Wood Nymph.

These same species will readily come to a mixture of mashed rotten bananas, molasses, sugar, stale beer, and fruit juice in water. This concoction can be spread on rocks and tree trunks. Rags soaked in it can be hung from tree limbs. Or a sponge can be floated in a plate of it.

For those butterflies that draw "nectar" from dung and urine, your family pet can supply the bait, provided you don't feel compelled to clean up after the animal's every use.

Puddles in the butterfly garden are the equivalent of bird baths in the bird watcher's backyard. Butterflies cannot drink directly from open water, but they will make regular visits to – and even congregate at – "puddles" of wet sand or earth. Several of these scattered about the natural depressions of your garden, with small rocks and sticks placed on top of them, will further enhance the garden's attractiveness to the butterflies.

Shelter to a butterfly means protection from two things, the wind and predators. Vine-covered walls, fences, or trellises; borders of small trees or shrubs; or any combination of these will fulfill both of the insects' needs.

Some widely attractive species are hops, passion flower, and pipevine for vine locations; honeysuckle and butterfly bush for low- to mid-range shrubs; and poplar, willow, aspen, and wild cherry for trees.

Gardens surrounded by windbreaks are not recommended, but a healthy amount of protection will draw more butterflies. Attractive gardens result from a terraced or layering approach, ranging from the open, sunlit space in the front to successively taller plants as the back edge is approached. This scheme also allows maximum viewing of the garden and all the activity it will attract.

A relatively recent addition to the butterfly garden is a device called the butterfly box. This elongated version of a nestbox for birds has several long, thin openings in its face to allow butterflies to enter so they can hibernate. The makers recommend that it be attached to a tree or post in a shady spot.

SPECIAL PLACES

If space permits, you might want to include a few specialized niches in the garden in an attempt to attract additional species not normally drawn to open-space

Right: A White Admiral takes nectar from a blossom of a boneset plant.

Right The Buckeye is one of many butterfly species that require wooded areas as a major part of their environment.

environments. The Mourning Cloak and several Satyr species, for example, prefer wooded areas, while the Red-spotted Purple and Buckeye frequent openings within those wooded areas.

If, on the other hand, space is substantially limited, potted plants and window boxes that incorporate a variety of the plant species on our list will attract butterflies. With just a little imagination, every aspect of a garden can be duplicated in these micro-environments.

A quick, easy, and effective way to fill your garden with butterflies is to stock it much the same as fishermen often stock favorite lakes or streams with fish. You can capture the eggs, larvae, and chrysalises from the wild and transplant them into the garden.

In the case of eggs or chrysalises, they should not be detached from the leaf or branch on which they are found. Instead, bring the entire arrangement back to the garden. A few species can also be purchased from butterfly farmers, such as those discussed earlier.

Exotic species should never be introduced into the wild state outside of their natural home areas. In all likelihood, they will have no natural enemies to act as a check on their numbers. Thus, they are likely to multiply until they become pests and may even cause damage to the local gene pools of their native counterparts.

One of the most common butterflies across North America didn't even exist here until 1860. In that year a few Cabbage Whites were accidentally introduced from Europe to Canada. Farmers and gardeners have been cursing them ever since, as they continue to expand their conquest of this new land.

The United States Department of Agriculture, as well as state and local agencies, have promulgated strict regulations on the import and interstate transport of potential pest species to prevent similar problems.

LAWS OF NATURE

Many books on butterfly gardening discuss various means for protecting the insects from the many predators waiting to pounce on them, particularly birds. Books about attracting birds into the backyard fall into the same trap, offering suggestions on minimizing the loss of the "desired" songbird species to birds of prey and the loss of bird seed to competitors such as squirrels. All this is nothing more than pandering to human misconceptions about the natural world. Nothing will ever change the fact that birds eat butterflies and are in turn eaten by other predators.

Nor can the wildlife gardener ignore the fact that nothing done in the garden is done in a vacuum. Many plants attract a wide variety of creatures. A garden that has been furnished with all the elements necessary for survival of butterflies will also have all the elements necessary for survival of birds, and so on.

Accept these facts. Welcome all creatures into the garden, each into its own niche, predator or prey. You'll be richer for it, despite the occasional predatory loss of a favored individual or two.

If feasible, maintain records for every creature and every event that you observe in your garden. Answer the basic newspaper reporter questions – Who? What? When? Where? Why? How? – and in a short time you'll have useful guidelines to the further development of your backyard Garden of Eden. You'll also find that this journal, packed with natural history, will be a pleasure in and of itself.

RAISING YOUR OWN

IN TIME YOU may feel that you want a more intimate understanding of the life of a butterfly. Perhaps you will want to try your hand at raising a butterfly, which actually is a fairly simple thing to do.

We'll use the Monarch as the example because both the butterfly and its host plant, milkweed, are generally familiar and easily recognized by the average person. However, nearly any common species and its appropriate host plant can be used. With all specimens, before taking them from the wild, be certain you know all regulations governing such practice in your local area.

• Find the Monarch's eggs on milkweed plants. The adult female will usually lay a single egg on the underside of each leaf she visits. Since the eggs are quite small, you will probably find that a magnifying glass is helpful in identifying the ribbed, conical, greenish-white eggs.

• Cut out the area of the leaf around the egg, leaving at least an inch on all sides of the egg.

• Repeat the first two steps several times to give yourself an ample number of eggs to ensure hatching.

• Take your specimens indoors and place the fresh leaf bits on a moist paper towel on a plate. To further retain the moisture, wrap a polyethylene plastic bag around the plate, paper towel, and leaf bits. Other types of plastic bags are often harmful to the caterpillar.

• When an egg is ready to hatch, the tiny black head of the baby caterpillar will show through at the tip of the egg. Now is the time to remove all other eggs to other containers. Perform this procedure in a warm location to prevent chilling of the eggs.

• Shortly the newborn caterpillar will eat its way out of the egg. It will finish off the egg as its first meal and follow it up with any other nearby, unhatched eggs. This is the reason for removing all others when signs of hatching appear and is the reason why the female generally lays only one egg per leaf.

• The tiny caterpillar will do only two things from this point on: eat and rest, with emphasis on eating. Keep it supplied with plenty of fresh milkweed.

• Elevate the top of the plastic bag to trap air inside.

• About a week after hatching, the caterpillar can be moved to a large rearing cage. This can be a plastic-sided or mesh-screened enclosure, or a jumbo glass jar. Place a small jar of water enclosed in a plastic bag in the cage and poke the base of a stalk of milkweed through the plastic and into the water. The small plastic bag is a protection against the caterpillar drowning.

• Being ever gentle with the caterpillar, replace the milkweed leaves and remove its tiny, dark droppings every other day.

• Under optimum conditions like these, the caterpillar will molt four times. After the fourth molt – about two weeks after hatching – the caterpillar will be fully grown at about two inches.

• Place a twig with a long, arching, horizontal branch into the container.

• The caterpillar will explore the twig for a bit, find a spot, attach itself, and molt one last time. The result of this fifth molt will be the chrysalis, which should not be handled.

• The chrysalis will hang for 9 to 14 days.

• Thirty-six hours before the adult butterfly is ready to emerge, the chrysalis will change to teal blue.

• Twenty-four hours before emergence, the chrysalis will become clear enough for you to see the wings through it.

• Within 10 minutes after emerging, the wings will be fully expanded. They still must dry before the insect can fly.

• Now is the first time you will be able to determine the sex of your prodigy. A male Monarch has a small black dot near the center of each hind wing, in addition to the black veins that radiate through the wings.

• Release the butterfly outside the next morning, unless it's raining.

• If it's raining, keep the butterfly caged until the following morning. Offer it a shallow saucer of sugar water with a small sponge floating in it. The butterfly may or may not take the offering. Either way don't be concerned. Just release it as soon as possible.

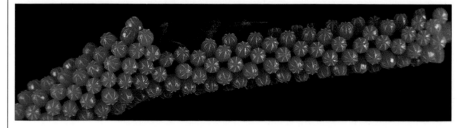

Left The egg mass of a Mourning Cloak which has been laid on a twig.

SMILE, PLEASE

PHOTOGRAPHY OF BUTTERFLIES will also help you to gain a more thorough understanding of their world and their lives, because satisfactory photos will result only after a great deal of patience and time spent with the insects.

A 35-millimeter, single lens reflex (SLR) camera that allows for interchangeable lenses is the basic piece of equipment needed. The recommended, all-around lens for close-up butterfly photography is a 200-millimeter macro, which will enable you to produce fairly large images of your subjects without needing to get so close as to scare them off.

A low-power flash will help you to produce very sharp studies of the butterflies while avoiding jet black backgrounds, if you strike the proper balance between the natural light of the sun and your artificial light source.

To find this balance point, set your camera at the fastest shutter speed at which it will synchronize with your flash. For most modern SLR cameras this is $\frac{1}{60}$, $\frac{1}{125}$, or $\frac{1}{250}$ of a second. Take an exposure reading of your subject, or some object that closely matches the lighting situation of your subject, and note the f-stop at which the meter registers proper lighting. Next determine the setting required for the flash at the flash-to-subject distance you intend to shoot.

Most often these two f-stops will not match, and you will need to reduce the light output of the flash to come closer to the sunlight setting. This is a simple task with a variable power flash that can be dialed to the required ratio. With other units, diffusion material can be placed over the face of the unit.

If the flash and sunlight f-stops are the same, any movement in your subject or the background will cause ghost images in your photos. To avoid this, the flash must be $\frac{1}{2}$ to $\frac{3}{4}$ of an f-stop more powerful than the natural light. Such a setting will also make the butterfly stand out from the background.

When using flash in what you hope will appear to be a natural-looking photo, remember that sunlight comes from above. To produce realistic shadows, your flash should also be slightly above your subject.

Film speed is the final mechanical decision. This speed is represented by an ASA or ISO number, including popular selections such as 25, 64, 100, 200, 400, and 1,000. The higher the number, the faster it is said to be, meaning it requires less light to produce images. However, the lower the number, the less grain it will have and the sharper the images it will produce. The general professional choice is most often 25 or 64.

In close-up photography you will be facing the inherent problem of narrow depth of field. In other words, only a small portion of your final image will be in sharp focus. The larger the aperture (represented by small f-stop numbers), the less depth of field you will have. Electronic flash eliminates this problem some-

Left *Close-up photography of butterflies requires great patience, but the rewards are ample: brilliantly colored photographs and an in-depth knowledge of the subjects.*

what by supplying a constant, strong source of light that allows you to use smaller apertures. To compensate still further, make certain that the eye of your subject is very sharp and the entire photo will appear to be more in focus.

With all of these techniques, and the hundreds more offered in many how-to photography books, the key is practice. Experiment on common subjects, learn from that experimentation, and be ready when the once-in-a-lifetime shot presents itself.

The early morning hours of a day following a cloudless, cool night in late spring or summer are optimum for butterfly photography. The resulting dew will have coated the insects, while the cool environmental temperatures will have lowered their body temperatures. They will need to warm up and dry out their wings before they are able to make any quick escapes, thus allowing you an easier approach.

Generally it is much more productive to set up your equipment at flowers frequented by butterflies and wait for your subject to come to you. However, if you do choose to follow a butterfly for your shot, keep your body and head no higher than the butterfly and avoid rapid movement and casting a shadow over the insect. When the subject settles on a flower, kneel several feet away from it and move toward it very gradually with your camera ready. You may want to snap a shot or two from less than optimum distance, in case the butterfly flees before you can get that close.

Above The early morning, after a cool, wet night in late spring or summer, is prime butterfly-watching time; the insects are chilled and coated with dew, making them slow to escape.

BUTTERFLY WATCHING

Aside from raising butterflies and photographing them, the simple pastime (or for some the passion) of butterfly watching is growing rapidly in popularity. While butterflies have not attracted the millions of fans that birds have won over, there is every indication that someday butterfly watching will be every bit as popular as bird watching.

Tools for the sport are simple. A comprehensive field guide that you are comfortable using is a must. If you can't get the feel of a particular guide and have trouble trying to use it quickly, try another, and another, until you have found the one that suits your method of identification.

Tuck a notebook into your pocket or pack to record all the things you are about to observe. At a minimum, keep track of the species you see, the plants they visit, their behavior, time, and date. Behavior of some species remains only poorly recorded, and amateurs have made important contributions in this area through the comprehensive notes they maintained.

You may even want to borrow the concept of a "life list" from the bird watching fraternity, trying to add as many different species as possible to it over the years. To measure your butterfly accomplishments, remember that geography generally limits the total number of species in even the best locale to less than 100.

A net for temporary capture can help to gently hold a specimen in place while you flip through your field guide at close range. With just a bit of practice, you'll be able to net the insects without doing them any harm.

You might want to add binoculars to your pack. They can be quite handy in observing intimate details of the butterfly's life without having to get too close to it. A pair that focuses quickly and closely is the only type to consider for butterfly watching.

When trying to locate specimens for observation, remember that the greatest diversity of species will be found in open, sun-bathed areas that have abundant flowers. Look particularly in meadows, weedy fields, and river valleys. And the greatest butterfly activity will occur during that part of the year when the daily high temperatures are above 60°F.

HOW TO USE THE DIRECTORY

The identifier section of this book is organized so that you can dive into the appropriate section the first time you glimpse a butterfly. The butterflies are grouped by major coloration, so if you see a blue butterfly, for example, you can turn immediately to the blue section and begin making closer observations for the details that will reveal the exact species.

Each species page points out the most noticeable aspects of that butterfly's coloring to assist you in making a quick identification. This description is followed by interesting items of information on the life or history of that butterfly and then a few notes on the non-adult stages of the butterfly's life.

The "Facts and Features" section of each entry gives the essential details of the species. Wingspan: Measured from apex to apex. Habitat: The general type of area where the species is usually found. Flight: The number of broods generated in a single year and the months in which the adult butterflies are generally observed. Lifecycle notes: Details to help identify the egg, caterpillar, and chrysalis stages. Host plant: Those plants on which the caterpillar feeds. Nectar sources: Those plants and other sources where the adult obtains nectar.

You will notice that for some species not all of the information has been provided. In these cases, the missing information has not been formally described and published. There are many of these gaps, and amateur lepidopterists can play an important part in filling them in.

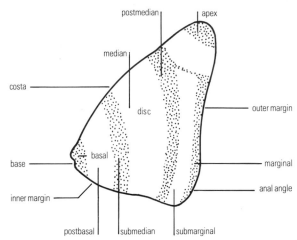

SPECIAL TERMS USED IN THE DIRECTORY

Apex	Outer tip of wing
Above	Refers to upper wings
Below	Refers to underside of wings
Cell	Central area of wing
Costa	Front margin of wing
Cremaster	Point at tail end of chrysalis which attaches to host plant
Dimorphism	The occurence of two different forms notably varying in some characteristic, such as coloration, within a species. Sexually dimorphic: Female and male vary along sexual lines.
♀	Female
Instar	Period between molts in the caterpillar stage
♂	Male
Margin	Outer wing edge
Median	Area halfway between base and apex of wing
Post-median line	Band below submarginal band on wing
Submargin	Band below marginal band on wing
Stigma	Scent scales on wing

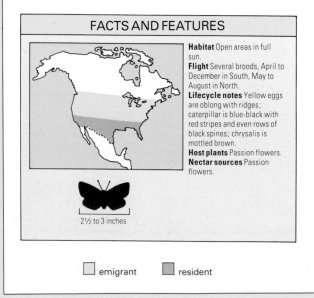

FACTS AND FEATURES

Habitat Open areas in full sun.
Flight Several broods, April to December in South, May to August in North.
Lifecycle notes Yellow eggs are oblong with ridges; caterpillar is blue-black with red stripes and even rows of black spines; chrysalis is mottled brown.
Host plants Passion flowers.
Nectar sources Passion flowers.

2½ to 3 inches

☐ emigrant   ■ resident

PIPEVINE SWALLOWTAIL
BATTUS PHILENOR

This butterfly is also known as the Blue Swallowtail for its hind wings, which are mostly shimmering blue above. The forewings are black.

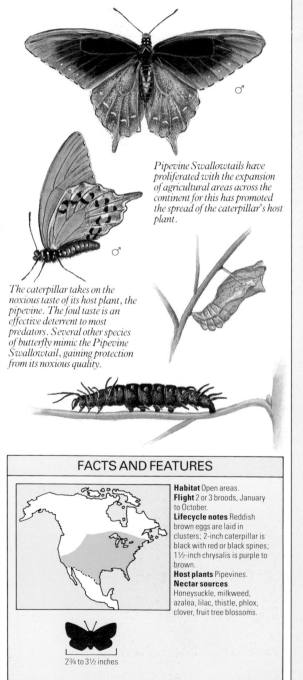

Pipevine Swallowtails have proliferated with the expansion of agricultural areas across the continent for this has promoted the spread of the caterpillar's host plant.

The caterpillar takes on the noxious taste of its host plant, the pipevine. The foul taste is an effective deterrent to most predators. Several other species of butterfly mimic the Pipevine Swallowtail, gaining protection from its noxious quality.

FACTS AND FEATURES

Habitat Open areas.
Flight 2 or 3 broods, January to October.
Lifecycle notes Reddish brown eggs are laid in clusters; 2-inch caterpillar is black with red or black spines; 1½-inch chrysalis is purple to brown.
Host plants Pipevines.
Nectar sources Honeysuckle, milkweed, azalea, lilac, thistle, phlox, clover, fruit tree blossoms.

2¾ to 3½ inches

POLYDAMAS SWALLOWTAIL
BATTUS POLYDAMAS

The single band of yellow checks near the margins of the wings above has earned the species its other name of Gold Rim Swallowtail. Red "Vs" are aligned along the rim of the hind wing below. This is the only tailless black species in the United States.

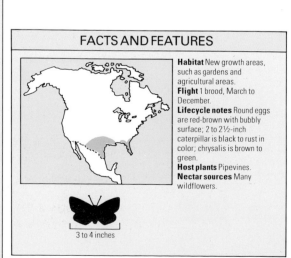

One year there may be almost none of this species to be seen in its normal range, while the next year it might be abundant.

The caterpillar takes on the noxious taste of its host plant, the pipevine, and thus acquires some protection from predators. The chrysalis varies in color from brown to green.

FACTS AND FEATURES

Habitat New growth areas, such as gardens and agricultural areas.
Flight 1 brood, March to December.
Lifecycle notes Round eggs are red-brown with bubbly surface; 2 to 2½-inch caterpillar is black to rust in color; chrysalis is brown to green.
Host plants Pipevines.
Nectar sources Many wildflowers.

3 to 4 inches

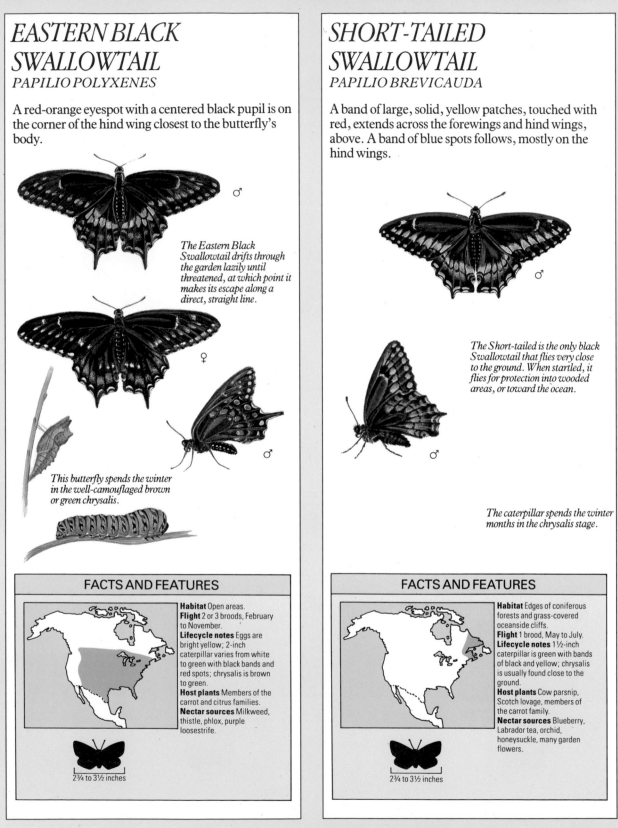

EASTERN BLACK SWALLOWTAIL
PAPILIO POLYXENES

A red-orange eyespot with a centered black pupil is on the corner of the hind wing closest to the butterfly's body.

♂

The Eastern Black Swallowtail drifts through the garden lazily until threatened, at which point it makes its escape along a direct, straight line.

♀

♂

This butterfly spends the winter in the well-camouflaged brown or green chrysalis.

FACTS AND FEATURES

Habitat Open areas.
Flight 2 or 3 broods, February to November.
Lifecycle notes Eggs are bright yellow; 2-inch caterpillar varies from white to green with black bands and red spots; chrysalis is brown to green.
Host plants Members of the carrot and citrus families.
Nectar sources Milkweed, thistle, phlox, purple loosestrife.

2¾ to 3½ inches

SHORT-TAILED SWALLOWTAIL
PAPILIO BREVICAUDA

A band of large, solid, yellow patches, touched with red, extends across the forewings and hind wings, above. A band of blue spots follows, mostly on the hind wings.

♂

The Short-tailed is the only black Swallowtail that flies very close to the ground. When startled, it flies for protection into wooded areas, or toward the ocean.

♂

The caterpillar spends the winter months in the chrysalis stage.

FACTS AND FEATURES

Habitat Edges of coniferous forests and grass-covered oceanside cliffs.
Flight 1 brood, May to July.
Lifecycle notes 1½-inch caterpillar is green with bands of black and yellow; chrysalis is usually found close to the ground.
Host plants Cow parsnip, Scotch lovage, members of the carrot family.
Nectar sources Blueberry, Labrador tea, orchid, honeysuckle, many garden flowers.

2¾ to 3½ inches

WESTERN BLACK SWALLOWTAIL
PAPILIO BAIRDII

One orange eyespot with an off-center black pupil appears on the corner of each hind wing closest to the body above.

Although the Western and Eastern Black Swallowtails share portions of their ranges near the middle of the continent, only the eastern species will be found in suburban gardens. The chrysalis ranges from green to brown and looks like a twig.

FACTS AND FEATURES

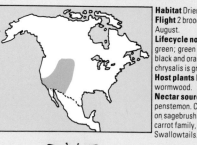

Habitat Drier mountain areas.
Flight 2 broods, May to August.
Lifecycle notes Eggs are green; green caterpillar has black and orange bands; chrysalis is green or brown.
Host plants Dragon wormwood.
Nectar sources Mint, penstemon. Caterpillars feed on sagebrush and not the carrot family, as do Black Swallowtails.

3 to 3½ inches

OLD WORLD SWALLOWTAIL
PAPILIO MACHAON

A broad band of pale yellow spots covers most of the wings above and even more below. Much of the black on the wings above is clouded over in yellow or pale blue. The eyespots on the hind wing are red but have no pupils. The butterfly appears almost completely yellow from underneath.

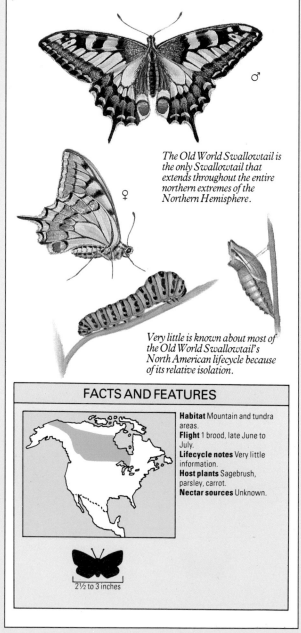

The Old World Swallowtail is the only Swallowtail that extends throughout the entire northern extremes of the Northern Hemisphere.

Very little is known about most of the Old World Swallowtail's North American lifecycle because of its relative isolation.

FACTS AND FEATURES

Habitat Mountain and tundra areas.
Flight 1 brood, late June to July.
Lifecycle notes Very little information.
Host plants Sagebrush, parsley, carrot.
Nectar sources Unknown.

2½ to 3 inches

ANISE SWALLOWTAIL
PAPILIO ZELICAON

A band of bright yellow spots with straight edges extends across the midwings above. Eyespots on the corner of the hind wing closest to the body are red with large, black, centered pupils.

This is the most common Swallowtail west of the Rocky Mountains. Male Anise Swallowtails are attracted to elevated spots, such as hilltops, particularly during courtship.

The caterpillar eats both the leaves and flowers of many plants, including fennel, cow parsnip, and members of the carrot and citrus families.

FACTS AND FEATURES

Habitat Very widespread, except for dense woodlands.
Flight 1 brood, June or July, at higher elevations; varying numbers of broods, year round, at lower elevations.
Lifecycle notes Eggs are yellow; caterpillar is green with black bands and orange spots; chrysalis is green or brown and resembles a stick.
Host plants Fennel, cow parsnip, members of the carrot and citrus families.
Nectar sources Mints, zinnia, butterfly bush, penstemon.

2½ to 3 inches

SHORT-TAILED BLACK SWALLOWTAIL
PAPILIO INDRA

A thin band of cream-colored spots extends across the wings near the rim above. The large black area of the wings appears frosted with scattered cream specks.

The Short-tailed Black Swallowtail, also called the Mountain Swallowtail, has more subspecies than other Swallowtails.

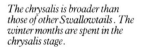

The chrysalis is broader than those of other Swallowtails. The winter months are spent in the chrysalis stage.

FACTS AND FEATURES

Habitat Dry areas such as deserts, canyons, and foothills.
Flight 1 brood, late spring to summer, over much of the range; second brood, late summer, in isolated pockets.
Lifecycle notes Light yellow eggs; white or light-shaded caterpillar has orange spots; chrysalis is dull gray or tan.
Host plants Members of the carrot family.
Nectar sources Mints.

2 to 3½ inches

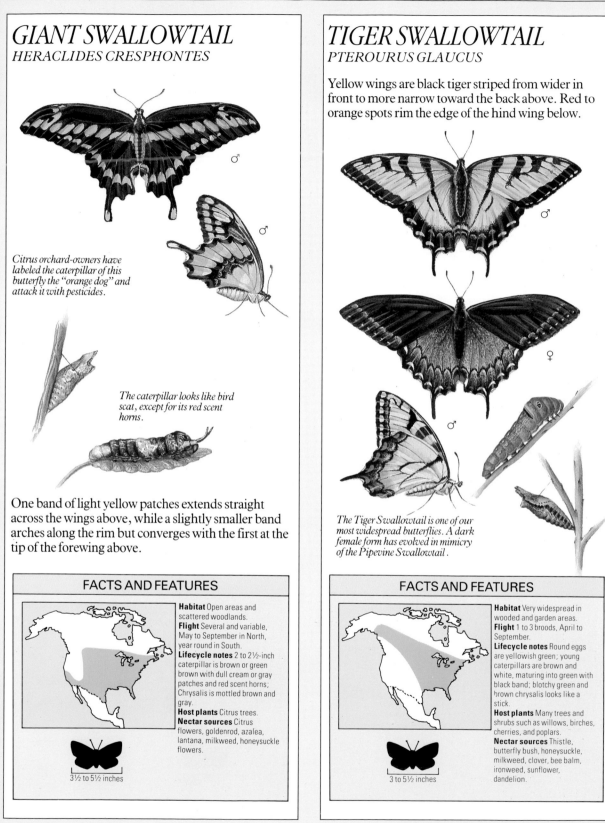

GIANT SWALLOWTAIL
HERACLIDES CRESPHONTES

♂

♂

Citrus orchard-owners have labeled the caterpillar of this butterfly the "orange dog" and attack it with pesticides.

The caterpillar looks like bird scat, except for its red scent horns.

One band of light yellow patches extends straight across the wings above, while a slightly smaller band arches along the rim but converges with the first at the tip of the forewing above.

FACTS AND FEATURES

Habitat Open areas and scattered woodlands.
Flight Several and variable, May to September in North, year round in South.
Lifecycle notes 2 to 2½-inch caterpillar is brown or green brown with dull cream or gray patches and red scent horns; Chrysalis is mottled brown and gray.
Host plants Citrus trees.
Nectar sources Citrus flowers, goldenrod, azalea, lantana, milkweed, honeysuckle flowers.

3½ to 5½ inches

TIGER SWALLOWTAIL
PTEROURUS GLAUCUS

Yellow wings are black tiger striped from wider in front to more narrow toward the back above. Red to orange spots rim the edge of the hind wing below.

♂

♀

♂

The Tiger Swallowtail is one of our most widespread butterflies. A dark female form has evolved in mimicry of the Pipevine Swallowtail.

FACTS AND FEATURES

Habitat Very widespread in wooded and garden areas.
Flight 1 to 3 broods, April to September.
Lifecycle notes Round eggs are yellowish green; young caterpillars are brown and white, maturing into green with black band; blotchy green and brown chrysalis looks like a stick.
Host plants Many trees and shrubs such as willows, birches, cherries, and poplars.
Nectar sources Thistle, butterfly bush, honeysuckle, milkweed, clover, bee balm, ironweed, sunflower, dandelion.

3 to 5½ inches

WESTERN TIGER SWALLOWTAIL
PTEROURUS RUTULUS

Black tiger stripes extend over bright yellow wings from front to back above. Bright red eyespots are curved along the edges of the hind wings closest to the body; there are no black pupils.

The Western Tiger Swallowtail is the most noticeable butterfly in the West.

The caterpillar has a bulging head with huge yellow and black eyespots.

FACTS AND FEATURES

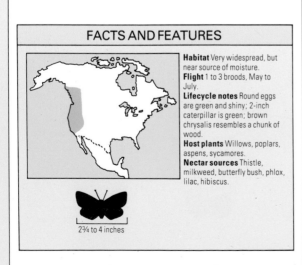

Habitat Very widespread, but near source of moisture.
Flight 1 to 3 broods, May to July.
Lifecycle notes Round eggs are green and shiny; 2-inch caterpillar is green; brown chrysalis resembles a chunk of wood.
Host plants Willows, poplars, aspens, sycamores.
Nectar sources Thistle, milkweed, butterfly bush, phlox, lilac, hibiscus.

2¾ to 4 inches

TWO-TAILED TIGER SWALLOWTAIL
PTEROURUS MULTICAUDATUS

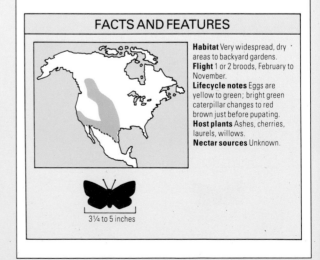

The Two-tailed Tiger Swallowtail is the largest Tiger Swallowtail in the West. It is very widespread.

The caterpillar transforms from bright green to red-brown before pupating.

As the name implies, this Swallowtail has two tails on each hind wing. The black tiger stripes are very narrow and short.

FACTS AND FEATURES

Habitat Very widespread, dry areas to backyard gardens.
Flight 1 or 2 broods, February to November.
Lifecycle notes Eggs are yellow to green; bright green caterpillar changes to red brown just before pupating.
Host plants Ashes, cherries, laurels, willows.
Nectar sources Unknown.

3¼ to 5 inches

PALE TIGER SWALLOWTAIL
PTEROURUS EURYMEDON

The pale yellow to off-white wings have broad tiger stripes running front to back above. Borders of the hind wing are marked in orange, pale blue, and off-white.

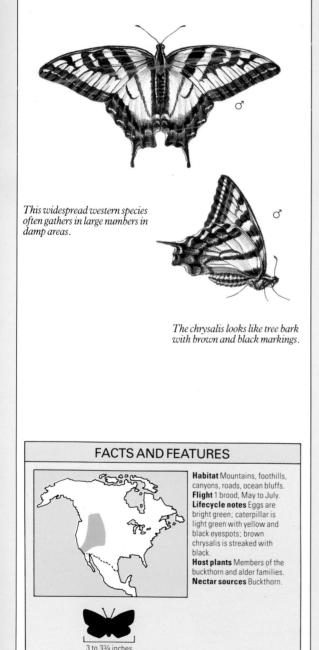

This widespread western species often gathers in large numbers in damp areas.

The chrysalis looks like tree bark with brown and black markings.

FACTS AND FEATURES

Habitat Mountains, foothills, canyons, roads, ocean bluffs.
Flight 1 brood, May to July.
Lifecycle notes Eggs are bright green; caterpillar is light green with yellow and black eyespots; brown chrysalis is streaked with black.
Host plants Members of the buckthorn and alder families.
Nectar sources Buckthorn.

3 to 3¾ inches

SPICEBUSH SWALLOWTAIL
PTEROURUS TROILUS

Also called the Green-clouded Swallowtail because of the shimmering blue-green "clouding" over the hind wing above. Two rows of orange patches curve across the hind wing below.

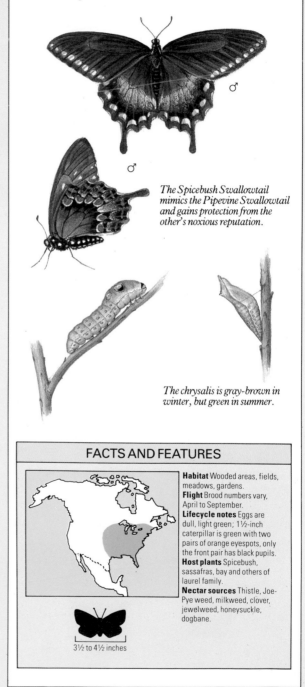

The Spicebush Swallowtail mimics the Pipevine Swallowtail and gains protection from the other's noxious reputation.

The chrysalis is gray-brown in winter, but green in summer.

FACTS AND FEATURES

Habitat Wooded areas, fields, meadows, gardens.
Flight Brood numbers vary, April to September.
Lifecycle notes Eggs are dull, light green; 1½-inch caterpillar is green with two pairs of orange eyespots, only the front pair has black pupils.
Host plants Spicebush, sassafras, bay and others of laurel family.
Nectar sources Thistle, Joe-Pye weed, milkweed, clover, jewelweed, honeysuckle, dogbane.

3½ to 4½ inches

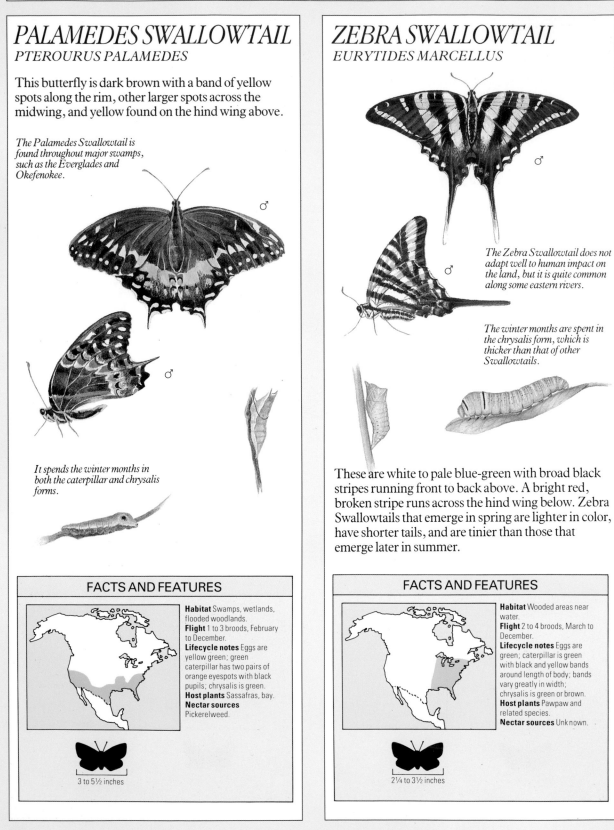

PALAMEDES SWALLOWTAIL
PTEROURUS PALAMEDES

This butterfly is dark brown with a band of yellow spots along the rim, other larger spots across the midwing, and yellow found on the hind wing above.

The Palamedes Swallowtail is found throughout major swamps, such as the Everglades and Okefenokee.

It spends the winter months in both the caterpillar and chrysalis forms.

FACTS AND FEATURES

Habitat Swamps, wetlands, flooded woodlands.
Flight 1 to 3 broods, February to December.
Lifecycle notes Eggs are yellow green; green caterpillar has two pairs of orange eyespots with black pupils; chrysalis is green.
Host plants Sassafras, bay.
Nectar sources Pickerelweed.

3 to 5½ inches

ZEBRA SWALLOWTAIL
EURYTIDES MARCELLUS

The Zebra Swallowtail does not adapt well to human impact on the land, but it is quite common along some eastern rivers.

The winter months are spent in the chrysalis form, which is thicker than that of other Swallowtails.

These are white to pale blue-green with broad black stripes running front to back above. A bright red, broken stripe runs across the hind wing below. Zebra Swallowtails that emerge in spring are lighter in color, have shorter tails, and are tinier than those that emerge later in summer.

FACTS AND FEATURES

Habitat Wooded areas near water.
Flight 2 to 4 broods, March to December.
Lifecycle notes Eggs are green; caterpillar is green with black and yellow bands around length of body; bands vary greatly in width; chrysalis is green or brown.
Host plants Pawpaw and related species.
Nectar sources Unknown.

2¼ to 3½ inches

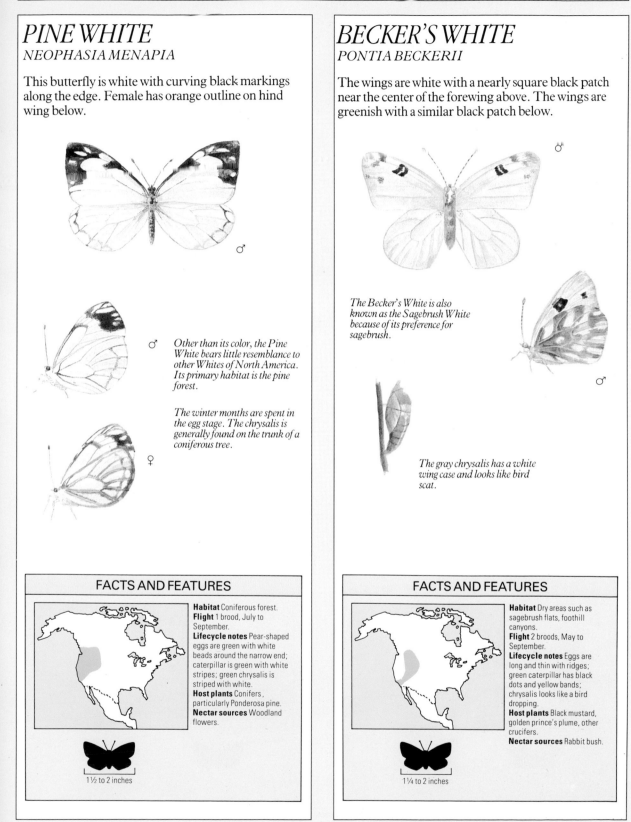

PINE WHITE
NEOPHASIA MENAPIA

This butterfly is white with curving black markings along the edge. Female has orange outline on hind wing below.

♂

♂

Other than its color, the Pine White bears little resemblance to other Whites of North America. Its primary habitat is the pine forest.

The winter months are spent in the egg stage. The chrysalis is generally found on the trunk of a coniferous tree.

♀

FACTS AND FEATURES

Habitat Coniferous forest.
Flight 1 brood, July to September.
Lifecycle notes Pear-shaped eggs are green with white beads around the narrow end; caterpillar is green with white stripes; green chrysalis is striped with white.
Host plants Conifers, particularly Ponderosa pine.
Nectar sources Woodland flowers.

1½ to 2 inches

BECKER'S WHITE
PONTIA BECKERII

The wings are white with a nearly square black patch near the center of the forewing above. The wings are greenish with a similar black patch below.

♂

The Becker's White is also known as the Sagebrush White because of its preference for sagebrush.

♂

The gray chrysalis has a white wing case and looks like bird scat.

FACTS AND FEATURES

Habitat Dry areas such as sagebrush flats, foothill canyons.
Flight 2 broods, May to September.
Lifecycle notes Eggs are long and thin with ridges; green caterpillar has black dots and yellow bands; chrysalis looks like a bird dropping.
Host plants Black mustard, golden prince's plume, other crucifers.
Nectar sources Rabbit bush.

1¼ to 2 inches

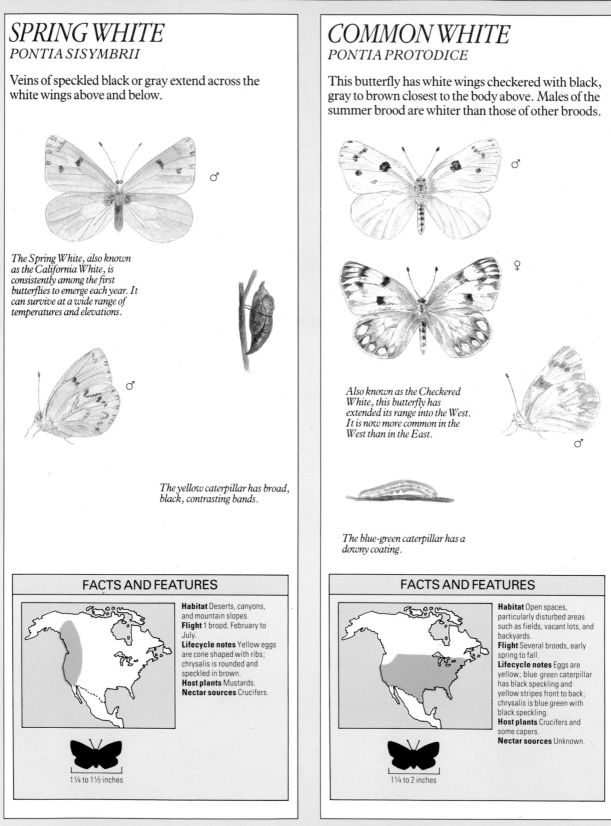

SPRING WHITE
PONTIA SISYMBRII

Veins of speckled black or gray extend across the white wings above and below.

♂

The Spring White, also known as the California White, is consistently among the first butterflies to emerge each year. It can survive at a wide range of temperatures and elevations.

♂

The yellow caterpillar has broad, black, contrasting bands.

FACTS AND FEATURES

Habitat Deserts, canyons, and mountain slopes.
Flight 1 brood, February to July.
Lifecycle notes Yellow eggs are cone shaped with ribs; chrysalis is rounded and speckled in brown.
Host plants Mustards.
Nectar sources Crucifers.

1¼ to 1½ inches

COMMON WHITE
PONTIA PROTODICE

This butterfly has white wings checkered with black, gray to brown closest to the body above. Males of the summer brood are whiter than those of other broods.

♂

♀

Also known as the Checkered White, this butterfly has extended its range into the West. It is now more common in the West than in the East.

♂

The blue-green caterpillar has a downy coating.

FACTS AND FEATURES

Habitat Open spaces, particularly disturbed areas such as fields, vacant lots, and backyards.
Flight Several broods, early spring to fall.
Lifecycle notes Eggs are yellow; blue green caterpillar has black speckling and yellow stripes front to back; chrysalis is blue green with black speckling.
Host plants Crucifers and some capers.
Nectar sources Unknown.

1¼ to 2 inches

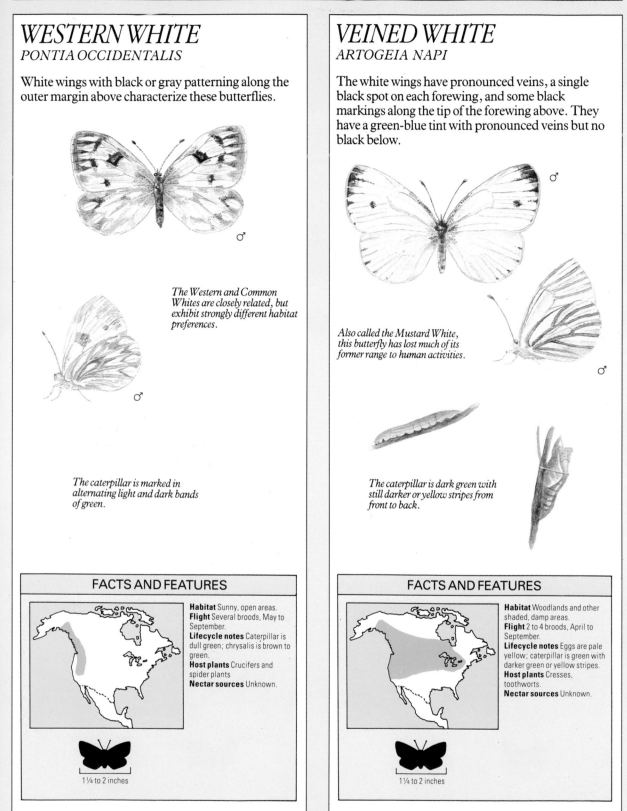

WESTERN WHITE
PONTIA OCCIDENTALIS

White wings with black or gray patterning along the outer margin above characterize these butterflies.

♂

The Western and Common Whites are closely related, but exhibit strongly different habitat preferences.

♂

The caterpillar is marked in alternating light and dark bands of green.

FACTS AND FEATURES

Habitat Sunny, open areas.
Flight Several broods, May to September.
Lifecycle notes Caterpillar is dull green; chrysalis is brown to green.
Host plants Crucifers and spider plants
Nectar sources Unknown.

1¼ to 2 inches

VEINED WHITE
ARTOGEIA NAPI

The white wings have pronounced veins, a single black spot on each forewing, and some black markings along the tip of the forewing above. They have a green-blue tint with pronounced veins but no black below.

♂

Also called the Mustard White, this butterfly has lost much of its former range to human activities.

♂

The caterpillar is dark green with still darker or yellow stripes from front to back.

FACTS AND FEATURES

Habitat Woodlands and other shaded, damp areas.
Flight 2 to 4 broods, April to September.
Lifecycle notes Eggs are pale yellow; caterpillar is green with darker green or yellow stripes.
Host plants Cresses, toothworts.
Nectar sources Unknown.

1¼ to 2 inches

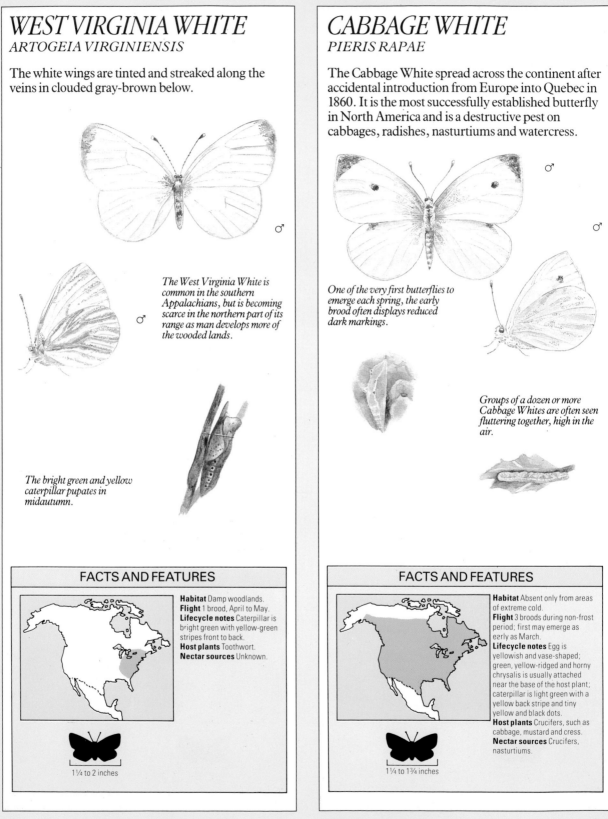

WEST VIRGINIA WHITE
ARTOGEIA VIRGINIENSIS

The white wings are tinted and streaked along the veins in clouded gray-brown below.

♂

The West Virginia White is common in the southern Appalachians, but is becoming scarce in the northern part of its range as man develops more of the wooded lands.

♂

The bright green and yellow caterpillar pupates in midautumn.

FACTS AND FEATURES

Habitat Damp woodlands.
Flight 1 brood, April to May.
Lifecycle notes Caterpillar is bright green with yellow-green stripes front to back.
Host plants Toothwort.
Nectar sources Unknown.

1¼ to 2 inches

CABBAGE WHITE
PIERIS RAPAE

The Cabbage White spread across the continent after accidental introduction from Europe into Quebec in 1860. It is the most successfully established butterfly in North America and is a destructive pest on cabbages, radishes, nasturtiums and watercress.

♂

♂

One of the very first butterflies to emerge each spring, the early brood often displays reduced dark markings.

Groups of a dozen or more Cabbage Whites are often seen fluttering together, high in the air.

FACTS AND FEATURES

Habitat Absent only from areas of extreme cold.
Flight 3 broods during non-frost period; first may emerge as early as March.
Lifecycle notes Egg is yellowish and vase-shaped; green, yellow-ridged and horny chrysalis is usually attached near the base of the host plant; caterpillar is light green with a yellow back stripe and tiny yellow and black dots.
Host plants Crucifers, such as cabbage, mustard and cress.
Nectar sources Crucifers, nasturtiums.

1¼ to 1¾ inches

GREAT SOUTHERN WHITE
ASCIA MONUSTE

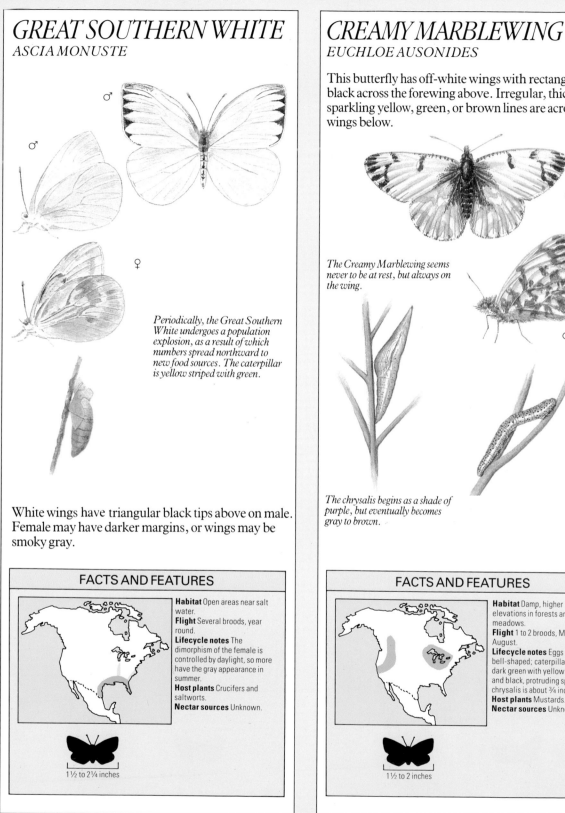

Periodically, the Great Southern White undergoes a population explosion, as a result of which numbers spread northward to new food sources. The caterpillar is yellow striped with green.

White wings have triangular black tips above on male. Female may have darker margins, or wings may be smoky gray.

FACTS AND FEATURES

Habitat Open areas near salt water.
Flight Several broods, year round.
Lifecycle notes The dimorphism of the female is controlled by daylight, so more have the gray appearance in summer.
Host plants Crucifers and saltworts.
Nectar sources Unknown.

1½ to 2¼ inches

CREAMY MARBLEWING
EUCHLOE AUSONIDES

This butterfly has off-white wings with rectangular black across the forewing above. Irregular, thick, sparkling yellow, green, or brown lines are across the wings below.

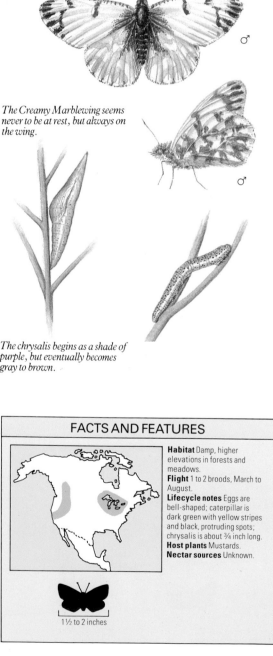

The Creamy Marblewing seems never to be at rest, but always on the wing.

The chrysalis begins as a shade of purple, but eventually becomes gray to brown.

FACTS AND FEATURES

Habitat Damp, higher elevations in forests and meadows.
Flight 1 to 2 broods, March to August.
Lifecycle notes Eggs are bell-shaped; caterpillar is dark green with yellow stripes and black, protruding spots; chrysalis is about ¾ inch long.
Host plants Mustards.
Nectar sources Unknown.

1½ to 2 inches

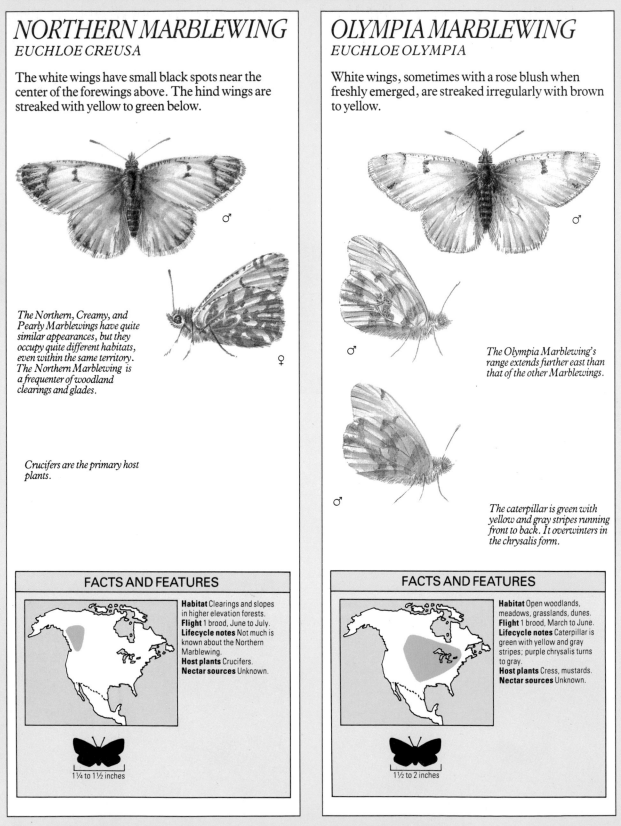

NORTHERN MARBLEWING
EUCHLOE CREUSA

The white wings have small black spots near the center of the forewings above. The hind wings are streaked with yellow to green below.

The Northern, Creamy, and Pearly Marblewings have quite similar appearances, but they occupy quite different habitats, even within the same territory. The Northern Marblewing is a frequenter of woodland clearings and glades.

Crucifers are the primary host plants.

♂

♀

FACTS AND FEATURES

Habitat Clearings and slopes in higher elevation forests.
Flight 1 brood, June to July.
Lifecycle notes Not much is known about the Northern Marblewing.
Host plants Crucifers.
Nectar sources Unknown.

1¼ to 1½ inches

OLYMPIA MARBLEWING
EUCHLOE OLYMPIA

White wings, sometimes with a rose blush when freshly emerged, are streaked irregularly with brown to yellow.

The Olympia Marblewing's range extends further east than that of the other Marblewings.

The caterpillar is green with yellow and gray stripes running front to back. It overwinters in the chrysalis form.

♂

♂

♂

FACTS AND FEATURES

Habitat Open woodlands, meadows, grasslands, dunes.
Flight 1 brood, March to June.
Lifecycle notes Caterpillar is green with yellow and gray stripes; purple chrysalis turns to gray.
Host plants Cress, mustards.
Nectar sources Unknown.

1½ to 2 inches

PEARLY MARBLEWING
EUCHLOE HYANTIS

White wings with speckled black doughnuts at the tips and pearly blue sheen over the entire wing above mark this butterfly.

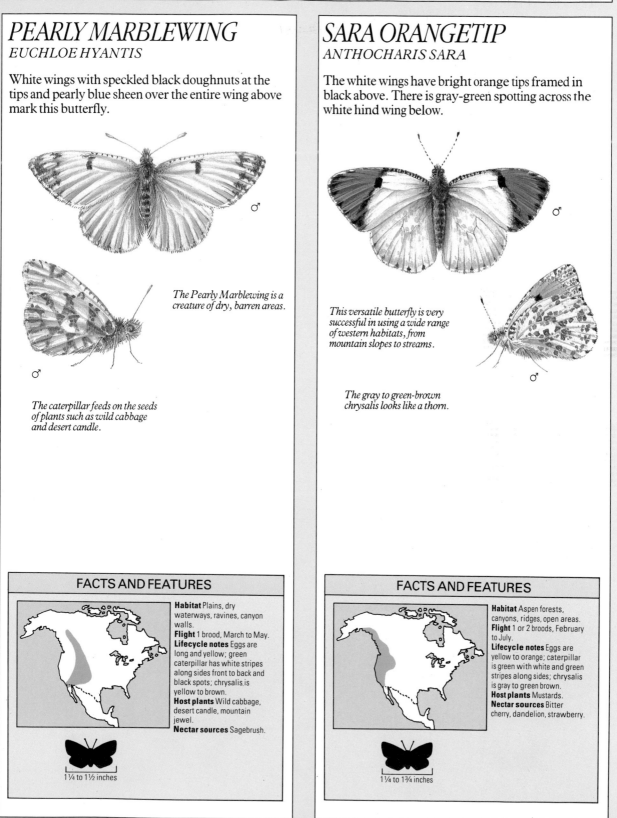

The Pearly Marblewing is a creature of dry, barren areas.

♂

The caterpillar feeds on the seeds of plants such as wild cabbage and desert candle.

SARA ORANGETIP
ANTHOCHARIS SARA

The white wings have bright orange tips framed in black above. There is gray-green spotting across the white hind wing below.

♂

This versatile butterfly is very successful in using a wide range of western habitats, from mountain slopes to streams.

♂

The gray to green-brown chrysalis looks like a thorn.

FACTS AND FEATURES

Habitat Plains, dry waterways, ravines, canyon walls.
Flight 1 brood, March to May.
Lifecycle notes Eggs are long and yellow; green caterpillar has white stripes along sides front to back and black spots; chrysalis is yellow to brown.
Host plants Wild cabbage, desert candle, mountain jewel.
Nectar sources Sagebrush.

1¼ to 1½ inches

FACTS AND FEATURES

Habitat Aspen forests, canyons, ridges, open areas.
Flight 1 or 2 broods, February to July.
Lifecycle notes Eggs are yellow to orange; caterpillar is green with white and green stripes along sides; chrysalis is gray to green brown.
Host plants Mustards.
Nectar sources Bitter cherry, dandelion, strawberry.

1¼ to 1¾ inches

FALCATE ORANGETIP
ANTHOCHARIS MIDEA

The white wings have an orange tip on the forewings of the male above. The female does not have the orange tip.

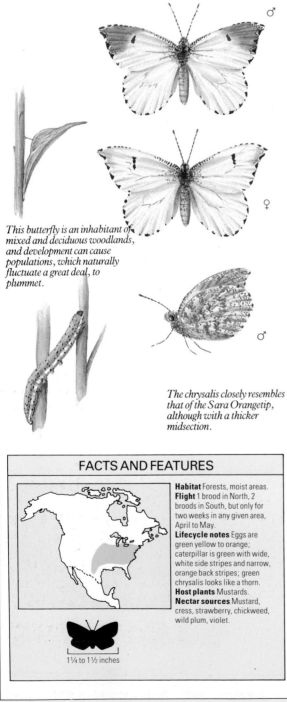

This butterfly is an inhabitant of mixed and deciduous woodlands, and development can cause populations, which naturally fluctuate a great deal, to plummet.

The chrysalis closely resembles that of the Sara Orangetip, although with a thicker midsection.

FACTS AND FEATURES

Habitat Forests, moist areas.
Flight 1 brood in North, 2 broods in South, but only for two weeks in any given area, April to May.
Lifecycle notes Eggs are green yellow to orange; caterpillar is green with wide, white side stripes and narrow, orange back stripes; green chrysalis looks like a thorn.
Host plants Mustards.
Nectar sources Mustard, cress, strawberry, chickweed, wild plum, violet.

1¼ to 1½ inches

CLODIUS PARNASSIAN
PARNASSIUS CLODIUS

The hind wings have red spots both above and below that vary through different geographical populations.

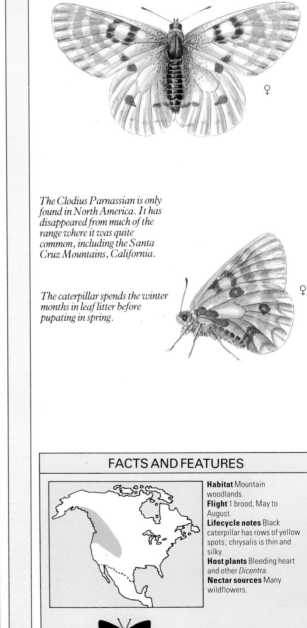

The Clodius Parnassian is only found in North America. It has disappeared from much of the range where it was quite common, including the Santa Cruz Mountains, California.

The caterpillar spends the winter months in leaf litter before pupating in spring.

FACTS AND FEATURES

Habitat Mountain woodlands.
Flight 1 brood, May to August.
Lifecycle notes Black caterpillar has rows of yellow spots; chrysalis is thin and silky.
Host plants Bleeding heart and other *Dicentra*.
Nectar sources Many wildflowers.

2¼ to 3 inches

COMMON SULPHUR
COLIAS PHILODICE

The pale yellow wings have black borders and one black dot on each forewing above. The greenish yellow wings below have a row of red-brown, irregular dots.

♂

♀

♂

The Common or Clouded Sulphur occasionally crosses with the Orange Sulphur, resulting in a butterfly with orange wing markings.

The Common Sulphur spends the winter months in its green chrysalis form.

FACTS AND FEATURES

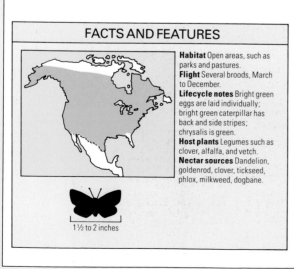

Habitat Open areas, such as parks and pastures.
Flight Several broods, March to December.
Lifecycle notes Bright green eggs are laid individually; bright green caterpillar has back and side stripes; chrysalis is green.
Host plants Legumes such as clover, alfalfa, and vetch.
Nectar sources Dandelion, goldenrod, clover, tickseed, phlox, milkweed, dogbane.

1½ to 2 inches

ORANGE SULPHUR
COLIAS EURYTHEME

♂

♀

The butterfly spends the winter months in its green chrysalis form.

The Orange Sulphur inhabits large areas of the continent due to the species' successful use of both wild and cultivated legumes.

♂

The gold to orange wings have a pinkish tint and black edges above. The orange or yellow wings have a red-circled silver spot on the hind wing and a row of brown spots below.

FACTS AND FEATURES

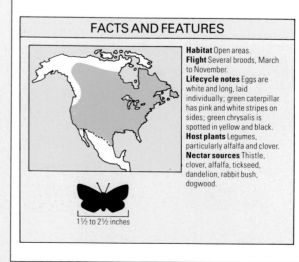

Habitat Open areas.
Flight Several broods, March to November.
Lifecycle notes Eggs are white and long, laid individually; green caterpillar has pink and white stripes on sides; green chrysalis is spotted in yellow and black.
Host plants Legumes, particularly alfalfa and clover.
Nectar sources Thistle, clover, alfalfa, tickseed, dandelion, rabbit bush, dogwood.

1½ to 2½ inches

QUEEN ALEXANDRA'S SULPHUR
COLIAS ALEXANDRA

The male is bright yellow with a brown fringe along the wing border above. The female is yellow or white with a noncontinuous border above. Both are shades of green below with a single, small cell spot on the hind wing.

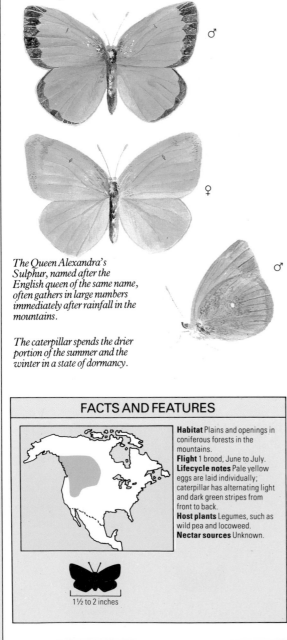

The Queen Alexandra's Sulphur, named after the English queen of the same name, often gathers in large numbers immediately after rainfall in the mountains.

The caterpillar spends the drier portion of the summer and the winter in a state of dormancy.

FACTS AND FEATURES

Habitat Plains and openings in coniferous forests in the mountains.
Flight 1 brood, June to July.
Lifecycle notes Pale yellow eggs are laid individually; caterpillar has alternating light and dark green stripes from front to back.
Host plants Legumes, such as wild pea and locoweed.
Nectar sources Unknown.

1½ to 2 inches

GREENLAND SULPHUR
COLIAS HECLA

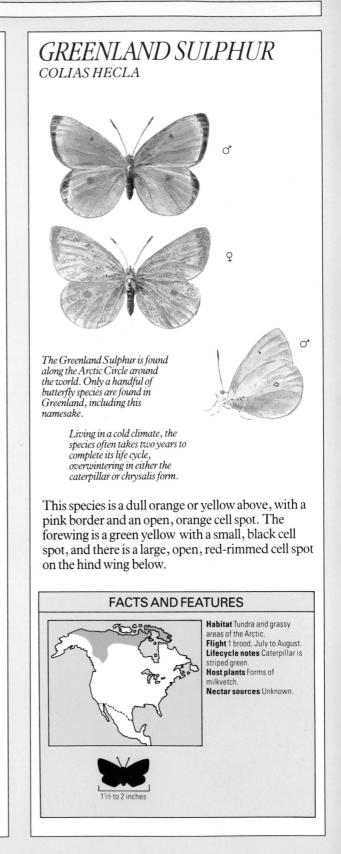

The Greenland Sulphur is found along the Arctic Circle around the world. Only a handful of butterfly species are found in Greenland, including this namesake.

Living in a cold climate, the species often takes two years to complete its life cycle, overwintering in either the caterpillar or chrysalis form.

This species is a dull orange or yellow above, with a pink border and an open, orange cell spot. The forewing is a green yellow with a small, black cell spot, and there is a large, open, red-rimmed cell spot on the hind wing below.

FACTS AND FEATURES

Habitat Tundra and grassy areas of the Arctic.
Flight 1 brood, July to August.
Lifecycle notes Caterpillar is striped green.
Host plants Forms of milkvetch.
Nectar sources Unknown.

1½ to 2 inches

LABRADOR SULPHUR
COLIAS NASTES

The male is pale green with a black and yellow border above. The female is yellow green with a paler border above. Both are dull yellow green with a cream cell spot on the hind wing below.

The Labrador Sulphur is strictly a northern species, found below the U.S.-Canadian border only in Washington and Montana.

The species spends the winter months in its caterpillar stage.

FACTS AND FEATURES

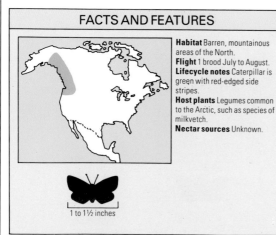

Habitat Barren, mountainous areas of the North.
Flight 1 brood July to August.
Lifecycle notes Caterpillar is green with red-edged side stripes.
Host plants Legumes common to the Arctic, such as species of milkvetch.
Nectar sources Unknown.

1 to 1½ inches

PINK-EDGED SULPHUR
COLIAS INTERIOR

This butterfly is yellow to yellow green with pink borders and an orange cell spot on the hind wing above and below.

Males of the Pink-edged Sulphur often gather in large numbers in damp areas.

The caterpillar is yellow green with red and pale blue stripes.

FACTS AND FEATURES

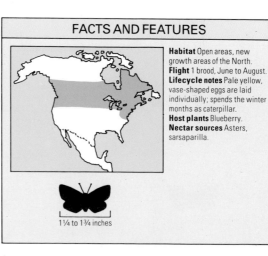

Habitat Open areas, new growth areas of the North.
Flight 1 brood, June to August.
Lifecycle notes Pale yellow, vase-shaped eggs are laid individually; spends the winter months as caterpillar.
Host plants Blueberry.
Nectar sources Asters, sarsaparilla.

1¼ to 1¾ inches

BLUEBERRY SULPHUR
COLIAS PELIDNE

A light to orange-yellow, with a pale pink edge and a white, pink-outlined cell spot on the hind wing above and below, characterize this butterfly.

♂

♀

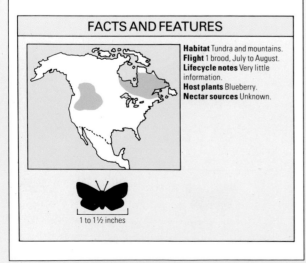

♂

Very little has been recorded about the Blueberry Sulphur, which can be observed in several national parks in the Western United States.

The caterpillar and chrysalis have not been described at this point.

FACTS AND FEATURES

Habitat Tundra and mountains.
Flight 1 brood, July to August.
Lifecycle notes Very little information.
Host plants Blueberry.
Nectar sources Unknown.

1 to 1½ inches

GREAT NORTHERN SULPHUR
COLIAS GIGANTEA

This butterfly is yellow with a gray border above; the border is interrupted in females. It is yellow with a pink border and a pink-rimmed cell spot on the hind wing below.

♂

♂

The Great Northern Sulphur, as the name implies, is larger than most, with the exception of the Giant Sulphurs.

Winter months are spent in the green-brown caterpillar stage.

FACTS AND FEATURES

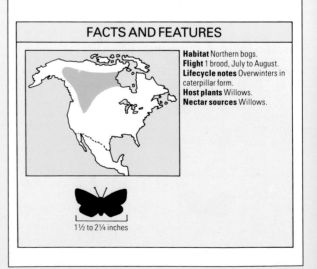

Habitat Northern bogs.
Flight 1 brood, July to August.
Lifecycle notes Overwinters in caterpillar form.
Host plants Willows.
Nectar sources Willows.

1½ to 2¼ inches

DOGFACE BUTTERFLY
ZERENE CESONIA

A pair of yellow-orange poodles or cocker spaniels, each with black eye, face out from the body on the otherwise black forewing above. Late autumn and winter forms of adults are rose-flushed beneath.

Looking like its close cousin, the California Dogface, the Dogface Butterfly is widespread throughout the South, while the former is restricted to the Western United States.

The caterpillar is striped green and black from front to back, with lateral bands of yellow.

FACTS AND FEATURES

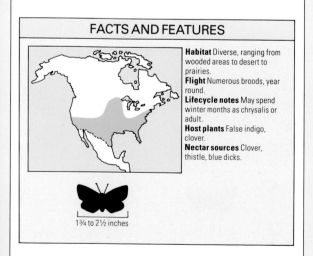

Habitat Diverse, ranging from wooded areas to desert to prairies.
Flight Numerous broods, year round.
Lifecycle notes May spend winter months as chrysalis or adult.
Host plants False indigo, clover.
Nectar sources Clover, thistle, blue dicks.

1¾ to 2½ inches

CLOUDLESS GIANT SULPHUR
PHOEBIS SENNAE

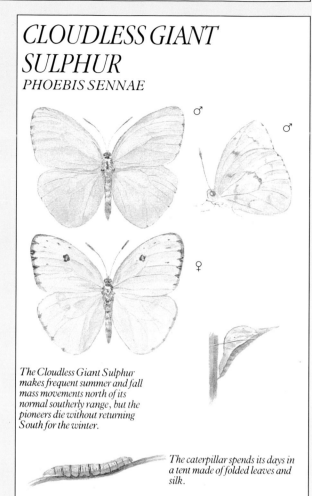

The Cloudless Giant Sulphur makes frequent summer and fall mass movements north of its normal southerly range, but the pioneers die without returning South for the winter.

The caterpillar spends its days in a tent made of folded leaves and silk.

The male is yellow above and yellow with brown intermixed below. The female is yellow or white above and below, with a black-rimmed, open diamond or square in the forewing cell.

FACTS AND FEATURES

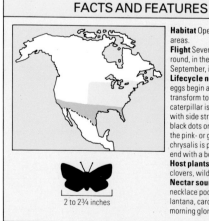

Habitat Open spaces, shore areas.
Flight Several broods, year round, in the South; 2, June to September, in the North.
Lifecycle notes Vase-shaped eggs begin as white but transform to orange; the caterpillar is yellow green with side stripes and rows of black dots on the back; the pink- or green-striped chrysalis is pointed at each end with a bend in the middle.
Host plants Legumes, clovers, wild peas.
Nectar sources Milkweed, necklace pod, firebush, lantana, cardinal flower, morning glory.

2 to 2¾ inches

ORANGE GIANT SULPHUR
PHOEBIS AGARITHE

The male is yellow orange above and below. The female is yellow orange to pink with brown dots above and below. Both have an irregular brown line through the middle of the forewing below.

Although the Orange Giant Sulphur frequents puddles and flowers, it is not often seen.

The caterpillar is green with lighter stripes on the sides. The chrysalis is green with yellow and purple stripes.

FACTS AND FEATURES

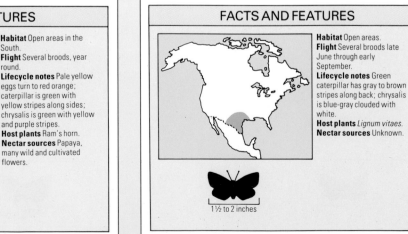

Habitat Open areas in the South.
Flight Several broods, year round.
Lifecycle notes Pale yellow eggs turn to red orange; caterpillar is green with yellow stripes along sides; chrysalis is green with yellow and purple stripes.
Host plants Ram's horn.
Nectar sources Papaya, many wild and cultivated flowers.

2¼ to 2¾ inches

LYSIDE
KRICOGONIA LYSIDE

The Lyside is white, cream, or yellow above, and green below with a gold hint near the body on the forewing.

The Lyside is commonly found in Texas, but it makes regular forays into wet areas to the north.

The caterpillar is green with gray to silver stripes rimmed in brown along the back. The chrysalis is a clouded blue gray.

FACTS AND FEATURES

Habitat Open areas.
Flight Several broods late June through early September.
Lifecycle notes Green caterpillar has gray to brown stripes along back; chrysalis is blue-gray clouded with white.
Host plants *Lignum vitaes.*
Nectar sources Unknown.

1½ to 2 inches

LITTLE YELLOW
EUREMA LISA

This butterfly is lemon yellow (sometimes white in the female) with a double border of purple and pink above. It is yellow splotched with purple and pink below, and has a large pink eyespot near the border of the hind wing and the same double border.

The Little Yellow is common throughout the eastern U.S., migrating to northern states after the winter.

The caterpillar is green with very fine hairs covering its body.

FACTS AND FEATURES

Habitat Widespread over open areas.
Flight Several broods, year round in South, May to October in North.
Lifecycle notes Eggs are so small as to be nearly impossible to identify; caterpillar has white side stripes and very fine hairs.
Host plants Legumes, clovers.
Nectar sources Unknown.

1 to 1½ inches

SLEEPY ORANGE
EUREMA NICIPPE

Yellow orange with a thick gray to black border (that is shortened in many females) and a black cell spot on the forewing above, mark this butterfly. It is lighter, with irregular red-brown patches below,

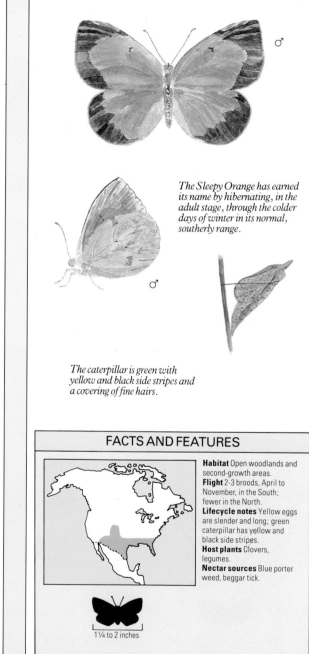

The Sleepy Orange has earned its name by hibernating, in the adult stage, through the colder days of winter in its normal, southerly range.

The caterpillar is green with yellow and black side stripes and a covering of fine hairs.

FACTS AND FEATURES

Habitat Open woodlands and second-growth areas.
Flight 2-3 broods, April to November, in the South; fewer in the North.
Lifecycle notes Yellow eggs are slender and long; green caterpillar has yellow and black side stripes.
Host plants Clovers, legumes.
Nectar sources Blue porter weed, beggar tick.

1¼ to 2 inches

FAIRY YELLOW
EUREMA DAIRA

The Fairy Yellow is pale yellow with black tips and borders above. It has a red-brown hind wing in the wet season (winter) form below.

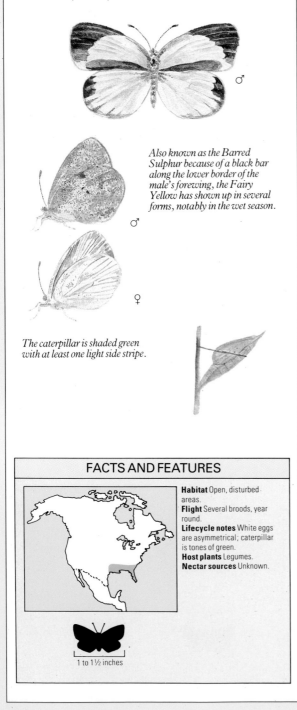

♂

Also known as the Barred Sulphur because of a black bar along the lower border of the male's forewing, the Fairy Yellow has shown up in several forms, notably in the wet season.

♂

♀

The caterpillar is shaded green with at least one light side stripe.

FACTS AND FEATURES

Habitat Open, disturbed areas.
Flight Several broods, year round.
Lifecycle notes White eggs are asymmetrical; caterpillar is tones of green.
Host plants Legumes.
Nectar sources Unknown.

1 to 1½ inches

DWARF YELLOW
NATHALIS IOLE

This butterfly is yellow with black tips on the forewings and black bars along the borders above; black is more pronounced on the female.

♂

♂

The Dwarf Yellow makes long migrations from Mexico into mid-Canada each year, only to have its northerly populations die off each fall.

The caterpillar is green with purple stripes on its back, and black and yellow stripes on its sides. The green chrysalis is smooth skinned.

FACTS AND FEATURES

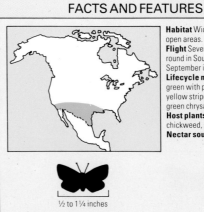

Habitat Widespread across open areas.
Flight Several broods year round in South; June to September in North.
Lifecycle notes Caterpillar is green with purple, black, and yellow stripes front to back; green chrysalis.
Host plants Marigold, chickweed, sneezeweed.
Nectar sources Marigold.

½ to 1¼ inches

LITTLE METALMARK
CALEPHELIS VIRGINIENSIS

♂

♂

The Little Metalmark is widespread throughout the Deep South, but in scattered, localized populations.

The caterpillar is green with a relatively flat shape. The chrysalis is brown, buried in leaf litter.

The male is deep burnt orange with many irregular scalloped bands of bluish black, a regular curving submarginal band of silvery white bordered in black, and a similar zigzagging band near the middle of the wing above. The female is a lighter shade above. Both are light orange with black speckling below.

FACTS AND FEATURES

Habitat Open areas and edges of wooded areas, generally damp.
Flight Several broods, year round in South, May to August in North.
Lifecycle notes Eggs are yellow green and flattened; caterpillar is green and flattened; chrysalis is brown.
Host plants Thistle.
Nectar sources Unknown.

½ to ¾ inch

SWAMP METALMARK
CALEPHELIS MUTICUM

This butterfly is reddish orange with scalloped bands of gray and black, and submarginal bands of metallic silver-white with an inner band, somewhat zigzagging, above. It is orange with black speckling below.

♂

♂

While the very similar Northern Metalmark prefers the dry, open areas, the Swamp Metalmark is true to its name in choice of habitat.

The flattened caterpillar is green with long, fine hairs. The chrysalis is also quite hairy.

FACTS AND FEATURES

Habitat Wet, wooded, and weedy areas.
Flight 1 brood, July to August.
Lifecycle notes Eggs are highly ribbed; caterpillar is flattened and green with few black spots; chrysalis is hairy.
Host plants Thistle.
Nectar sources Unknown.

¾ to 1¼ inches

SNOUT BUTTERFLY
LIBYTHEANA BACHMANII

The long, pointed snout (palpi), jutting forward from the head is the distinguishing feature. The butterfly is pale orange fading into black and white patches, giving the appearance of curved feathers, with varying wide borders of pale gray, above. The forewing is orange at the body, followed by a white patch encircled by a wide black band and ending in gray; the hindwing is gray, below.

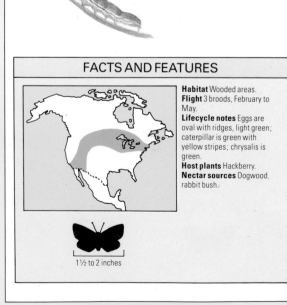

The Snout Butterfly is one of only two representatives of its family in North America. The other is the Southern Snout, which is restricted to the extreme Southwest.

The winter months are spent in the green chrysalis stage. The caterpillar is green with yellow stripes.

FACTS AND FEATURES

Habitat Wooded areas.
Flight 3 broods, February to May.
Lifecycle notes Eggs are oval with ridges, light green; caterpillar is green with yellow stripes; chrysalis is green.
Host plants Hackberry.
Nectar sources Dogwood, rabbit bush.

1½ to 2 inches

GULF FRITILLARY
AGRAULIS VANILLAE

This butterfly is brilliant orange with tadpolelike streaks of black (the head of the tadpole at the trailing edge) throughout; with several white, black-edged spots near the costa of the forewing, above. The orange forewing is tan at the apex corner, with distinct white, black-edged patches; it is tan with distinct white, black-edged patches on the hindwing, below.

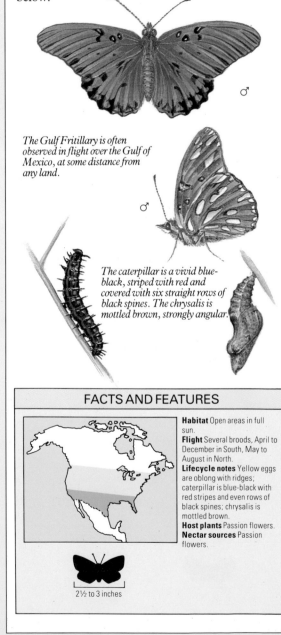

The Gulf Fritillary is often observed in flight over the Gulf of Mexico, at some distance from any land.

The caterpillar is a vivid blue-black, striped with red and covered with six straight rows of black spines. The chrysalis is mottled brown, strongly angular.

FACTS AND FEATURES

Habitat Open areas in full sun.
Flight Several broods, April to December in South, May to August in North.
Lifecycle notes Yellow eggs are oblong with ridges; caterpillar is blue-black with red stripes and even rows of black spines; chrysalis is mottled brown.
Host plants Passion flowers.
Nectar sources Passion flowers.

2½ to 3 inches

VARIEGATED FRITILLARY
EUPTOIETA CLAUDIA

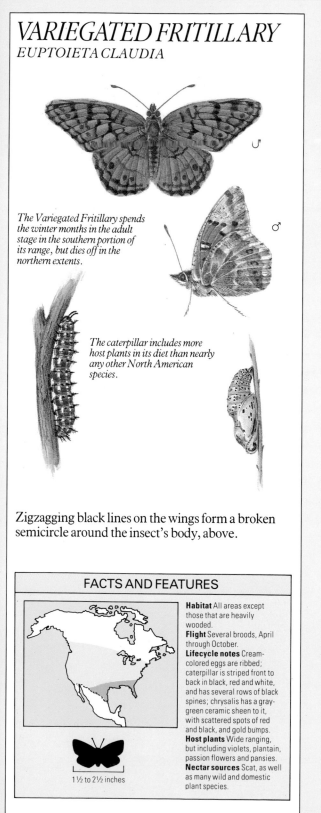

The Variegated Fritillary spends the winter months in the adult stage in the southern portion of its range, but dies off in the northern extents.

The caterpillar includes more host plants in its diet than nearly any other North American species.

Zigzagging black lines on the wings form a broken semicircle around the insect's body, above.

FACTS AND FEATURES

Habitat All areas except those that are heavily wooded.
Flight Several broods, April through October.
Lifecycle notes Cream-colored eggs are ribbed; caterpillar is striped front to back in black, red and white, and has several rows of black spines; chrysalis has a gray-green ceramic sheen to it, with scattered spots of red and black, and gold bumps.
Host plants Wide ranging, but including violets, plantain, passion flowers and pansies.
Nectar sources Scat, as well as many wild and domestic plant species.

1½ to 2½ inches

DIANA
SPEYERIA DIANA

The male is black with a broad border of brilliant orange, with small black dots inside, along the margins, above. The female is duller black to dark gray with bands of white and pale orange patches on the forewing and bands of light blue patches on the hindwing, above. The male is duller orange with black patches, below. The female is black to brown-black with white patches, below.

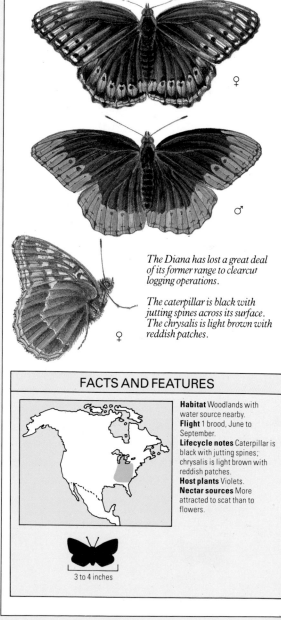

The Diana has lost a great deal of its former range to clearcut logging operations.

The caterpillar is black with jutting spines across its surface. The chrysalis is light brown with reddish patches.

FACTS AND FEATURES

Habitat Woodlands with water source nearby.
Flight 1 brood, June to September.
Lifecycle notes Caterpillar is black with jutting spines; chrysalis is light brown with reddish patches.
Host plants Violets.
Nectar sources More attracted to scat than to flowers.

3 to 4 inches

GREAT SPANGLED FRITILLARY
SPEYERIA CYBELE

Above, this butterfly is light orange to yellow, and brown to gray-brown in a rough circle nearest the body, with several zigzagging black bands, followed by a band of black dots and a band of curving black patches. Below, it is orange to red-brown with bands similar to those above on the forewing, and bands of yellow then silver next to a margin border of brown.

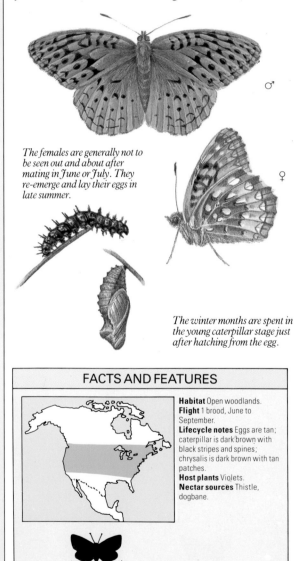

The females are generally not to be seen out and about after mating in June or July. They re-emerge and lay their eggs in late summer.

The winter months are spent in the young caterpillar stage just after hatching from the egg.

FACTS AND FEATURES

Habitat Open woodlands.
Flight 1 brood, June to September.
Lifecycle notes Eggs are tan; caterpillar is dark brown with black stripes and spines; chrysalis is dark brown with tan patches.
Host plants Violets.
Nectar sources Thistle, dogbane.

2 to 3 inches

APHRODITE
SPEYERIA APHRODITE

This butterfly is dull orange above with irregular and broken bands of black, followed by a row of black dots and scalloped black and orange bands along the outer margins. It is brown to brown orange with broken bands of black on the forewing and bands of bright white patches on both wings below.

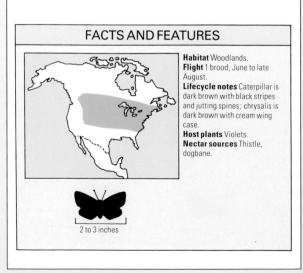

Aphrodites often gather in large numbers at nectar sources, such as thistle and dogbane.

The winter months are spent in the caterpillar stage.

FACTS AND FEATURES

Habitat Woodlands.
Flight 1 brood, June to late August.
Lifecycle notes Caterpillar is dark brown with black stripes and jutting spines; chrysalis is dark brown with cream wing case.
Host plants Violets.
Nectar sources Thistle, dogbane.

2 to 3 inches

REGAL FRITILLARY
SPEYERIA IDALIA

This butterfly is orange with several black zigzagging patches near the costa of the forewing and two bands of black patches across the entire forewing; there is blue gray with two bands of white patches on the hind wing above. There are similar markings on the forewing, and the hind wing is brown with a profusion of large white patches below.

Agriculture is destroying much of the Regal Fritillary's grassy habitat and thus shrinking its once large range.

The winter months are spent in the light brown caterpillar stage. The chrysalis is also light brown.

FACTS AND FEATURES

Habitat Moist woodland and grassland areas.
Flight 1 brood, June to September.
Lifecycle notes Eggs are light brown; caterpillar is light brown with black patches and orange spines; chrysalis is light brown with darker patches.
Host plants Violets.
Nectar sources Milkweed, thistle.

2¾ to 3¾ inches

EDWARDS' FRITILLARY
SPEYERIA EDWARDSII

The Edwards' Fritillary is a common species across its range in the West.

Very little information has been documented on the various life stages of the Edwards' Fritillary.

The butterfly is yellow orange with zigzagging bands of black and a scalloped border of brown, with an orange spot in each scallop above. It is pale gray-tan below with many large blue-white patches across both wings and a few cream patches near the costa of the forewing.

FACTS AND FEATURES

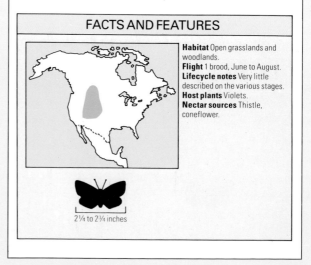

Habitat Open grasslands and woodlands.
Flight 1 brood, June to August.
Lifecycle notes Very little described on the various stages.
Host plants Violets.
Nectar sources Thistle, coneflower.

2¼ to 2¾ inches

ZERENE FRITILLARY
SPEYERIA ZERENE

This butterfly is red orange with brown shading near its body, looping black bands that resemble musical notes near the center of the wings, and scattered black patches and bars throughout above. Below, there is orange fading into brown as the distance from body increases, with black markings similar to those above.

The markings of the Zerene Fritillary vary strongly from one local population to the next.

The winter months are spent in the newly hatched caterpillar stage.

FACTS AND FEATURES

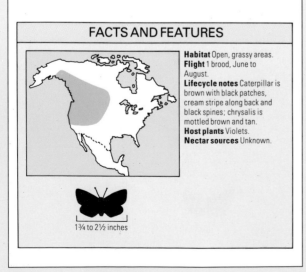

Habitat Open, grassy areas.
Flight 1 brood, June to August.
Lifecycle notes Caterpillar is brown with black patches, cream stripe along back and black spines; chrysalis is mottled brown and tan.
Host plants Violets.
Nectar sources Unknown.

1¾ to 2½ inches

CALLIPPE FRITILLARY
SPEYERIA CALLIPPE

The Callippe Fritillary is orange to yellow orange with broken but regular bands of black patches, dots, and bars above. It has black zigzagging bands and a few metallic silver patches near the apex of the forewing, and curving bands of metallic silver patches across the hind wing below.

The males of the Callippe Fritillary defend hilltop territories from all comers.

The winter months are spent in the newly hatched caterpillar stage.

FACTS AND FEATURES

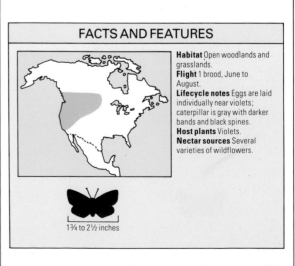

Habitat Open woodlands and grasslands.
Flight 1 brood, June to August.
Lifecycle notes Eggs are laid individually near violets; caterpillar is gray with darker bands and black spines.
Host plants Violets.
Nectar sources Several varieties of wildflowers.

1¾ to 2½ inches

ATLANTIS FRITILLARY
SPEYERIA ATLANTIS

Above, this butterfly is bright orange with broken bands of black, a black submarginal border, and a thin marginal border of white bars. There are shades of brown orange with a scalloped band of silver patches along the margins below.

The Atlantis Fritillary is a widespread species, with many color variations across the continent in a confusing assortment of localized populations.

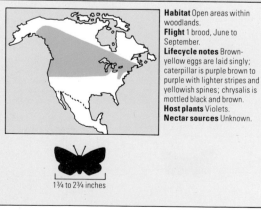

The winter months are spent in the caterpillar stage. The chrysalis is mottled black and brown.

FACTS AND FEATURES

Habitat Open areas within woodlands.
Flight 1 brood, June to September.
Lifecycle notes Brown-yellow eggs are laid singly; caterpillar is purple brown to purple with lighter stripes and yellowish spines; chrysalis is mottled black and brown.
Host plants Violets.
Nectar sources Unknown.

1¾ to 2¾ inches

MORMON FRITILLARY
SPEYERIA MORMONIA

This butterfly is orange with irregular bands of black, some forming circular, enclosed shapes near the costa of the forewing; the colors are more vivid in the female above. It has a greenish tint with a black pattern from above repeated on the forewing, and there are large silver patches across the hind wing below.

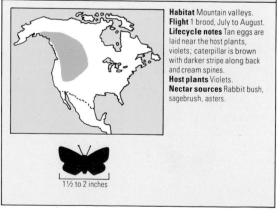

The Mormon Fritillary is often seen in large congregations at its various nectar sources in mountain valleys.

The caterpillar is brown with a darker stripe along its back and cream spines.

FACTS AND FEATURES

Habitat Mountain valleys.
Flight 1 brood, July to August.
Lifecycle notes Tan eggs are laid near the host plants, violets; caterpillar is brown with darker stripe along back and cream spines.
Host plants Violets.
Nectar sources Rabbit bush, sagebrush, asters.

1½ to 2 inches

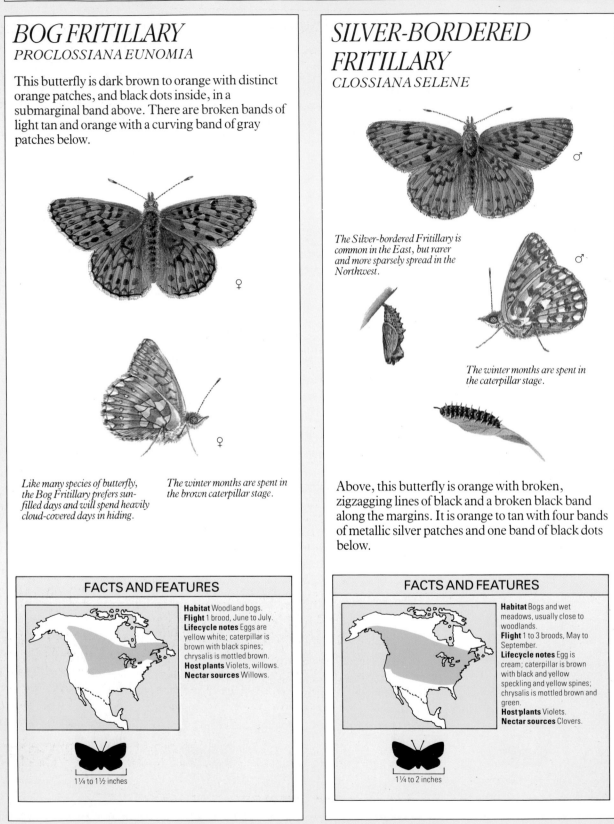

BOG FRITILLARY
PROCLOSSIANA EUNOMIA

This butterfly is dark brown to orange with distinct orange patches, and black dots inside, in a submarginal band above. There are broken bands of light tan and orange with a curving band of gray patches below.

♀

♀

Like many species of butterfly, the Bog Fritillary prefers sun-filled days and will spend heavily cloud-covered days in hiding.

The winter months are spent in the brown caterpillar stage.

FACTS AND FEATURES

Habitat Woodland bogs.
Flight 1 brood, June to July.
Lifecycle notes Eggs are yellow white; caterpillar is brown with black spines; chrysalis is mottled brown.
Host plants Violets, willows.
Nectar sources Willows.

1¼ to 1½ inches

SILVER-BORDERED FRITILLARY
CLOSSIANA SELENE

♂

The Silver-bordered Fritillary is common in the East, but rarer and more sparsely spread in the Northwest.

♂

The winter months are spent in the caterpillar stage.

Above, this butterfly is orange with broken, zigzagging lines of black and a broken black band along the margins. It is orange to tan with four bands of metallic silver patches and one band of black dots below.

FACTS AND FEATURES

Habitat Bogs and wet meadows, usually close to woodlands.
Flight 1 to 3 broods, May to September.
Lifecycle notes Egg is cream; caterpillar is brown with black and yellow speckling and yellow spines; chrysalis is mottled brown and green.
Host plants Violets.
Nectar sources Clovers.

1¼ to 2 inches

MEADOW FRITILLARY
CLOSSIANA BELLONA

This butterfly is orange with zigzagging bands of solid black, and it also has spots and patches. The tip of the forewing bulges outward above, and is orange with the same black pattern and a metallic brown to tan tip. The hind wing below is orange to tan-gray with metallic dusting.

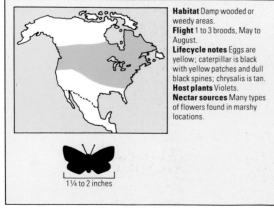

The Meadow Fritillary has a fast, darting flight.

The winter months are spent in the black caterpillar stage.

FACTS AND FEATURES

Habitat Damp wooded or weedy areas.
Flight 1 to 3 broods, May to August.
Lifecycle notes Eggs are yellow; caterpillar is black with yellow patches and dull black spines; chrysalis is tan.
Host plants Violets.
Nectar sources Many types of flowers found in marshy locations.

1¼ to 2 inches

FRIGGA'S FRITILLARY
CLOSSIANA FRIGGA

Orange with zigzagging bands of black, this butterfly is marked with curved bands of black dots and patches near the margins above. It is orange with a similar but paler black pattern and a few cream patches at the outer margin on the forewing; it is orange with large cream patches and a purplish tint on the hind wing below.

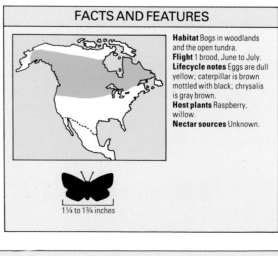

The name of the Frigga's Fritillary is derived from that of Frigga, wife of the Nordic god Odin.

The winter months are spent in the gray-brown chrysalis stage. The caterpillar is brown, mottled with black.

FACTS AND FEATURES

Habitat Bogs in woodlands and the open tundra.
Flight 1 brood, June to July.
Lifecycle notes Eggs are dull yellow; caterpillar is brown mottled with black; chrysalis is gray brown.
Host plants Raspberry, willow.
Nectar sources Unknown.

1¼ to 1¾ inches

65

DINGY ARCTIC FRITILLARY
CLOSSIANA IMPROBA

This butterfly is characterized by shades of brown with distinct, darker bands, most noticeable near the costa of the forewing above. It is pale orange on the forewing with almost imperceptible brown bands and dull orange brown to yellow with a white patch near the costa on the hind wing below.

♂

♂

One of the less colorful Fritillaries, the aptly named Dingy Arctic Fritillary does most of its traveling on the ground.

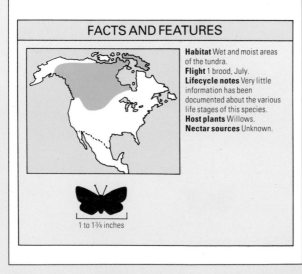

Very little is known about this butterfly of the far North, but the winter months are spent in the caterpillar stage.

FACTS AND FEATURES

Habitat Wet and moist areas of the tundra.
Flight 1 brood, July.
Lifecycle notes Very little information has been documented about the various life stages of this species.
Host plants Willows.
Nectar sources Unknown.

1 to 1¾ inches

WESTERN MEADOW FRITILLARY
CLOSSIANA EPITHORE

This butterfly is bright orange with zigzagging bands of dull black, with one circular patch open in the middle near the body on the forewing, and a broken band of thin white along the margins above. It is brown orange with a similar black pattern on the forewing and there are mottled shades of brown on the hind wing below.

♀

The Western Meadow Fritillary is a successful colonizer, able to utilize many different habitats.

♂

Very little information has been collected about the various life stages of this butterfly.

FACTS AND FEATURES

Habitat Damp, open areas in woodlands or meadows.
Flight 1 brood, May to August.
Lifecycle notes Very little has been described about the life stages of this species; winter months are spent in the caterpillar stage.
Host plants Violets.
Nectar sources Several species of wildflowers, varying by locale.

1¼ to 1¾ inches

FREYA'S FRITILLARY
CLOSSIANA FREIJA

Above, this butterfly is brown orange with zigzagging bands of black and bands of black spots. It has an orange forewing; yellow brown with scalloped bands of red-brown and white; there is a large, white patch near the center and a submarginal band of white patches below.

Freya's Fritillary is named for the Nordic goddess of love and beauty.

The harsh winter months of the North are spent in the mottled brown caterpillar stage.

FACTS AND FEATURES

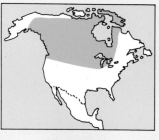

Habitat Moist areas in woodlands and on the tundra.
Flight 1 brood, May to June.
Lifecycle notes Eggs are light brown; caterpillar is mottled brown with darker spines; chrysalis is mottled brown.
Host plants Blueberry, bearberry.
Nectar sources Blueberry.

1 to 1½ inches

TITANIA'S FRITILLARY
CLOSSIANA TITANIA

Titania's Fritillary is burnt orange with dull brown next to its body; there are broken zigzagging bands of black, bands of black spots and patches, and thin white bars along the outer margins above. The forewing is similar to the above; the hind wing is red brown with a yellow-white band below.

In medieval folklore, Titania was the queen of the fairies. Her namesake is a widespread species, well able to take advantage of localized conditions. This species is also known as the Purple Lesser Fritillary.

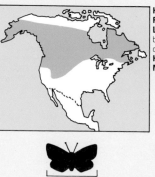

The winter months are spent in the mottled brown caterpillar stage.

FACTS AND FEATURES

Habitat Moist areas.
Flight 1 brood, June to July.
Lifecycle notes Egg is yellow brown with strong ridges; caterpillar is mottled brown.
Host plants Willows, violets.
Nectar sources Unknown.

1¼ to 1¾ inches

QUESTION MARK
POLYGONIA INTERROGATIONIS

The Question Mark is orange with scattered black patches and spots; there is a thin but brilliant purple blue border along the outer edges of the heavily angled wings above. There are shades of tan and brown with a drabber purple blue border along the outer edges and the namesake cream question mark in the cell of the hind wing below.

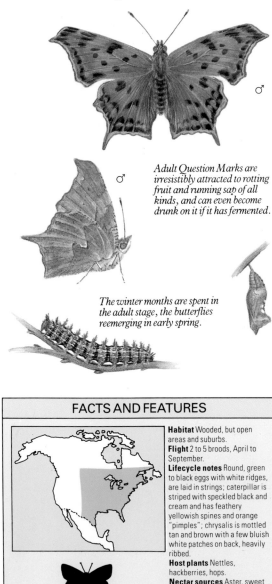

Adult Question Marks are irresistibly attracted to rotting fruit and running sap of all kinds, and can even become drunk on it if it has fermented.

The winter months are spent in the adult stage, the butterflies reemerging in early spring.

FACTS AND FEATURES

Habitat Wooded, but open areas and suburbs.
Flight 2 to 5 broods, April to September.
Lifecycle notes Round, green to black eggs with white ridges, are laid in strings; caterpillar is striped with speckled black and cream and has feathery yellowish spines and orange "pimples"; chrysalis is mottled tan and brown with a few bluish white patches on back, heavily ribbed.
Host plants Nettles, hackberries, hops.
Nectar sources Aster, sweet pepperbush, rotting fruit, running sap.

2¼ to 2¾ inches

COMMA
POLYGONIA COMMA

The Comma is orange with sparsely scattered black patches and spots; it has a brilliant purple blue border, most noticeable along the hind wing's outer edge above. It is tan with a duller purple blue border on both wings and its namesake, a cream, black-edged comma, is in the cell of the hind wing below.

The male Comma is quick to attack anything that moves into its territory, but the attack is totally a bluff. It is also called the Hop Merchant.

The winter months are spent in the adult stage.

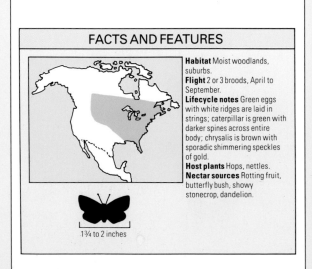

FACTS AND FEATURES

Habitat Moist woodlands, suburbs.
Flight 2 or 3 broods, April to September.
Lifecycle notes Green eggs with white ridges are laid in strings; caterpillar is green with darker spines across entire body; chrysalis is brown with sporadic shimmering speckles of gold.
Host plants Hops, nettles.
Nectar sources Rotting fruit, butterfly bush, showy stonecrop, dandelion.

1¾ to 2 inches

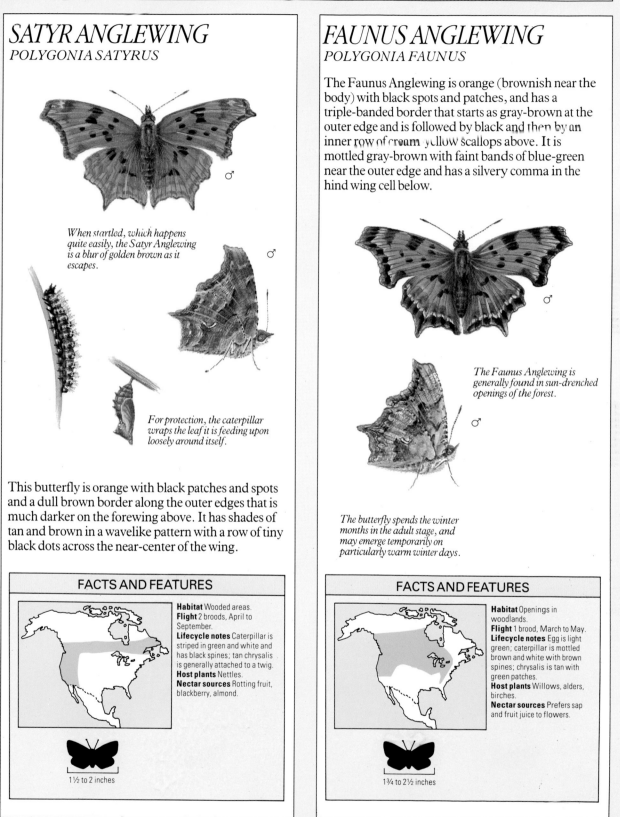

SATYR ANGLEWING
POLYGONIA SATYRUS

When startled, which happens quite easily, the Satyr Anglewing is a blur of golden brown as it escapes.

♂

♂

For protection, the caterpillar wraps the leaf it is feeding upon loosely around itself.

This butterfly is orange with black patches and spots and a dull brown border along the outer edges that is much darker on the forewing above. It has shades of tan and brown in a wavelike pattern with a row of tiny black dots across the near-center of the wing.

FACTS AND FEATURES

Habitat Wooded areas.
Flight 2 broods, April to September.
Lifecycle notes Caterpillar is striped in green and white and has black spines; tan chrysalis is generally attached to a twig.
Host plants Nettles.
Nectar sources Rotting fruit, blackberry, almond.

1½ to 2 inches

FAUNUS ANGLEWING
POLYGONIA FAUNUS

The Faunus Anglewing is orange (brownish near the body) with black spots and patches, and has a triple-banded border that starts as gray-brown at the outer edge and is followed by black and then by an inner row of cream-yellow scallops above. It is mottled gray-brown with faint bands of blue-green near the outer edge and has a silvery comma in the hind wing cell below.

♂

The Faunus Anglewing is generally found in sun-drenched openings of the forest.

♂

The butterfly spends the winter months in the adult stage, and may emerge temporarily on particularly warm winter days.

FACTS AND FEATURES

Habitat Openings in woodlands.
Flight 1 brood, March to May.
Lifecycle notes Egg is light green; caterpillar is mottled brown and white with brown spines; chrysalis is tan with green patches.
Host plants Willows, alders, birches.
Nectar sources Prefers sap and fruit juice to flowers.

1¾ to 2½ inches

ZEPHYR ANGLEWING
POLYGONIA ZEPHYRUS

This butterfly is yellow orange with a few black patches and spots near the cell of the forewing and has a tan border along the outer edge of the hind wing above. It is gray-brown with a silver, black-edged crescent in the cell of the hind wing and submarginal broken black bands along the curves of the outer edges.

The Zephyr Anglewing is easily frightened from its perch into the nearest wooded areas, but soon returns to nearly the same place.

The caterpillar is black with red and white spines. The chrysalis is pink and green.

GRAY COMMA
POLYGONIA PROGNE

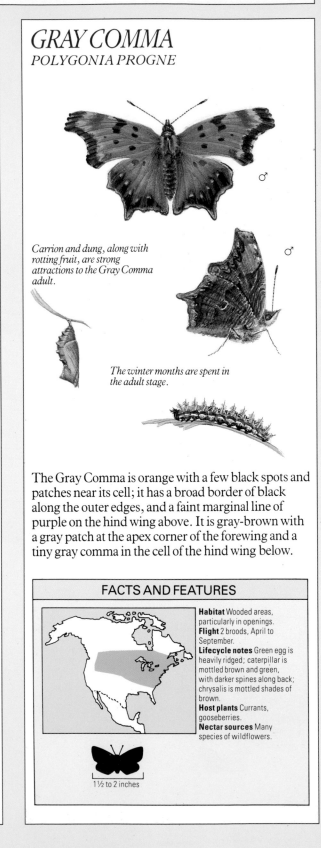

Carrion and dung, along with rotting fruit, are strong attractions to the Gray Comma adult.

The winter months are spent in the adult stage.

The Gray Comma is orange with a few black spots and patches near its cell; it has a broad border of black along the outer edges, and a faint marginal line of purple on the hind wing above. It is gray-brown with a gray patch at the apex corner of the forewing and a tiny gray comma in the cell of the hind wing below.

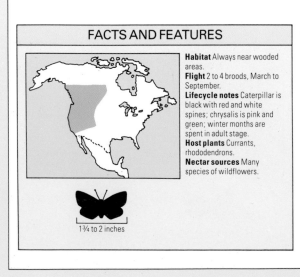

FACTS AND FEATURES

Habitat Always near wooded areas.
Flight 2 to 4 broods, March to September.
Lifecycle notes Caterpillar is black with red and white spines; chrysalis is pink and green; winter months are spent in adult stage.
Host plants Currants, rhododendrons.
Nectar sources Many species of wildflowers.

1¾ to 2 inches

FACTS AND FEATURES

Habitat Wooded areas, particularly in openings.
Flight 2 broods, April to September.
Lifecycle notes Green egg is heavily ridged; caterpillar is mottled brown and green, with darker spines along back; chrysalis is mottled shades of brown.
Host plants Currants, gooseberries.
Nectar sources Many species of wildflowers.

1½ to 2 inches

MILBERT'S TORTOISESHELL
AGLAIS MILBERTI

This butterfly is black with two orange patches along the costa of the forewing, followed on both the forewing and the hind wing by a sunburst effect of yellow fading into orange, and then a border of black with blue-white patches above. Brown replaces black and mottled tan replaces the sunburst band below.

The Milbert's Tortoiseshell has adapted to take advantage of every type of habitat that it encounters, and is possibly the longest lived of all North American butterflies.

The caterpillars begin this stage as communal-nest creatures but mature into loners that tend to roll leaves of host plants about themselves.

FACTS AND FEATURES

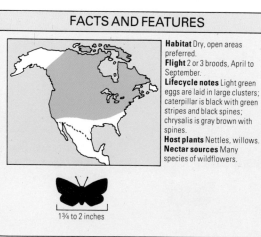

Habitat Dry, open areas preferred.
Flight 2 or 3 broods, April to September.
Lifecycle notes Light green eggs are laid in large clusters; caterpillar is black with green stripes and black spines; chrysalis is gray brown with spines.
Host plants Nettles, willows.
Nectar sources Many species of wildflowers.

1¾ to 2 inches

COMPTON TORTOISESHELL
NYMPHALIS VAU-ALBUM

This butterfly is shimmering yellow orange (rust brown near the body) with distinct black patches; it has one small white patch near the forward angle of each wing and an outlining submarginal band of black above. It is mottled gray-brown with an irregular band of blue-silver across the middle of both wings below.

Gatherings of the Compton Tortoiseshell are sometimes to be found around rotting fruit.

The green caterpillars feed in groups. The winter months are spent in the adult stage.

FACTS AND FEATURES

Habitat Woodland openings.
Flight 1 brood, year round.
Lifecycle notes Orange eggs are laid in groups; caterpillar is green with brighter green spots and black spines; chrysalis is brown.
Host plants Birches, willows, poplars.
Nectar sources Rotting fruit and running sap are particular favorites.

2½ to 3 inches

AMERICAN PAINTED LADY
VANESSA VIRGINIENSIS

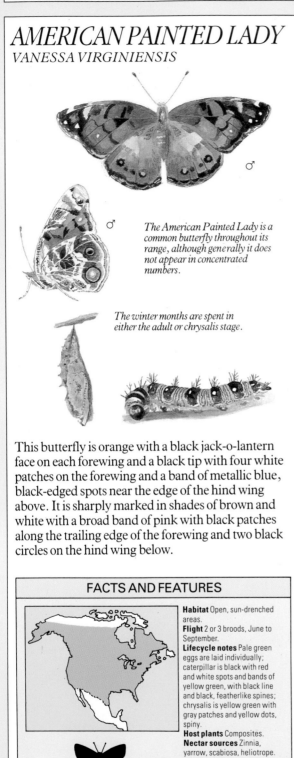

The American Painted Lady is a common butterfly throughout its range, although generally it does not appear in concentrated numbers.

The winter months are spent in either the adult or chrysalis stage.

This butterfly is orange with a black jack-o-lantern face on each forewing and a black tip with four white patches on the forewing and a band of metallic blue, black-edged spots near the edge of the hind wing above. It is sharply marked in shades of brown and white with a broad band of pink with black patches along the trailing edge of the forewing and two black circles on the hind wing below.

FACTS AND FEATURES

Habitat Open, sun-drenched areas.
Flight 2 or 3 broods, June to September.
Lifecycle notes Pale green eggs are laid individually; caterpillar is black with red and white spots and bands of yellow green, with black line and black, featherlike spines; chrysalis is yellow green with gray patches and yellow dots, spiny.
Host plants Composites.
Nectar sources Zinnia, yarrow, scabiosa, heliotrope.

1¾ to 2¼ inches

PAINTED LADY
VANESSA CARDUI

The Painted Lady is clouded tan next to its body, followed by a wide lateral band of orange with black patches and black tips with white patches above. It is orange with black and white patches and an apex of mottled gray, and tan and light blue on the forewing; it is mottled gray-brown, white, and blue-white on the hind wing with circles of black, white, and orange below.

The Painted Lady is found in every temperate zone continent world wide. Formerly known as the Thistle Butterfly.

This species is found throughout most of North America in the warmer months, but it dies off each fall except in its southwestern stronghold. The next spring many of the southwestern butterflies will emigrate northward.

FACTS AND FEATURES

Habitat Nearly universal.
Flight Several broods, year round in Southwest, April to September in North and East.
Lifecycle notes Light green eggs are laid individually; caterpillar is covered in thin bands of black, green, and yellow, and bands of sharp, gray spines; chrysalis is blue-green with patches of olive, black dots, and spines.
Host plants Thistles, many species of wildflowers.
Nectar sources Many species of wildflowers.

2 to 2¼ inches

VICEROY
BASILARCHIA ARCHIPPUS

The Viceroy's most noticeable feature is a black postmedian line across the hind wing above and below. It is very similar above and below: orange, veined with black, with a black border dotted with white spots above and white crescents below.

The Viceroy mimics the Monarch over much of its range, but in the South it mimics the deeper-colored but similarly distasteful Queen, thus gaining some protection from predators.

The Viceroy is a master of camouflage. The caterpillar hibernates in leaf shreddings attached to a small branch. The chrysalis resembles a bird dropping.

FACTS AND FEATURES

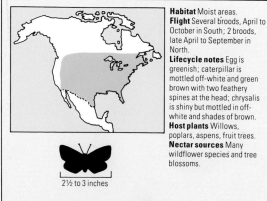

Habitat Moist areas.
Flight Several broods, April to October in South; 2 broods, late April to September in North.
Lifecycle notes Egg is greenish; caterpillar is mottled off-white and green brown with two feathery spines at the head; chrysalis is shiny but mottled in off-white and shades of brown.
Host plants Willows, poplars, aspens, fruit trees.
Nectar sources Many wildflower species and tree blossoms.

2½ to 3 inches

GOATWEED BUTTERFLY
ANAEA ANDRIA

The apex of the forewing is angled and pointed. It is bright burnt orange with a few gray veins and an indistinct black border along the outer edges above. It is gray-brown with hints of purple or blue near the body and across the hind wing below.

The Goatweed Butterfly is the northernmost member of a family of otherwise tropical butterflies, whose wings resemble plant leaves.

The winter months are spent in the adult stage. The caterpillar bends host plant leaves about itself and bundles them with silk for protection.

FACTS AND FEATURES

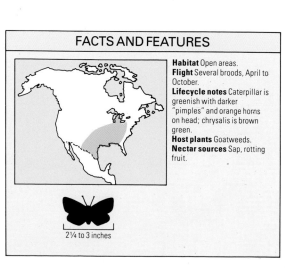

Habitat Open areas.
Flight Several broods, April to October.
Lifecycle notes Caterpillar is greenish with darker "pimples" and orange horns on head; chrysalis is brown green.
Host plants Goatweeds.
Nectar sources Sap, rotting fruit.

2¼ to 3 inches

HACKBERRY BUTTERFLY
ASTEROCAMPA CELTIS

The Hackberry Butterfly is tan and orange above with a black apex on the forewing and bands of black dots, crescents, and looping bars on the hind wing. It is light gray-brown below with a distinct band of black and white spots across the hind wing.

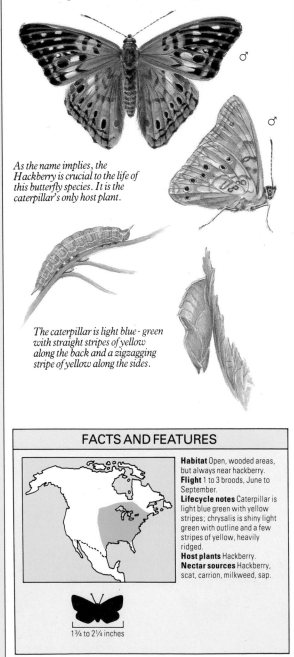

As the name implies, the Hackberry is crucial to the life of this butterfly species. It is the caterpillar's only host plant.

The caterpillar is light blue-green with straight stripes of yellow along the back and a zigzagging stripe of yellow along the sides.

FACTS AND FEATURES

Habitat Open, wooded areas, but always near hackberry.
Flight 1 to 3 broods, June to September.
Lifecycle notes Caterpillar is light blue green with yellow stripes; chrysalis is shiny light green with outline and a few stripes of yellow, heavily ridged.
Host plants Hackberry.
Nectar sources Hackberry, scat, carrion, milkweed, sap.

1¾ to 2¼ inches

HARVESTER
FENISECA TARQUINIUS

The Harvester is orange brown with black to brown borders and patches above, and orange brown with dusty white-edged patches below.

As its common name implies, the Harvester is the only carnivorous (meat-eating) butterfly in North America. Like its tropical relatives, it eats smaller insects.

The caterpillar preys entirely on various species of aphids.

FACTS AND FEATURES

Habitat Moist areas that include the plants that support the caterpillar's hosts, aphids.
Flight Several broods, as far north as Pennsylvania; 1 or 2, further north; April to September.
Lifecycle notes Eggs laid singly among aphids. Caterpillars eat aphids and live in silk web covered with aphid carcasses; chrysalis displays face of monkey on its back.
Host plants Aphids.
Nectar sources Aphids.

1 to 1¼ inches

TAILED COPPER
THARSALEA AROTA

♀

♂

♀

The pattern and darkness of the wing coloration below varies considerably according to geographic location.

The caterpillar is green with two white back lines and a yellow side line. The chrysalis is a yellow brown.

The male is dull brown with some black spots and faint orange patches on its hind wing above. The female is orange with brown patches above. Both are brown gray with an orange tint on the forewing. They are gray blue to white with bands on the hind wing, and black patches and curved lines on both wings below. Both have a short, pointed tail extending from the rear of the hind wing.

FACTS AND FEATURES

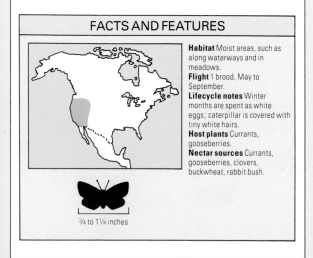

Habitat Moist areas, such as along waterways and in meadows.
Flight 1 brood, May to September.
Lifecycle notes Winter months are spent as white eggs; caterpillar is covered with tiny white hairs.
Host plants Currants, gooseberries.
Nectar sources Currants, gooseberries, clovers, buckwheat, rabbit bush.

¾ to 1¼ inches

AMERICAN COPPER
LYCAENA PHLAEAS

This butterfly is orange with a distinct gray-brown border and black patches on the forewing; it is mostly gray-brown with distinct orange patches at the rear on the hind wing above. It is gray-brown with a shading of orange on the forewing, and there is a distinct orange band on the hind wing and black dots throughout below.

♂

♂

The American Copper is widespread, although more common in the North and East.

The caterpillar is covered with fine hairs. The winter months are spent in the chrysalis form.

FACTS AND FEATURES

Habitat Open and disturbed areas.
Flight 2 to 4 broods, April to October.
Lifecycle notes Green eggs have prominent modeling; caterpillar is green with pink patches along sides.
Host plants Sorrels, dock.
Nectar sources Yarrow, daisies, goldenrod.

¾ to 1¼ inches

LUSTROUS COPPER
LYCAENA CUPREUS

The male is bright red orange with black patches and border above. The female is not as bright and has less distinct patches and border above. Both are pink to a gray-brown with an orange hint and have black dots below.

Populations of the Lustrous Copper show tremendous variety in coloration.

Very little is known of the caterpillar and chrysalis stages of the Lustrous Copper, but it spends the winter months in the egg stage.

FACTS AND FEATURES

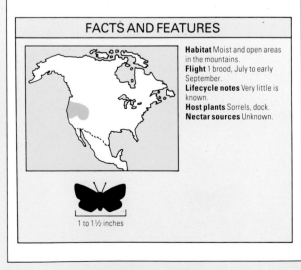

Habitat Moist and open areas in the mountains.
Flight 1 brood, July to early September.
Lifecycle notes Very little is known.
Host plants Sorrels, dock.
Nectar sources Unknown.

1 to 1½ inches

RUDDY COPPER
CHALCERIA RUBIDUS

The male is bright red orange with thin borders of white and then black along its margins above. The female is olive brown with dull orange and black patches above. Both are white to faint yellow green with black dots on the forewing below.

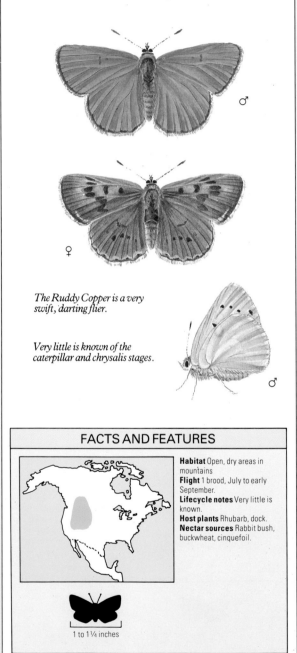

The Ruddy Copper is a very swift, darting flier.

Very little is known of the caterpillar and chrysalis stages.

FACTS AND FEATURES

Habitat Open, dry areas in mountains
Flight 1 brood, July to early September.
Lifecycle notes Very little is known.
Host plants Rhubarb, dock.
Nectar sources Rabbit bush, buckwheat, cinquefoil.

1 to 1¼ inches

BLUE COPPER
CHALCERIA HETERONEA

The male is blue with black borders above. The female is grayer with shades of brown above. Both are off-white with black spots below.

Looking more like a Blue than a Copper, the Blue Copper's configuration nevertheless clearly labels it a Copper.

The caterpillar and chrysalis both bear strong resemblances to plant leaves.

FACTS AND FEATURES

Habitat Canyons, plateaus, river valleys.
Flight 1 brood, late June to August.
Lifecycle notes Spends the winter months in egg stage; caterpillar is green with tiny white hairs; chrysalis is green with brown splattering.
Host plants Buckwheat.
Nectar sources Buckwheat.

1 to 1¼ inches

GREAT GRAY COPPER
GAEIDES XANTHOIDES

The male is gray with white and then black borders and faint, orange-edged black patches at the rear of the hind wings above. The female has orange patches at the rear of the hind wings and forewings above. Both are pale gray with black dots and orange patches on the hind wings below.

The Great Gray Copper is the largest member of its family in North America.

The chrysalis is found in a silk-and-soil cocoon near dock.

FACTS AND FEATURES

Habitat Damp and moist areas in East, dry areas in West.
Flight 1 brood, May to August.
Lifecycle notes Eggs are white; caterpillar is green with orange stripes from front to back; chrysalis is pale pink.
Host plants Dock.
Nectar sources Milkweed.

1¼ to 2 inches

77

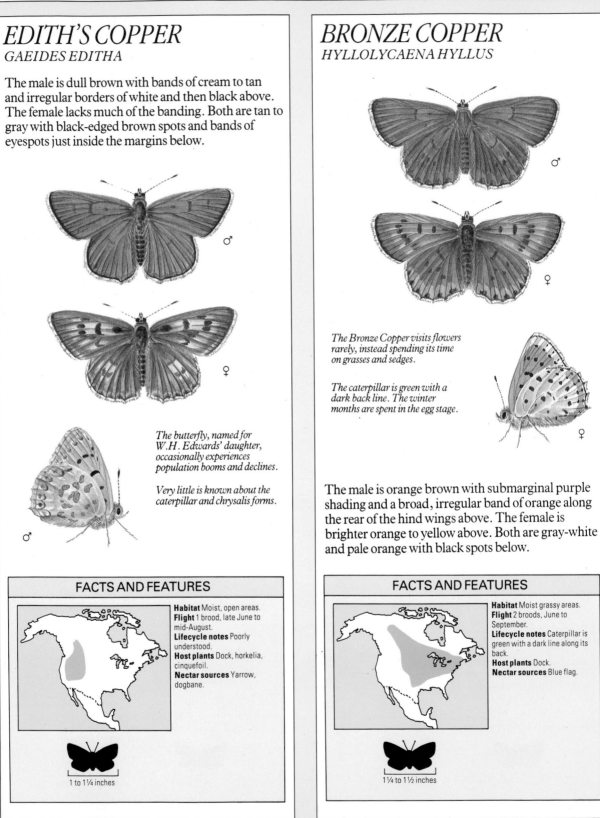

EDITH'S COPPER
GAEIDES EDITHA

The male is dull brown with bands of cream to tan and irregular borders of white and then black above. The female lacks much of the banding. Both are tan to gray with black-edged brown spots and bands of eyespots just inside the margins below.

♂

♀

The butterfly, named for W.H. Edwards' daughter, occasionally experiences population booms and declines.

Very little is known about the caterpillar and chrysalis forms.

♂

FACTS AND FEATURES

Habitat Moist, open areas.
Flight 1 brood, late June to mid-August.
Lifecycle notes Poorly understood.
Host plants Dock, horkelia, cinquefoil.
Nectar sources Yarrow, dogbane.

1 to 1¼ inches

BRONZE COPPER
HYLLOLYCAENA HYLLUS

♂

♀

The Bronze Copper visits flowers rarely, instead spending its time on grasses and sedges.

The caterpillar is green with a dark back line. The winter months are spent in the egg stage.

♀

The male is orange brown with submarginal purple shading and a broad, irregular band of orange along the rear of the hind wings above. The female is brighter orange to yellow above. Both are gray-white and pale orange with black spots below.

FACTS AND FEATURES

Habitat Moist grassy areas.
Flight 2 broods, June to September.
Lifecycle notes Caterpillar is green with a dark line along its back.
Host plants Dock.
Nectar sources Blue flag.

1¼ to 1½ inches

MARIPOSA COPPER
EPIDEMIA MARIPOSA

The male is orange brown with bands of black dots and a faint zigzag band of orange on the hind wing above. The female is darker with orange spots. Both are grayish with black markings below.

While the Mariposa Copper is a strongly scattered and localized species, it is also the most common butterfly in some of its range.

Very little about the various stages of the Mariposa Copper has been confirmed.

FACTS AND FEATURES

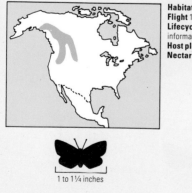

Habitat Moist, open areas.
Flight 1 brood, July to August.
Lifecycle notes Very little information.
Host plants Knotweed.
Nectar sources Unknown.

1 to 1¼ inches

NIVALIS COPPER
EPIDEMIA NIVALIS

The male is orange brown with a purple hint, black spots, and a band of orange at the rear of the hind wing above. The female is darker above. Both are pale orange with black spots on the forewing and a hint of pink or purple on the hind wing below.

The Nivalis Copper, also called the Lilac-bordered Copper, is a widely scattered species, prevalent in some areas but absent in other areas between.

The Nivalis Copper spends the winter months in its egg stage.

FACTS AND FEATURES

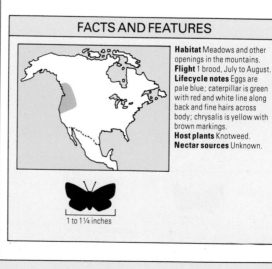

Habitat Meadows and other openings in the mountains.
Flight 1 brood, July to August.
Lifecycle notes Eggs are pale blue; caterpillar is green with red and white line along back and fine hairs across body; chrysalis is yellow with brown markings.
Host plants Knotweed.
Nectar sources Unknown.

1 to 1¼ inches

PURPLISH COPPER
EPIDEMIA HELLOIDES

The male is orange brown above with purple tints, black patches, and a zigzag band of orange at the rear of the hind wing above. The female lacks the purple tints above. Both are gray to tan with black patches and an orange band on the hind wing below.

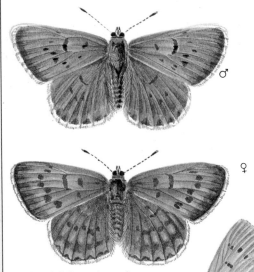

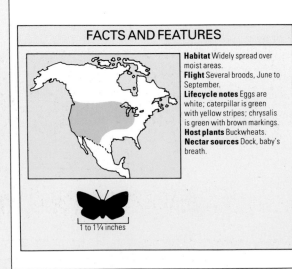

The Purplish Copper is one of only a handful of butterflies that occupy much of the northwest part of the continent, which otherwise has few species.

The caterpillar is green with yellow stripes along the back and sides. The chrysalis is green with brown markings.

FACTS AND FEATURES

Habitat Widely spread over moist areas.
Flight Several broods, June to September.
Lifecycle notes Eggs are white; caterpillar is green with yellow stripes; chrysalis is green with brown markings.
Host plants Buckwheats.
Nectar sources Dock, baby's breath.

1 to 1¼ inches

DORCAS COPPER
EPIDEMIA DORCAS

The male is dark orange brown with purple tints above. The female is brown with orange markings above. Both are yellow to brown with black spots below.

The Dorcas Copper is very similar to the Purplish Copper in appearance.

Little information has been gathered about the various stages of the Dorcas Copper.

FACTS AND FEATURES

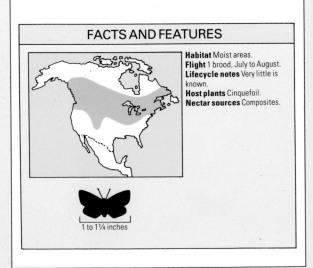

Habitat Moist areas.
Flight 1 brood, July to August.
Lifecycle notes Very little is known.
Host plants Cinquefoil.
Nectar sources Composites.

1 to 1¼ inches

JUNIPER HAIRSTREAK
MITOURA SIVA

The male is gray-brown with reddish spots above. The female has a reddish tint above. Both are greenish to orange brown below with a distinct band of white, black, and brown, and a dusting of white along the margin of the hind wing.

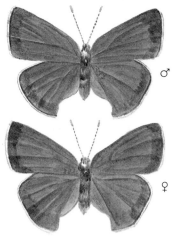

♂

♀

Many experts believe that several distinct species are currently described as the Juniper Hairstreak.

The caterpillar is green with yellow patches and many "pimples." The winter months are spent in the brown chrysalis stage.

FACTS AND FEATURES

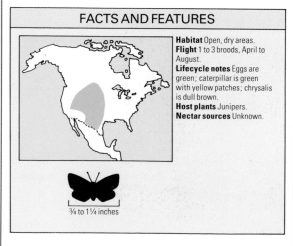

Habitat Open, dry areas.
Flight 1 to 3 broods, April to August.
Lifecycle notes Eggs are green; caterpillar is green with yellow patches; chrysalis is dull brown.
Host plants Junipers.
Nectar sources Unknown.

¾ to 1¼ inches

OLIVE HAIRSTREAK
MITOURA GRYNEUS

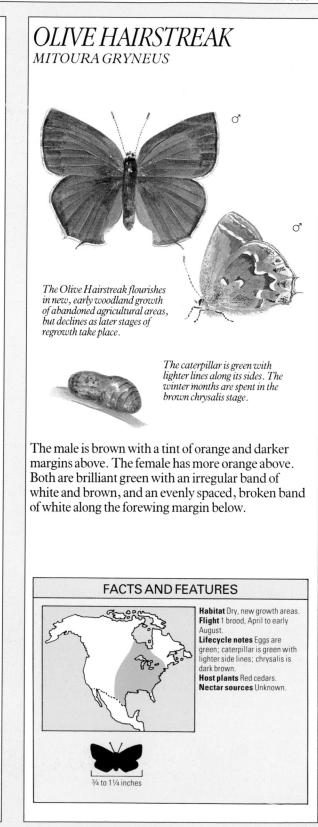

♂

♂

The Olive Hairstreak flourishes in new, early woodland growth of abandoned agricultural areas, but declines as later stages of regrowth take place.

The caterpillar is green with lighter lines along its sides. The winter months are spent in the brown chrysalis stage.

The male is brown with a tint of orange and darker margins above. The female has more orange above. Both are brilliant green with an irregular band of white and brown, and an evenly spaced, broken band of white along the forewing margin below.

FACTS AND FEATURES

Habitat Dry, new growth areas.
Flight 1 brood, April to early August.
Lifecycle notes Eggs are green; caterpillar is green with lighter side lines; chrysalis is dark brown.
Host plants Red cedars.
Nectar sources Unknown.

¾ to 1¼ inches

BRAMBLE GREEN HAIRSTREAK
CALLOPHRYS DUMETORUM

This butterfly is gray-brown to red-brown above, and light green with a nondistinct band of orange brown tinting on the forewing and a few irregular spots of white on the hind wing below. It is tailless.

Experts disagree over the correct number of species of Green Hairstreaks that actually exist. Exact identification of the different species is difficult.

The green caterpillar has yellow back lines and white side lines, with tiny hairs throughout. The winter months are spent in leaf litter in the brown chrysalis stage.

FACTS AND FEATURES

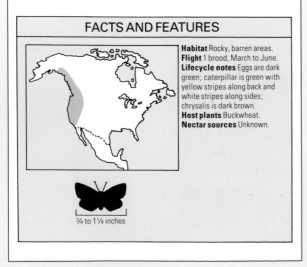

Habitat Rocky, barren areas.
Flight 1 brood, March to June.
Lifecycle notes Eggs are dark green; caterpillar is green with yellow stripes along back and white stripes along sides; chrysalis is dark brown.
Host plants Buckwheat.
Nectar sources Unknown.

¾ to 1¼ inches

DESERT GREEN HAIRSTREAK
CALLOPHRYS COMSTOCKI

This butterfly is gray-brown above, and gray-green with an irregular band of white, black-edged spots curved along the hind wing below. It is tailless.

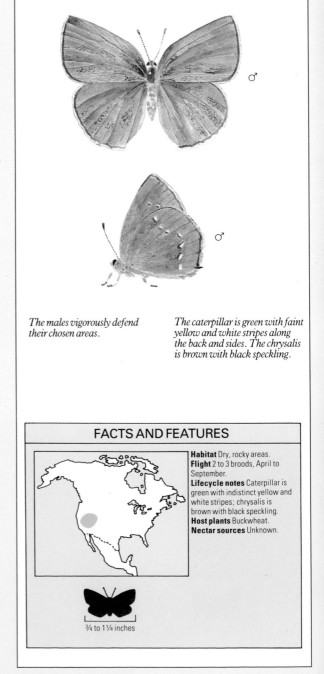

The males vigorously defend their chosen areas.

The caterpillar is green with faint yellow and white stripes along the back and sides. The chrysalis is brown with black speckling.

FACTS AND FEATURES

Habitat Dry, rocky areas.
Flight 2 to 3 broods, April to September.
Lifecycle notes Caterpillar is green with indistinct yellow and white stripes; chrysalis is brown with black speckling.
Host plants Buckwheat.
Nectar sources Unknown.

¾ to 1¼ inches

WHITE-LINED GREEN HAIRSTEAK

CALLOPHRYS SHERIDANII

This butterfly is gray above, and blue-green with an unbroken band of white, edged black, and marginal bands of white, gray, and white below. It is tailless.

Its characteristic unbroken white line combined with the blue-green below make the White-lined Green Hairstreak one of the easier Green Hairstreaks to identify.

The caterpillar is green with two broken, white stripes along the back. The winter months are spent in the dark brown chrysalis stage.

SOOTY HAIRSTREAK

SATYRIUM FULIGINOSUM

Newly emerged Sooty Hairstreaks are much more colorful than the description, with tints of blue, green, and purple. The coloration is soon lost, however.

Very little information has been documented about the various life stages of the Sooty Hairstreak.

This butterfly is gray to brown above, and gray to brown with a band of black, white-edged dots and a faint band of gray along the outer margin (wider on the hind wing) below. It is tailless.

FACTS AND FEATURES

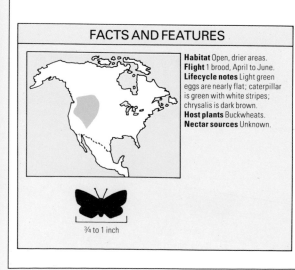

Habitat Open, drier areas.
Flight 1 brood, April to June.
Lifecycle notes Light green eggs are nearly flat; caterpillar is green with white stripes; chrysalis is dark brown.
Host plants Buckwheats.
Nectar sources Unknown.

¾ to 1 inch

FACTS AND FEATURES

Habitat Widespread across many environments, but generally close to lupines.
Flight 1 brood, June to August.
Lifecycle notes Very little information available.
Host plants Lupines.
Nectar sources Lupines, New Jersey tea, dogbane, milkweed.

1 to 1½ inches

ACADIAN HAIRSTREAK
SATYRIUM ACADICA

The color of this butterfly is gray to gray-brown with orange patches near the tail on the hind wing above. It is green-gray to silver-gray with a band of orange triangles framed in black and white and a band of black, with white-edged spots below.

The Acadian Hairstreak is a widespread species, but it is generally found quite near the wet and damp areas in its habitat.

The caterpillar is green with broken lines of yellow and white along its sides.

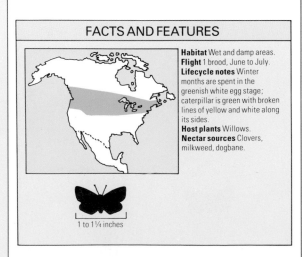

FACTS AND FEATURES

Habitat Wet and damp areas.
Flight 1 brood, June to July.
Lifecycle notes Winter months are spent in the greenish white egg stage; caterpillar is green with broken lines of yellow and white along its sides.
Host plants Willows.
Nectar sources Clovers, milkweed, dogbane.

1 to 1¼ inches

WESTERN PYGMY BLUE
BREPHIDIUM EXILIS

There is shaded blue fading into tan away from the body with blue borders along the outer margins above. There is blue gray near the body changing to tan mottled with blue gray away from the body, with a curving band of black patches near the outer margin of the hind wing below.

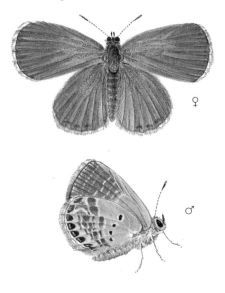

This smallest of Western butterflies extends its range northward each summer, but dies off outside its southern range each fall.

The light green caterpillar is covered with small brown "pimples".

FACTS AND FEATURES

Habitat Disturbed areas with new growth.
Flight Several broods, year round in South.
Lifecycle notes Winter months are spent in blue green egg stage; caterpillar is light green with yellow stripes on back and sides and brown "pimples" across its surface; chrysalis is tiny and mottled brown.
Host plants Various goosefoot species.
Nectar sources Various goosefoot species.

¼ to ¾ inch

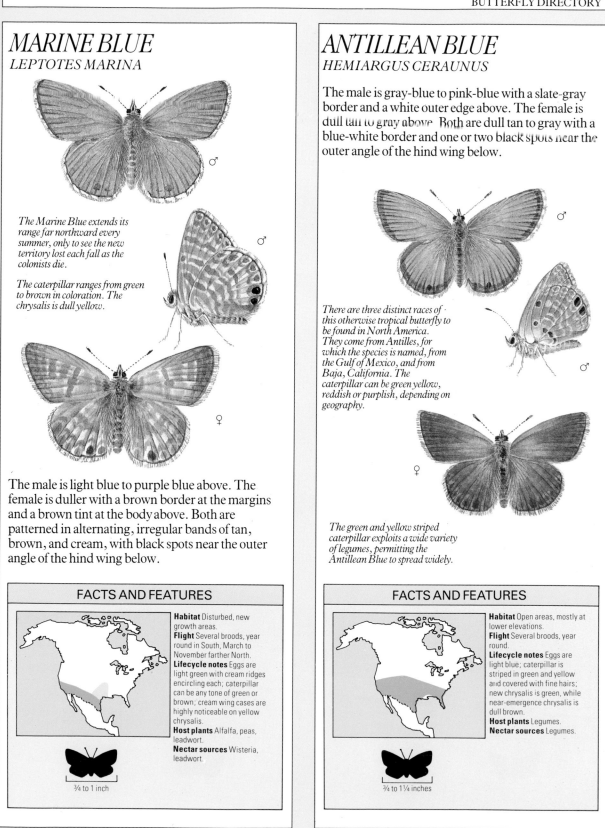

MARINE BLUE
LEPTOTES MARINA

♂

The Marine Blue extends its range far northward every summer, only to see the new territory lost each fall as the colonists die.

The caterpillar ranges from green to brown in coloration. The chrysalis is dull yellow.

♂

♀

The male is light blue to purple blue above. The female is duller with a brown border at the margins and a brown tint at the body above. Both are patterned in alternating, irregular bands of tan, brown, and cream, with black spots near the outer angle of the hind wing below.

FACTS AND FEATURES

Habitat Disturbed, new growth areas.
Flight Several broods, year round in South, March to November farther North.
Lifecycle notes Eggs are light green with cream ridges encircling each; caterpillar can be any tone of green or brown; cream wing cases are highly noticeable on yellow chrysalis.
Host plants Alfalfa, peas, leadwort.
Nectar sources Wisteria, leadwort.

¾ to 1 inch

ANTILLEAN BLUE
HEMIARGUS CERAUNUS

The male is gray-blue to pink-blue with a slate-gray border and a white outer edge above. The female is dull tan to gray above. Both are dull tan to gray with a blue-white border and one or two black spots near the outer angle of the hind wing below.

♂

There are three distinct races of this otherwise tropical butterfly to be found in North America. They come from Antilles, for which the species is named, from the Gulf of Mexico, and from Baja, California. The caterpillar can be green yellow, reddish or purplish, depending on geography.

♂

♀

The green and yellow striped caterpillar exploits a wide variety of legumes, permitting the Antillean Blue to spread widely.

FACTS AND FEATURES

Habitat Open areas, mostly at lower elevations.
Flight Several broods, year round.
Lifecycle notes Eggs are light blue; caterpillar is striped in green and yellow and covered with fine hairs; new chrysalis is green, while near-emergence chrysalis is dull brown.
Host plants Legumes.
Nectar sources Legumes.

¾ to 1¼ inches

85

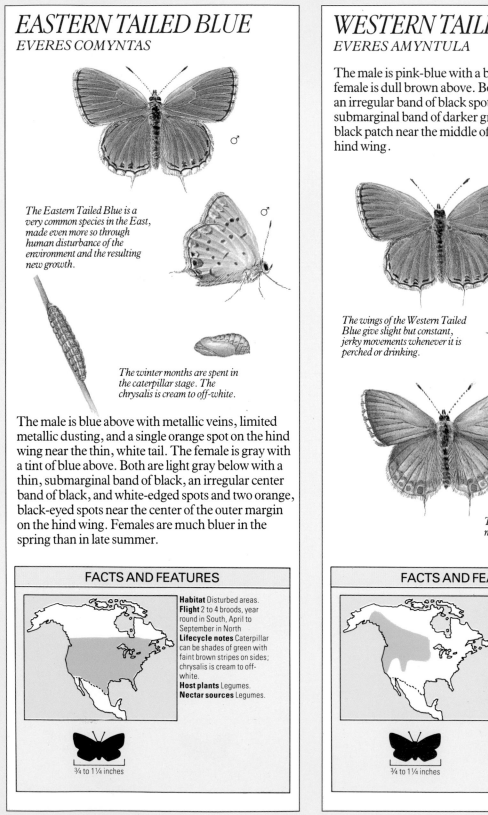

EASTERN TAILED BLUE
EVERES COMYNTAS

The Eastern Tailed Blue is a very common species in the East, made even more so through human disturbance of the environment and the resulting new growth.

The winter months are spent in the caterpillar stage. The chrysalis is cream to off-white.

The male is blue above with metallic veins, limited metallic dusting, and a single orange spot on the hind wing near the thin, white tail. The female is gray with a tint of blue above. Both are light gray below with a thin, submarginal band of black, an irregular center band of black, and white-edged spots and two orange, black-eyed spots near the center of the outer margin on the hind wing. Females are much bluer in the spring than in late summer.

FACTS AND FEATURES

Habitat Disturbed areas.
Flight 2 to 4 broods, year round in South, April to September in North
Lifecycle notes Caterpillar can be shades of green with faint brown stripes on sides; chrysalis is cream to off-white.
Host plants Legumes.
Nectar sources Legumes.

¾ to 1¼ inches

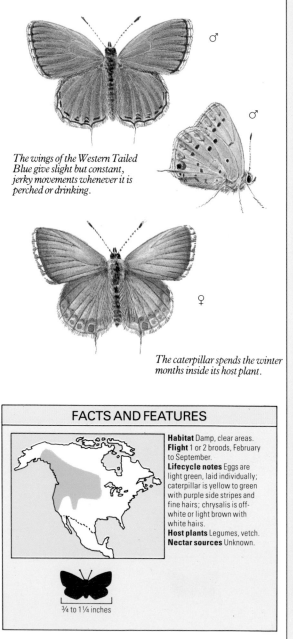

WESTERN TAILED BLUE
EVERES AMYNTULA

The male is pink-blue with a black border above. The female is dull brown above. Both are gray below with an irregular band of black spots, and an indistinct submarginal band of darker gray and an orange-and-black patch near the middle of the outer margin of the hind wing.

The wings of the Western Tailed Blue give slight but constant, jerky movements whenever it is perched or drinking.

The caterpillar spends the winter months inside its host plant.

FACTS AND FEATURES

Habitat Damp, clear areas.
Flight 1 or 2 broods, February to September.
Lifecycle notes Eggs are light green, laid individually; caterpillar is yellow to green with purple side stripes and fine hairs; chrysalis is off-white or light brown with white hairs.
Host plants Legumes, vetch.
Nectar sources Unknown.

¾ to 1¼ inches

SPRING AZURE
CELASTRINA LADON

The Spring Azure is purple blue above; the female has a black border around the forewing. Both are gray blue with irregular black and darker gray spots and patches, and a band of gray along the outer margin below. Later broods have much paler coloration.

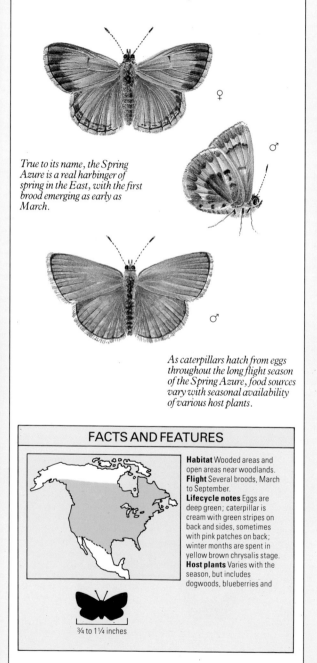

True to its name, the Spring Azure is a real harbinger of spring in the East, with the first brood emerging as early as March.

As caterpillars hatch from eggs throughout the long flight season of the Spring Azure, food sources vary with seasonal availability of various host plants.

FACTS AND FEATURES

Habitat Wooded areas and open areas near woodlands.
Flight Several broods, March to September.
Lifecycle notes Eggs are deep green; caterpillar is cream with green stripes on back and sides, sometimes with pink patches on back; winter months are spent in yellow brown chrysalis stage.
Host plants Varies with the season, but includes dogwoods, blueberries and

¾ to 1¼ inches

DOTTED BLUE
EUPHILOTES ENOPTES

The male is blue with black borders and an orange tint on the hind wing above. The female is brown with the same orange tint above. Below, both are white with irregular black patches throughout the wings; a thin black line connects black dots submarginally and there is a band of orange patches on the hind wing.

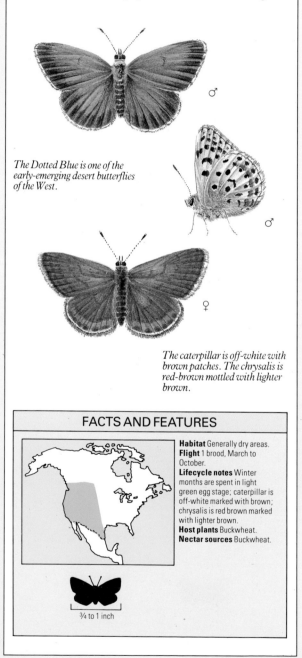

The Dotted Blue is one of the early-emerging desert butterflies of the West.

The caterpillar is off-white with brown patches. The chrysalis is red-brown mottled with lighter brown.

FACTS AND FEATURES

Habitat Generally dry areas.
Flight 1 brood, March to October.
Lifecycle notes Winter months are spent in light green egg stage; caterpillar is off-white marked with brown; chrysalis is red brown marked with lighter brown.
Host plants Buckwheat.
Nectar sources Buckwheat.

¾ to 1 inch

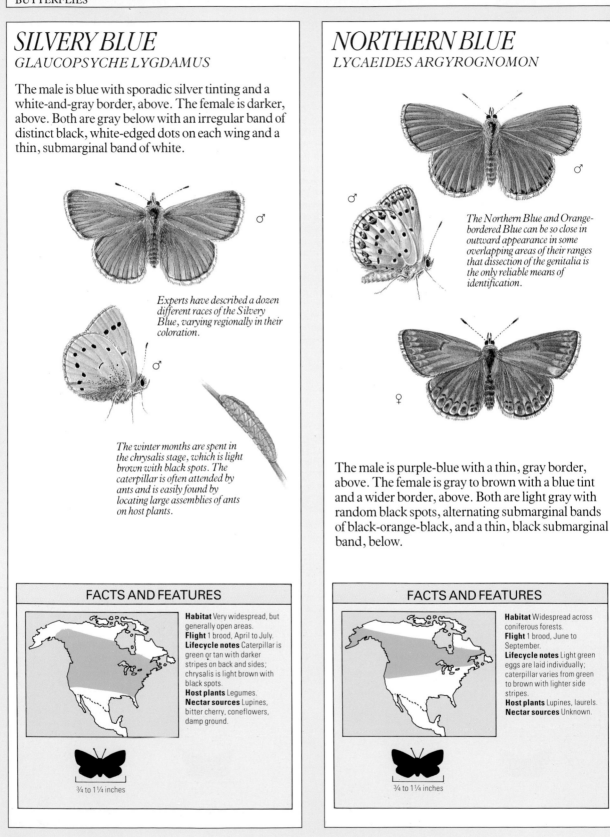

SILVERY BLUE
GLAUCOPSYCHE LYGDAMUS

The male is blue with sporadic silver tinting and a white-and-gray border, above. The female is darker, above. Both are gray below with an irregular band of distinct black, white-edged dots on each wing and a thin, submarginal band of white.

♂

Experts have described a dozen different races of the Silvery Blue, varying regionally in their coloration.

♂

The winter months are spent in the chrysalis stage, which is light brown with black spots. The caterpillar is often attended by ants and is easily found by locating large assemblies of ants on host plants.

FACTS AND FEATURES

Habitat Very widespread, but generally open areas.
Flight 1 brood, April to July.
Lifecycle notes Caterpillar is green or tan with darker stripes on back and sides; chrysalis is light brown with black spots.
Host plants Legumes.
Nectar sources Lupines, bitter cherry, coneflowers, damp ground.

¾ to 1¼ inches

NORTHERN BLUE
LYCAEIDES ARGYROGNOMON

♂

♂

The Northern Blue and Orange-bordered Blue can be so close in outward appearance in some overlapping areas of their ranges that dissection of the genitalia is the only reliable means of identification.

♀

The male is purple-blue with a thin, gray border, above. The female is gray to brown with a blue tint and a wider border, above. Both are light gray with random black spots, alternating submarginal bands of black-orange-black, and a thin, black submarginal band, below.

FACTS AND FEATURES

Habitat Widespread across coniferous forests.
Flight 1 brood, June to September.
Lifecycle notes Light green eggs are laid individually; caterpillar varies from green to brown with lighter side stripes.
Host plants Lupines, laurels.
Nectar sources Unknown.

¾ to 1¼ inches

ORANGE-BORDERED BLUE
LYCAEIDES MELISSA

The male is blue with a silver tint and distinct, thin black then white borders, above. The female is blue with an orange tint, particularly in the veins, fading to pale orange with gray and black spots and an off-white border, above. Both are off-white with black borders and orange-blue spots at the rear of the hindwing, below.

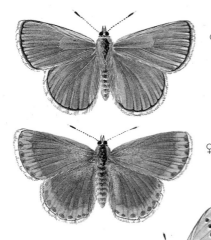

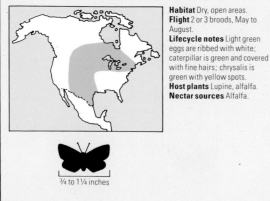

A subspecies of the Orange-bordered Blue, the Karner Blue, is protected in several states because of its relative scarcity.

The winter months are spent either in the light green egg stage or the green caterpillar stage.

FACTS AND FEATURES

Habitat Dry, open areas.
Flight 2 or 3 broods, May to August.
Lifecycle notes Light green eggs are ribbed with white; caterpillar is green and covered with fine hairs; chrysalis is green with yellow spots.
Host plants Lupine, alfalfa.
Nectar sources Alfalfa.

¾ to 1¼ inches

GREENISH BLUE
PLEBEJUS SAEPIOLUS

The male is blue with a silver to green tint and black borders, above; and gray to white with a blue tint and irregularly spaced black dots, below. The female is brown with orange patches on the hindwing, above; and light gray with irregular bands of black dots, below.

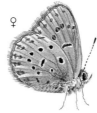

The Greenish Blue is a widespread species, benefiting from man's spread of such domestic species of nectar sources as white clover.

The winter months are spent in the green caterpillar stage.

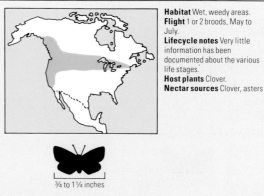

FACTS AND FEATURES

Habitat Wet, weedy areas.
Flight 1 or 2 broods, May to July.
Lifecycle notes Very little information has been documented about the various life stages.
Host plants Clover.
Nectar sources Clover, asters.

¾ to 1¼ inches

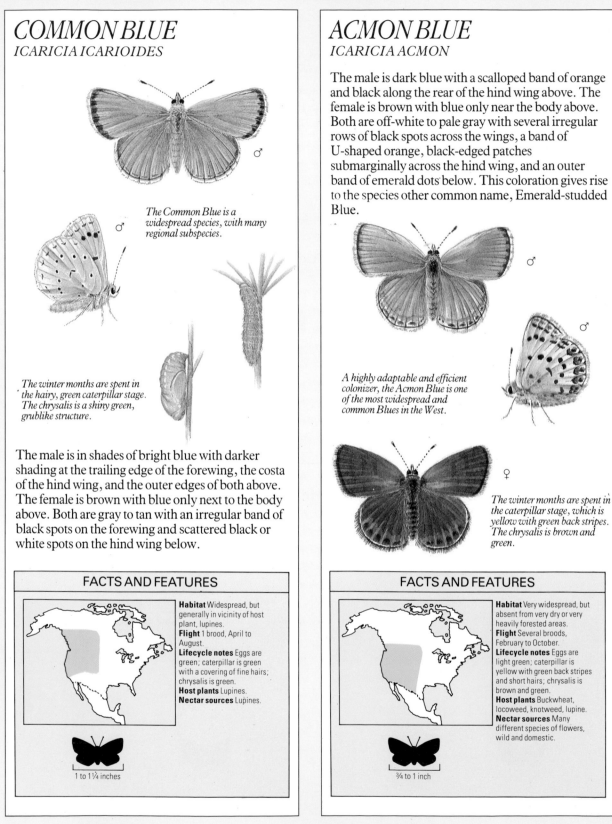

COMMON BLUE
ICARICIA ICARIOIDES

The Common Blue is a widespread species, with many regional subspecies.

♂

♂

The winter months are spent in the hairy, green caterpillar stage. The chrysalis is a shiny green, grublike structure.

The male is in shades of bright blue with darker shading at the trailing edge of the forewing, the costa of the hind wing, and the outer edges of both above. The female is brown with blue only next to the body above. Both are gray to tan with an irregular band of black spots on the forewing and scattered black or white spots on the hind wing below.

FACTS AND FEATURES

Habitat Widespread, but generally in vicinity of host plant, lupines.
Flight 1 brood, April to August.
Lifecycle notes Eggs are green; caterpillar is green with a covering of fine hairs; chrysalis is green.
Host plants Lupines.
Nectar sources Lupines.

1 to 1¼ inches

ACMON BLUE
ICARICIA ACMON

The male is dark blue with a scalloped band of orange and black along the rear of the hind wing above. The female is brown with blue only near the body above. Both are off-white to pale gray with several irregular rows of black spots across the wings, a band of U-shaped orange, black-edged patches submarginally across the hind wing, and an outer band of emerald dots below. This coloration gives rise to the species other common name, Emerald-studded Blue.

♂

♂

A highly adaptable and efficient colonizer, the Acmon Blue is one of the most widespread and common Blues in the West.

♀

The winter months are spent in the caterpillar stage, which is yellow with green back stripes. The chrysalis is brown and green.

FACTS AND FEATURES

Habitat Very widespread, but absent from very dry or very heavily forested areas.
Flight Several broods, February to October.
Lifecycle notes Eggs are light green; caterpillar is yellow with green back stripes and short hairs; chrysalis is brown and green.
Host plants Buckwheat, locoweed, knotweed, lupine.
Nectar sources Many different species of flowers, wild and domestic.

¾ to 1 inch

REAKIRT'S BLUE
HEMIARGUS ISOLA

The male is light blue with a sporadic dusting of white; there are black borders along the outer edges and a black dot near the rear of the hind wing above. The female is light blue at the body, fading into gray-brown, with a white-blue border and a black, white-edged dot near the rear of the hind wing above. Both are pale gray-brown below with a distinct band of black; and white-edged spots near the middle of the forewing.

♂

Reakirt's Blues are generally seen as lone individuals, giving rise to their other common name of Solitary Blue.

♂

Very little information has been documented about the life stages of the Reakirt's Blue.

♀

FACTS AND FEATURES

Habitat Disturbed, open areas.
Flight Several broods, year round in South, June to late September in North.
Lifecycle notes Very little information described.
Host plants Legumes.
Nectar sources Many species of wildflowers.

¾ to 1¼ inches

COLORADO HAIRSTREAK
HYPAUROTIS CRYSALUS

The wings are pale blue bordered by olive with a few orange spots above. They are brownish gray with a bluish hint and two narrow white and black bands below.

♂

The Colorado Hairstreak will regularly be seen after sunset and on overcast days.

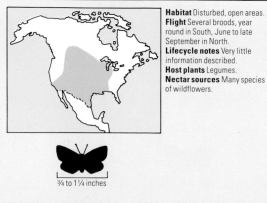

♂

The gambel oak plays an important part in the life of all stages of the Colorado Hairstreak.

FACTS AND FEATURES

Habitat Canyons and foothills with oak populations.
Flight 1 brood, July to September.
Lifecycle notes All stages have been observed in connection with the gambel oak.
Host plants Gambel oak.
Nectar sources Unknown.

1¼ to 1½ inches

CALIFORNIA HAIRSTREAK
SATYRIUM CALIFORNICA

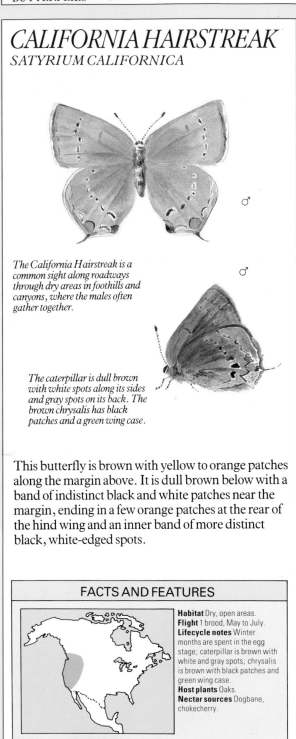

The California Hairstreak is a common sight along roadways through dry areas in foothills and canyons, where the males often gather together.

The caterpillar is dull brown with white spots along its sides and gray spots on its back. The brown chrysalis has black patches and a green wing case.

This butterfly is brown with yellow to orange patches along the margin above. It is dull brown below with a band of indistinct black and white patches near the margin, ending in a few orange patches at the rear of the hind wing and an inner band of more distinct black, white-edged spots.

FACTS AND FEATURES

Habitat Dry, open areas.
Flight 1 brood, May to July.
Lifecycle notes Winter months are spent in the egg stage; caterpillar is brown with white and gray spots; chrysalis is brown with black patches and green wing case.
Host plants Oaks.
Nectar sources Dogbane, chokecherry.

1 to 1¼ inches

NORTHERN HAIRSTREAK
EURISTRYMON ONTARIO

Above it is dull brown with orange patches; below it is gray to gray-brown with thin, irregular bands of brown, white, and black, ending in a double "M" near the outer angle of the hind wing. There are patches of orange and metallic blue near the outer angle of the hind wing.

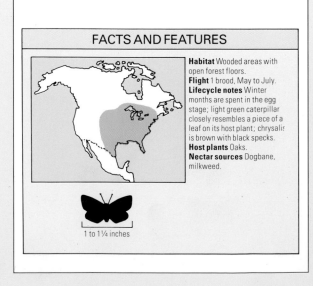

The inappropriately named Northern Hairstreak is actually much more common toward the southern portion of its range, where its orange patches are more distinct.

The chrysalis spins a loosely knit silken hammock amid the leaf litter on the forest floor.

FACTS AND FEATURES

Habitat Wooded areas with open forest floors.
Flight 1 brood, May to July.
Lifecycle notes Winter months are spent in the egg stage; light green caterpillar closely resembles a piece of a leaf on its host plant; chrysalis is brown with black specks.
Host plants Oaks.
Nectar sources Dogbane, milkweed.

1 to 1¼ inches

RED-BANDED HAIRSTREAK
CALYCOPIS CECROPS

This butterfly's hind wings are covered with blue gray patches (more widespread on the female) above. It is gray-brown with a broad band of red orange, edged with black and white along the outer edge across the middle of the wings, ending in a strong zigzag pattern near the trailing edge of the hind wing below.

Unlike many species of butterflies, the Red-banded Hairstreak is most active at sunset, preferring to remain hidden during the bright daylight hours.

The caterpillar hatches from the egg as a tiny, pale yellow creature, but matures into a much deeper shade of yellow with a green stripe along its back.

FACTS AND FEATURES

Habitat Open areas near woodlands.
Flight 3 broods, April to September.
Lifecycle notes Winter months are spent in white egg stage, buried amid litter on forest floor; caterpillar is yellow with green stripe along back; chrysalis is red brown, speckled with black.
Host plants Sumac, croton.
Nectar sources Sumac.

1 to 1¼ inches

GRAY HAIRSTREAK
STRYMON MELINUS

The Gray Hairstreak is gray to gray-brown with an orange patch near the outer angle on the hind wing above. It is green-gray below with two irregular black, white-edged bands across its wings, and slate gray outer edges and orange patches near the outer angle of the hind wing.

An extremely able colonizer, the Gray Hairstreak is one of North America's most widespread butterfly species. It also goes by the name of Common Hairstreak.

The caterpillar is also called the Cotton Borer because of the damage it has done to cotton crops in the South.

FACTS AND FEATURES

Habitat Very widespread across areas that are generally open or have open forest floors.
Flight 3 broods, April to early October.
Lifecycle notes Eggs are yellow-green; caterpillar is green with white stripes along sides; chrysalis is brown speckled with black.
Host plants Very wide-ranging, but including oaks, cotton, legumes, mints.
Nectar sources Many wild and domestic species.

1 to 1¼ inches

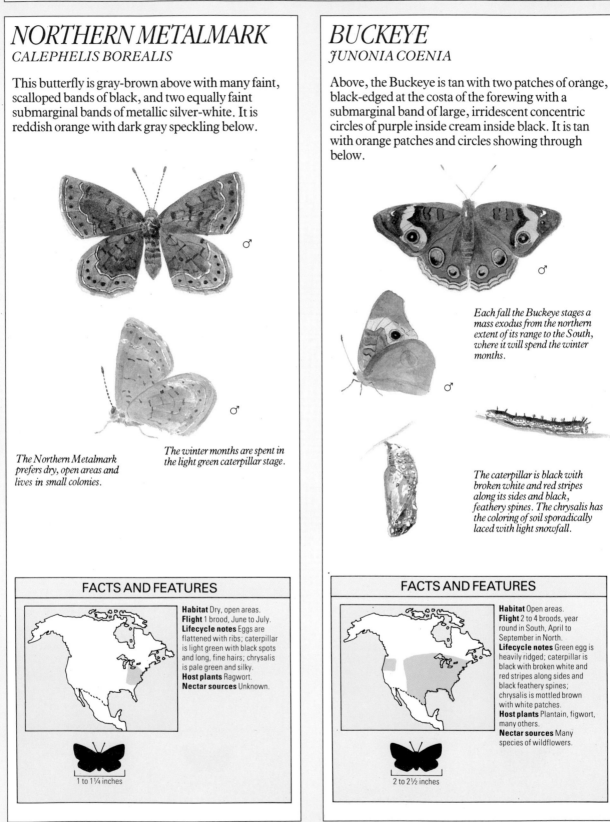

NORTHERN METALMARK
CALEPHELIS BOREALIS

This butterfly is gray-brown above with many faint, scalloped bands of black, and two equally faint submarginal bands of metallic silver-white. It is reddish orange with dark gray speckling below.

♂

♂

The Northern Metalmark prefers dry, open areas and lives in small colonies.

The winter months are spent in the light green caterpillar stage.

FACTS AND FEATURES

Habitat Dry, open areas.
Flight 1 brood, June to July.
Lifecycle notes Eggs are flattened with ribs; caterpillar is light green with black spots and long, fine hairs; chrysalis is pale green and silky.
Host plants Ragwort.
Nectar sources Unknown.

1 to 1¼ inches

BUCKEYE
JUNONIA COENIA

Above, the Buckeye is tan with two patches of orange, black-edged at the costa of the forewing with a submarginal band of large, irridescent concentric circles of purple inside cream inside black. It is tan with orange patches and circles showing through below.

♂

♂

Each fall the Buckeye stages a mass exodus from the northern extent of its range to the South, where it will spend the winter months.

The caterpillar is black with broken white and red stripes along its sides and black, feathery spines. The chrysalis has the coloring of soil sporadically laced with light snowfall.

FACTS AND FEATURES

Habitat Open areas.
Flight 2 to 4 broods, year round in South, April to September in North.
Lifecycle notes Green egg is heavily ridged; caterpillar is black with broken white and red stripes along sides and black feathery spines; chrysalis is mottled brown with white patches.
Host plants Plantain, figwort, many others.
Nectar sources Many species of wildflowers.

2 to 2½ inches

WHITE M HAIRSTREAK
PARRHASIUS M-ALBUM

As the common name implies, the White M Hairstreak has a very clear white and black "M" near the lower middle of its hind wing, which is accompanied by an orange-red patch below.

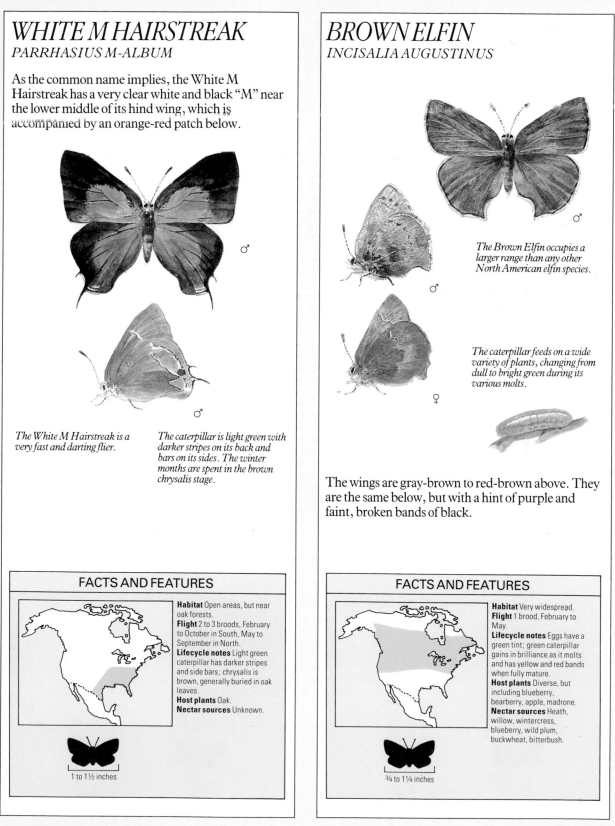

The White M Hairstreak is a very fast and darting flier.

The caterpillar is light green with darker stripes on its back and bars on its sides. The winter months are spent in the brown chrysalis stage.

FACTS AND FEATURES

Habitat Open areas, but near oak forests.
Flight 2 to 3 broods, February to October in South, May to September in North.
Lifecycle notes Light green caterpillar has darker stripes and side bars; chrysalis is brown, generally buried in oak leaves.
Host plants Oak.
Nectar sources Unknown.

1 to 1½ inches

BROWN ELFIN
INCISALIA AUGUSTINUS

The Brown Elfin occupies a larger range than any other North American elfin species.

The caterpillar feeds on a wide variety of plants, changing from dull to bright green during its various molts.

The wings are gray-brown to red-brown above. They are the same below, but with a hint of purple and faint, broken bands of black.

FACTS AND FEATURES

Habitat Very widespread.
Flight 1 brood, February to May.
Lifecycle notes Eggs have a green tint; green caterpillar gains in brilliance as it molts and has yellow and red bands when fully mature.
Host plants Diverse, but including blueberry, bearberry, apple, madrone.
Nectar sources Heath, willow, wintercress, blueberry, wild plum, buckwheat, bitterbush.

¾ to 1¼ inches

EARLY ELFIN
INCISALIA FOTIS

The wings are gray-brown to red-brown above. They are gray-brown with white speckling and an irregular, thin band of black and white below.

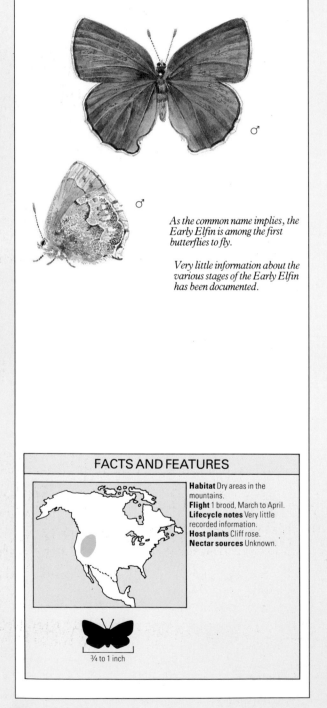

♂

♂

As the common name implies, the Early Elfin is among the first butterflies to fly.

Very little information about the various stages of the Early Elfin has been documented.

FACTS AND FEATURES

Habitat Dry areas in the mountains.
Flight 1 brood, March to April.
Lifecycle notes Very little recorded information.
Host plants Cliff rose.
Nectar sources Unknown.

¾ to 1 inch

HOARY ELFIN
INCISALIS POLIOS

This butterfly is clouded gray-brown above, and gray-brown with a thin, irregular band of darker brown and white, and a dusting of white along the outer margin below.

♂

♂

The Hoary Elfin is another early-emergence species.

The caterpillar changes from yellow to green as it matures. The winter months are spent in the brown chrysalis stage.

FACTS AND FEATURES

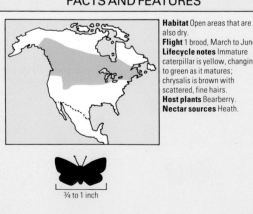

Habitat Open areas that are also dry.
Flight 1 brood, March to June.
Lifecycle notes Immature caterpillar is yellow, changing to green as it matures; chrysalis is brown with scattered, fine hairs.
Host plants Bearberry.
Nectar sources Heath.

¾ to 1 inch

FROSTED ELFIN
INCISALIA IRUS

The Frosted Elfin is gray-brown to red-brown above, and tan with a thin, irregular, faint band of black and white and a white frosting, mostly on the hind wing, below.

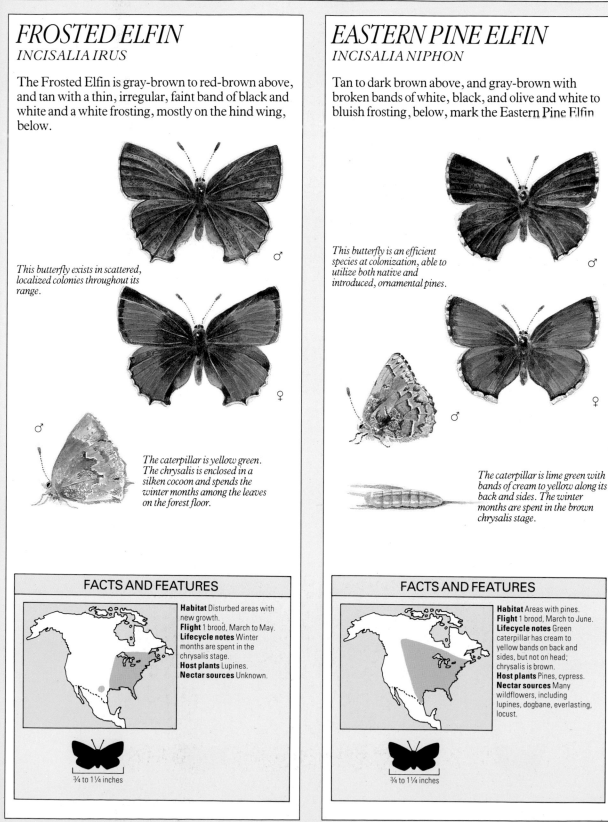

♂

This butterfly exists in scattered, localized colonies throughout its range.

♀

♂

The caterpillar is yellow green. The chrysalis is enclosed in a silken cocoon and spends the winter months among the leaves on the forest floor.

FACTS AND FEATURES

Habitat Disturbed areas with new growth.
Flight 1 brood, March to May.
Lifecycle notes Winter months are spent in the chrysalis stage.
Host plants Lupines.
Nectar sources Unknown.

¾ to 1¼ inches

EASTERN PINE ELFIN
INCISALIA NIPHON

Tan to dark brown above, and gray-brown with broken bands of white, black, and olive and white to bluish frosting, below, mark the Eastern Pine Elfin

♂

This butterfly is an efficient species at colonization, able to utilize both native and introduced, ornamental pines.

♀

♂

The caterpillar is lime green with bands of cream to yellow along its back and sides. The winter months are spent in the brown chrysalis stage.

FACTS AND FEATURES

Habitat Areas with pines.
Flight 1 brood, March to June.
Lifecycle notes Green caterpillar has cream to yellow bands on back and sides, but not on head; chrysalis is brown.
Host plants Pines, cypress.
Nectar sources Many wildflowers, including lupines, dogbane, everlasting, locust.

¾ to 1¼ inches

WESTERN PINE ELFIN
INCISALIA ERYPHON

This butterfly is brown to orange brown above, and orange brown with zigzagging bands of black, darker brown and white, and an oak-leaf outline on the hind wing below.

♂

♂

Unlike its eastern cousin, the Eastern Pine Elfin, the Western has not been able to take much advantage of introduced, ornamental pine species.

The caterpillar is silky green with cream to yellow stripes. The winter months are spent in the brown chrysalis stage.

FACTS AND FEATURES

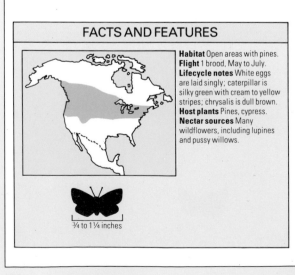

Habitat Open areas with pines.
Flight 1 brood, May to July.
Lifecycle notes White eggs are laid singly; caterpillar is silky green with cream to yellow stripes; chrysalis is dull brown.
Host plants Pines, cypress.
Nectar sources Many wildflowers, including lupines and pussy willows.

¾ to 1¼ inches

THICKET HAIRSTREAK
MITOURA SPINETORUM

Gray blue with white margins above, and shades of brown with a distinct band of white and black and a margin band of white on the forewing below, mark the Thicket Hairstreak.

♂

♂

Males claim territories along hilltops and canyon rims, where mating will take place.

The caterpillar is green with patches of red and white, and many "pimples." The winter months are spent in the gray-brown chrysalis stage.

FACTS AND FEATURES

Habitat Canyons and coniferous trees.
Flight 1 or 2 broods, April to September.
Lifecycle notes Greenish eggs are laid singly; caterpillar is green with patches of red and white; chrysalis is gray brown.
Host plants Mistletoe.
Nectar sources Buckwheat.

1 to 1¼ inches

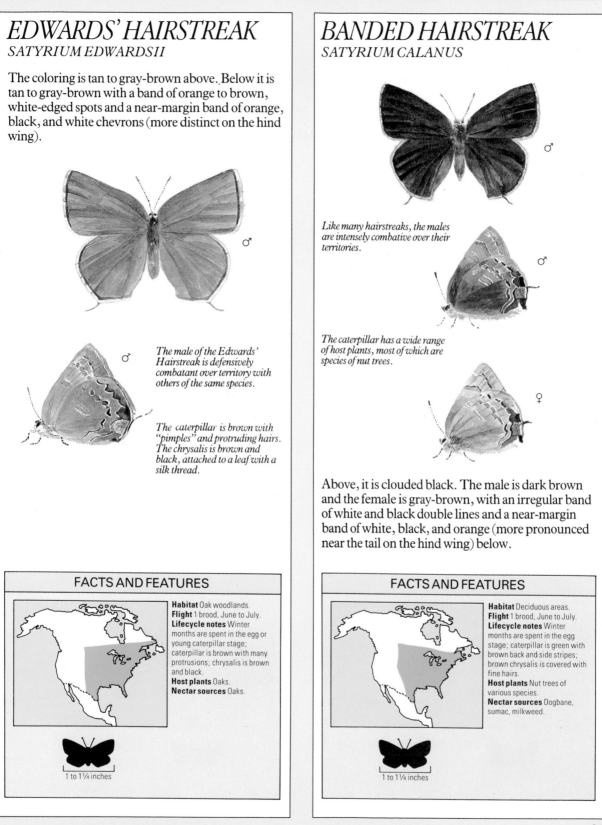

EDWARDS' HAIRSTREAK
SATYRIUM EDWARDSII

The coloring is tan to gray-brown above. Below it is tan to gray-brown with a band of orange to brown, white-edged spots and a near-margin band of orange, black, and white chevrons (more distinct on the hind wing).

♂

♂

The male of the Edwards' Hairstreak is defensively combatant over territory with others of the same species.

The caterpillar is brown with "pimples" and protruding hairs. The chrysalis is brown and black, attached to a leaf with a silk thread.

BANDED HAIRSTREAK
SATYRIUM CALANUS

♂

Like many hairstreaks, the males are intensely combative over their territories.

♂

The caterpillar has a wide range of host plants, most of which are species of nut trees.

♀

Above, it is clouded black. The male is dark brown and the female is gray-brown, with an irregular band of white and black double lines and a near-margin band of white, black, and orange (more pronounced near the tail on the hind wing) below.

FACTS AND FEATURES

Habitat Oak woodlands.
Flight 1 brood, June to July.
Lifecycle notes Winter months are spent in the egg or young caterpillar stage; caterpillar is brown with many protrusions; chrysalis is brown and black.
Host plants Oaks.
Nectar sources Oaks.

1 to 1¼ inches

FACTS AND FEATURES

Habitat Deciduous areas.
Flight 1 brood, June to July.
Lifecycle notes Winter months are spent in the egg stage; caterpillar is green with brown back and side stripes; brown chrysalis is covered with fine hairs.
Host plants Nut trees of various species.
Nectar sources Dogbane, sumac, milkweed.

1 to 1¼ inches

HICKORY HAIRSTREAK
SATYRIUM CARYAEVORUS

This butterfly is clouded brown to black above. Below, it is tan with two irregular bands that are brown, white- and black-edged across the middle of the wings and a band of orange that is black-edged (more distinct on the hind wing).

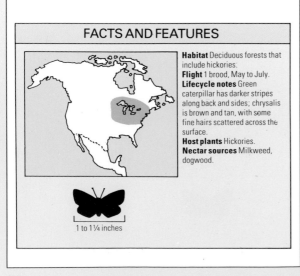

The Hickory Hairstreak experiences population booms and accompanying territorial expansions regularly, but the reasons for these are not fully understood.

As the name implies, the primary host plants for this green caterpillar are hickories.

FACTS AND FEATURES

Habitat Deciduous forests that include hickories.
Flight 1 brood, May to July.
Lifecycle notes Green caterpillar has darker stripes along back and sides; chrysalis is brown and tan, with some fine hairs scattered across the surface.
Host plants Hickories.
Nectar sources Milkweed, dogwood.

1 to 1¼ inches

KING'S HAIRSTREAK
SATYRIUM KINGI

Above, it is brown; below, it is gray-brown with very broken, scattered bands that are brown, with white and black edges, and orange, with black-edged patches along the margin of the hind wing.

The King's Hairstreak is a relatively recent addition to the list of discovered butterflies and was first described in 1952.

The King's Hairstreak occurs only in conjunction with its primary host plant, the horse sugar; the buds of this plant form the food base for the caterpillar.

FACTS AND FEATURES

Habitat Swamps near the ocean and deciduous forests
Flight 1 brood, May to July.
Lifecycle notes Winter months are spent in egg stage; caterpillar is green.
Host plants Horse sugar.
Nectar sources Chinquapin and related evergreens.

1 to 1¼ inches

HEDGEROW HAIRSTREAK
SATYRIUM SAEPIUM

♂

♂

Large gatherings of the Hedgerow Hairstreak are often found in the densely tangled growth from which it gained its common name.

The clouded green caterpillar and brown chrysalis are extremely well camouflaged, closely resembling a leaf of the host plant and an animal dropping, respectively.

The Hedgerow Hairstreak is light brown with darker margins above. It is tan clouded with white, with faint bands of brown to red-brown patches and a band of brown "Vs" near the margin of the hind wing below.

FACTS AND FEATURES

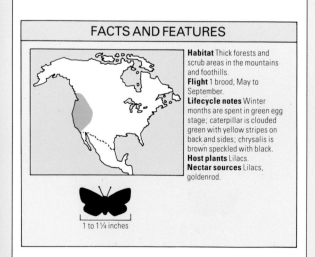

Habitat Thick forests and scrub areas in the mountains and foothills.
Flight 1 brood, May to September.
Lifecycle notes Winter months are spent in green egg stage; caterpillar is clouded green with yellow stripes on back and sides; chrysalis is brown speckled with black.
Host plants Lilacs.
Nectar sources Lilacs, goldenrod.

1 to 1¼ inches

SOUTHERN HAIRSTREAK
EURISTRYMON FAVONIUS

This butterfly is dark brown with orange along the costa and in patches near the rear of the hind wing above. It is a light olive brown with thin, forking bands of black and white on both wings, and with orange and metallic blue gray patches at the rear of the hind wing below. There are two long tails on the hind wing.

♂

♂

In areas where their ranges overlap, the Southern and Northern Hairstreaks appear to interbreed.

The caterpillar is green with darker stripes along its back and sides, and yellow stripes on the side.

FACTS AND FEATURES

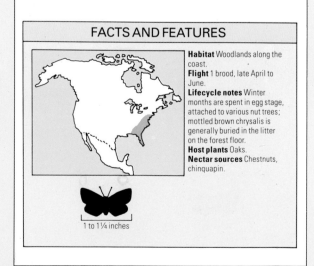

Habitat Woodlands along the coast.
Flight 1 brood, late April to June.
Lifecycle notes Winter months are spent in egg stage, attached to various nut trees; mottled brown chrysalis is generally buried in the litter on the forest floor.
Host plants Oaks.
Nectar sources Chestnuts, chinquapin.

1 to 1¼ inches

CORAL HAIRSTREAK
HARKENCLENUS TITUS

The Coral Hairstreak's Latin genus name is derived from that of lepidopterist Harry Kendon Clench, who spent many years studying the various Hairstreaks.

The caterpillar is green with a pink patch on its back and appears very soft.

The male is brown with red orange patches in an irregular band along the margin of the hind wing above. The female is lighter brown with less distinct red orange patches above. Both are gray-brown with a band of black, white-edged patches in an irregular band across the middle of both wings and a red orange band, edged with white and black near the outer margin of the hind wing below. It is tailless.

FACTS AND FEATURES

Habitat Densely foliated areas.
Flight 1 brood, June to July.
Lifecycle notes Winter months are spent in the egg stage; caterpillar is green with pink patch on its back.
Host plants Cherry, serviceberry.
Nectar sources Cherry.

1 to 1¼ inches

PEARLY EYE
ENODIA PORTLANDIA

This butterfly is brown (dusky in the male, brighter in the female) with zigzagging bands of darker brown and a band of darker spots on the hind wing above. It is cream-brown to gray-brown below with a band of concentric circles of orange brown and white on the hind wing, and one large, dark circle and three small, less distinct circles on the forewing.

Male Pearly Eyes claim tree trunks in their woodland territory, which they guard vigorously as their courtship grounds.

The red-horned caterpillar spends the winter months snuggled among tree bark.

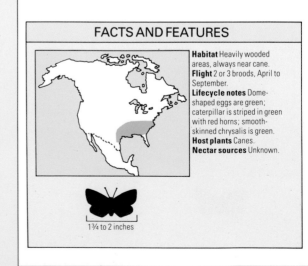

FACTS AND FEATURES

Habitat Heavily wooded areas, always near cane.
Flight 2 or 3 broods, April to September.
Lifecycle notes Dome-shaped eggs are green; caterpillar is striped in green with red horns; smooth-skinned chrysalis is green.
Host plants Canes.
Nectar sources Unknown.

1¾ to 2 inches

NORTHERN PEARLY EYE
ENODIA ANTHEDON

Above, this butterfly is brown with heavy zigzagging; there are thin bands of darker brown across both wings, a submarginal band of five darker circles on the hind wing, and four less distinct circles on the forewing. It is smooth gray-brown with a curving submarginal band of black spots, cream-edged with a white dot in the center on the hind wing, and four less distinct spots on the forewing below.

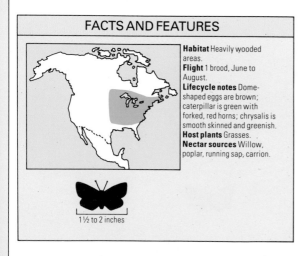

The Northern Pearly Eye is a butterfly species, although its penchant for comparatively shaded areas of a woodland tend to align its habitat preferences more closely to that of moths.

No stage of the Northern Pearly Eye relies on flowers. The caterpillar's host plants are grasses, and nectar preferences are willow and poplar.

FACTS AND FEATURES

Habitat Heavily wooded areas.
Flight 1 brood, June to August.
Lifecycle notes Dome-shaped eggs are brown; caterpillar is green with forked, red horns; chrysalis is smooth skinned and greenish.
Host plants Grasses.
Nectar sources Willow, poplar, running sap, carrion.

1½ to 2 inches

EYED BROWN
SATYRODES EURYDICE

The Eyed Brown butterfly is brown with bands of concentrically ringed spots of tan, cream, and black on the hind wing and less distinct spots on the forewing above. It is greenish brown to brown with a straight band of adjacent spots similar to the above on the forewing and a curving band on the hind wing below.

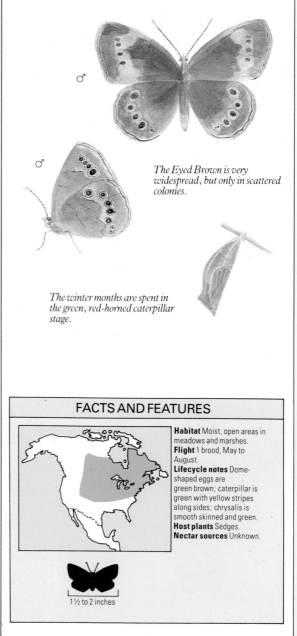

The Eyed Brown is very widespread, but only in scattered colonies.

The winter months are spent in the green, red-horned caterpillar stage.

FACTS AND FEATURES

Habitat Moist, open areas in meadows and marshes.
Flight 1 brood, May to August.
Lifecycle notes Dome-shaped eggs are green brown; caterpillar is green with yellow stripes along sides; chrysalis is smooth skinned and green.
Host plants Sedges.
Nectar sources Unknown.

1½ to 2 inches

APPALACHIAN BROWN
SATYRODES APPALACHIA

Above, the butterfly is dark brown with a curving, submarginal band of four black spots on the hind wing and a very indistinct band of spots on the forewing. Below, it is light brown with a purplish tint, a band of vivid, concentrically ringed spots of white and black that curves along the hind wing and two smaller but similarly colored spots on the forewing.

The Appalachian Brown, never an overly abundant species, has lost much of its habitat to human development.

The caterpillar is green with yellow stripes and a pair of red horns at both ends. The chrysalis is green.

FACTS AND FEATURES

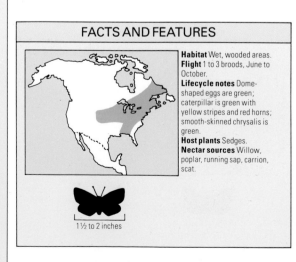

Habitat Wet, wooded areas.
Flight 1 to 3 broods, June to October.
Lifecycle notes Dome-shaped eggs are green; caterpillar is green with yellow stripes and red horns; smooth-skinned chrysalis is green.
Host plants Sedges.
Nectar sources Willow, poplar, running sap, carrion, scat.

1½ to 2 inches

CAROLINA SATYR
HERMEUPTYCHIA SOSYBIUS

This butterfly is brown with a very indistinct submarginal band of darker spots above. It is clouded brown with wavy, darker lines across the middle of the wings and a submarginal band of darker spots, some concentric circles of tan, black, and white, and some indistinct smudges of tan.

Not only is the Carolina Satyr the smallest Satyr, it also has the unsatyrlike habit of visiting several species of flower.

The caterpillar is green with darker side stripes and short, fine yellowish hairs. The chrysalis is greenish brown.

FACTS AND FEATURES

Habitat Wooded areas, particularly deciduous, with slow-moving or standing water.
Flight Several broods, year round in extreme South; 2 broods, April through August in North.
Lifecycle notes Dome-shaped eggs are greenish; caterpillar is green with darker side stripes and yellowish hairs; chrysalis is smooth skinned and greenish brown.
Host plants Grasses.
Nectar sources Several species of flowers, but also willows, poplars, running sap, carrion, scat.

1 to 1½ inches

GEORGIA SATYR
NEONYMPHA AREOLATUS

Above, the Georgia Satyr is dark brown with an indistinct band of darker patches near the center of the hind wing. Below, it is dark brown with wavy bands of red-brown or orange-brown on the hind wing and submarginal, straight bands of red-brown or orange-brown on the forewing; there are mottled patches of cream and black on the hind wing.

The Georgia Satyr is most often observed very near the ground in patches of tall grass. It is slow to take flight.

The winter months are spent in the light green caterpillar stage.

FACTS AND FEATURES

Habitat Moist, grassy areas.
Flight 1 to 3 broods, year round in extreme South, April to August in North.
Lifecycle notes Dome-shaped eggs are yellowish; caterpillar is light green with darker side stripes and short, fine hairs; chrysalis is green with cream patches.
Host plants Grasses.
Nectar sources This species does not share its cousin's preference for trees.

1½ to 2 inches

LITTLE WOOD SATYR
MEGISTO CYMELA

The widespread nature of the Little Wood Satyr's populations attest to its abilities to adapt to nearly any sufficiently moist area that is somewhat wooded and grassy.

The winter months are spent in the mottled brown and white caterpillar stage.

This butterfly is brown above with very evenly spaced submarginal black spots, circled in cream with two tiny dots of white in the center. It is gray-brown with a band of spots similar to those above, but nearly connected with small, less distinct patches of white below.

FACTS AND FEATURES

Habitat Moist, wooded, and grassy areas.
Flight 1 or 2 broods, March to September in South, April to July in North.
Lifecycle notes Dome-shaped eggs are yellowish; caterpillar is mottled brown and white; chrysalis is brown and curved.
Host plants Grasses.
Nectar sources Some wildflowers, running sap, carrion.

1¾ to 2 inches

GEMMED SATYR
CYLLOPSIS GEMMA

This butterfly is brown with a band of black spots along the margin of the hind wing above. Below, it is clouded brown with a band of four black, white-edged patches with white or gray centers at the margin of the hind wing.

The Gemmed Satyr is widespread throughout the South, but its populations are scattered and localized.

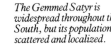

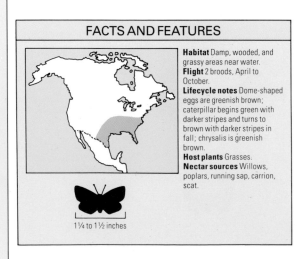

The winter months are spent in the brown caterpillar stage, into which the Gemmed Satyr changes after a few months as a green caterpillar.

FACTS AND FEATURES

Habitat Damp, wooded, and grassy areas near water.
Flight 2 broods, April to October.
Lifecycle notes Dome-shaped eggs are greenish brown; caterpillar begins green with darker stripes and turns to brown with darker stripes in fall; chrysalis is greenish brown.
Host plants Grasses.
Nectar sources Willows, poplars, running sap, carrion, scat.

1¼ to 1½ inches

HAYDEN'S RINGLET
COENONYMPHA HAYDENII

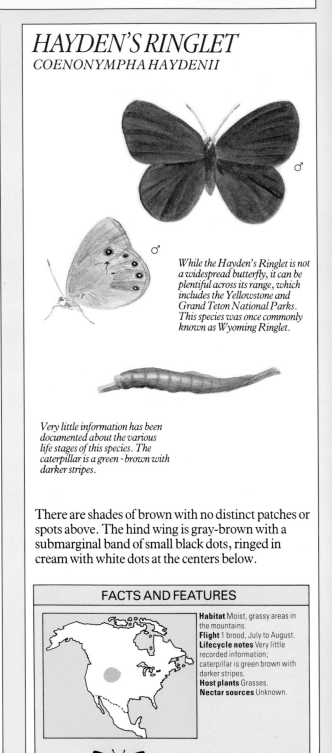

While the Hayden's Ringlet is not a widespread butterfly, it can be plentiful across its range, which includes the Yellowstone and Grand Teton National Parks. This species was once commonly known as Wyoming Ringlet.

Very little information has been documented about the various life stages of this species. The caterpillar is a green - brown with darker stripes.

There are shades of brown with no distinct patches or spots above. The hind wing is gray-brown with a submarginal band of small black dots, ringed in cream with white dots at the centers below.

FACTS AND FEATURES

Habitat Moist, grassy areas in the mountains.
Flight 1 brood, July to August.
Lifecycle notes Very little recorded information; caterpillar is green brown with darker stripes.
Host plants Grasses.
Nectar sources Unknown.

1½ to 2 inches

PRAIRIE RINGLET
COENONYMPHA INORNATA

This butterfly is light brown to red-brown with no distinct markings above. Below, it is light red-brown on the forewing, tan on the hind wing, and both are framed with a broad band of white gray to yellow gray, and a distinct black spot with a white center near the apex of the forewing.

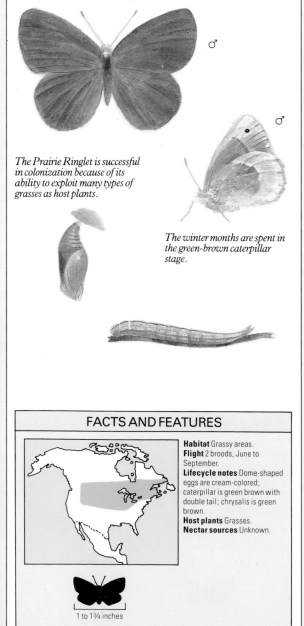

The Prairie Ringlet is successful in colonization because of its ability to exploit many types of grasses as host plants.

The winter months are spent in the green-brown caterpillar stage.

CALIFORNIA RINGLET
COENONYMPHA CALIFORNIA

This butterfly is dull off-white with no distinct markings above. It is off-white with a yellow tint and black-clouded near the body on the hind wing; there are small black dots in a band across the wings below.

The California Ringlet is an extremely poor flier that prefers hiding to flight.

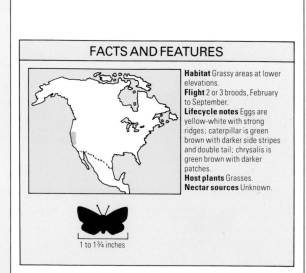

The winter months are spent in the green-brown caterpillar stage.

FACTS AND FEATURES

Habitat Grassy areas.
Flight 2 broods, June to September.
Lifecycle notes Dome-shaped eggs are cream-colored; caterpillar is green brown with double tail; chrysalis is green brown.
Host plants Grasses.
Nectar sources Unknown.

1 to 1¾ inches

FACTS AND FEATURES

Habitat Grassy areas at lower elevations.
Flight 2 or 3 broods, February to September.
Lifecycle notes Eggs are yellow-white with strong ridges; caterpillar is green brown with darker side stripes and double tail; chrysalis is green brown with darker patches.
Host plants Grasses.
Nectar sources Unknown.

1 to 1¾ inches

LARGE WOOD NYMPH
CERCYONIS PEGALA

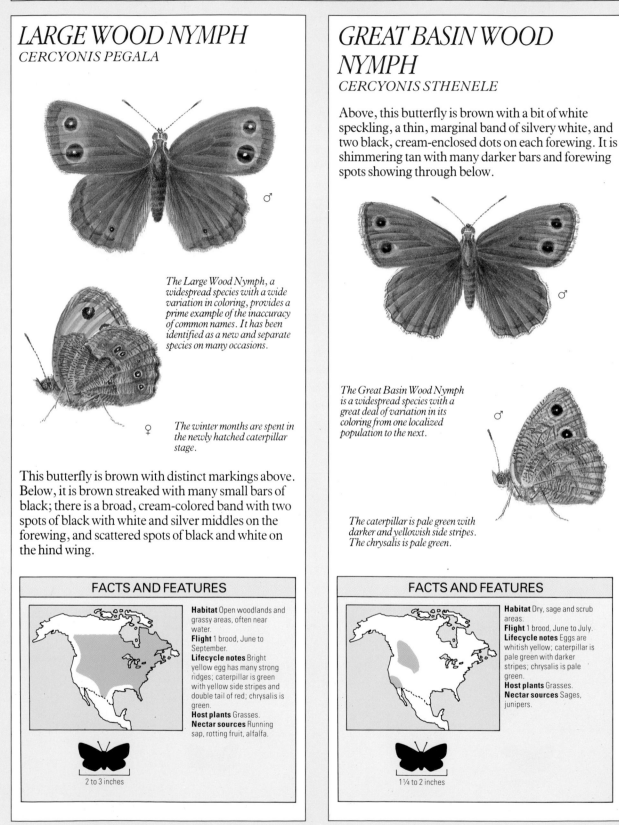

♂

The Large Wood Nymph, a widespread species with a wide variation in coloring, provides a prime example of the inaccuracy of common names. It has been identified as a new and separate species on many occasions.

♀

The winter months are spent in the newly hatched caterpillar stage.

This butterfly is brown with distinct markings above. Below, it is brown streaked with many small bars of black; there is a broad, cream-colored band with two spots of black with white and silver middles on the forewing, and scattered spots of black and white on the hind wing.

FACTS AND FEATURES

Habitat Open woodlands and grassy areas, often near water.
Flight 1 brood, June to September.
Lifecycle notes Bright yellow egg has many strong ridges; caterpillar is green with yellow side stripes and double tail of red; chrysalis is green.
Host plants Grasses.
Nectar sources Running sap, rotting fruit, alfalfa.

2 to 3 inches

GREAT BASIN WOOD NYMPH
CERCYONIS STHENELE

Above, this butterfly is brown with a bit of white speckling, a thin, marginal band of silvery white, and two black, cream-enclosed dots on each forewing. It is shimmering tan with many darker bars and forewing spots showing through below.

♂

The Great Basin Wood Nymph is a widespread species with a great deal of variation in its coloring from one localized population to the next.

♂

The caterpillar is pale green with darker and yellowish side stripes. The chrysalis is pale green.

FACTS AND FEATURES

Habitat Dry, sage and scrub areas.
Flight 1 brood, June to July.
Lifecycle notes Eggs are whitish yellow; caterpillar is pale green with darker stripes; chrysalis is pale green.
Host plants Grasses.
Nectar sources Sages, junipers.

1¼ to 2 inches

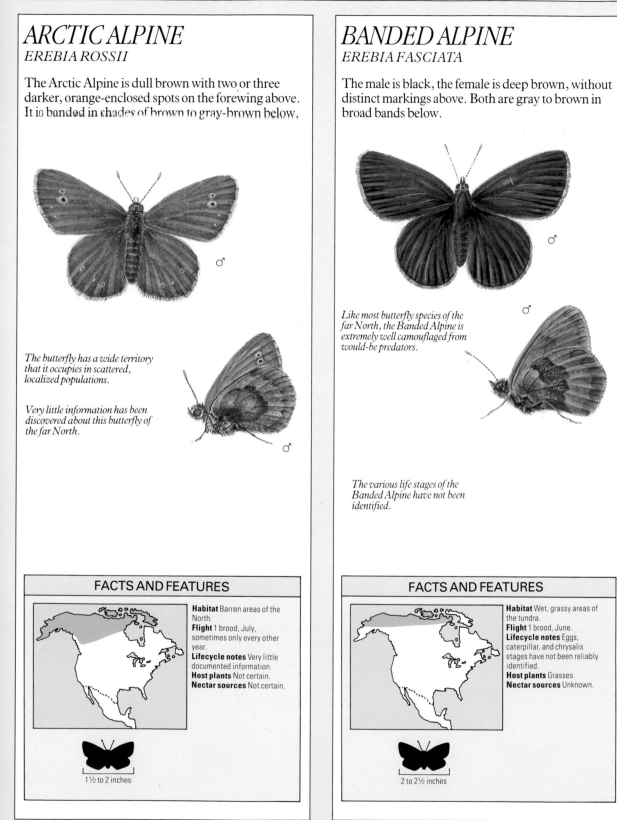

ARCTIC ALPINE
EREBIA ROSSII

The Arctic Alpine is dull brown with two or three darker, orange-enclosed spots on the forewing above. It is banded in shades of brown to gray-brown below,

The butterfly has a wide territory that it occupies in scattered, localized populations.

Very little information has been discovered about this butterfly of the far North.

FACTS AND FEATURES

Habitat Barren areas of the North.
Flight 1 brood, July, sometimes only every other year.
Lifecycle notes Very little documented information.
Host plants Not certain.
Nectar sources Not certain.

1½ to 2 inches

BANDED ALPINE
EREBIA FASCIATA

The male is black, the female is deep brown, without distinct markings above. Both are gray to brown in broad bands below.

Like most butterfly species of the far North, the Banded Alpine is extremely well camouflaged from would-be predators.

The various life stages of the Banded Alpine have not been identified.

FACTS AND FEATURES

Habitat Wet, grassy areas of the tundra.
Flight 1 brood, June.
Lifecycle notes Eggs, caterpillar, and chrysalis stages have not been reliably identified.
Host plants Grasses.
Nectar sources Unknown.

2 to 2½ inches

RED-DISKED ALPINE
EREBIA DISCOIDALIS

This butterfly is black or very dark brown with a reddish hint and longitudinal patches of red-brown on the forewing above. It is mostly black, with a reddish hint, and a small, lighter forewing disk of red-brown below.

The Red-disked Alpine has a wider range, both South and East, than other alpine butterflies. It has been recorded at the Great Lakes.

The Red-disked Alpine's flight season occurs earlier than any other alpine species: May to July.

FACTS AND FEATURES

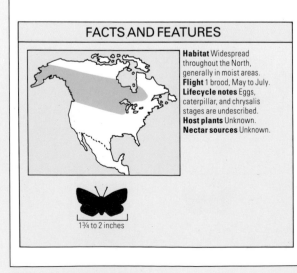

Habitat Widespread throughout the North, generally in moist areas.
Flight 1 brood, May to July.
Lifecycle notes Eggs, caterpillar, and chrysalis stages are undescribed.
Host plants Unknown.
Nectar sources Unknown.

1¾ to 2 inches

YUKON ALPINE
EREBIA YOUNGI

This butterfly is dark brown with several small reddish spots submarginally along the forewing above. Below, it is brown with reddish spots and a gray-brown band across the hind wing.

Like most butterflies of the far North, the Yukon Alpine has an extremely short flight season: late June into early July.

No life stages other than the adult have been documented.

FACTS AND FEATURES

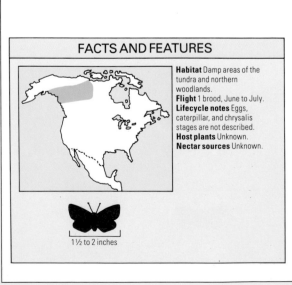

Habitat Damp areas of the tundra and northern woodlands.
Flight 1 brood, June to July.
Lifecycle notes Eggs, caterpillar, and chrysalis stages are not described.
Host plants Unknown.
Nectar sources Unknown.

1½ to 2 inches

COMMON ALPINE
EREBIA EPIPSODEA

The Common Alpine is green-brown with a strong greenish tint and submarginal patches of orange with black and white spots above. It is red-brown with a submarginal band of distinct black, white-eyed spots below.

A highly adaptable species, the Common Alpine is the most southerly of the Alpine butterflies, colonizing even lower altitudes.

The caterpillar pupates in a sack of silk and grass in the spring, after spending the winter in hibernation.

FACTS AND FEATURES

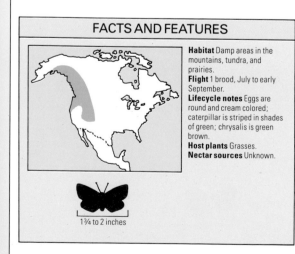

Habitat Damp areas in the mountains, tundra, and prairies.
Flight 1 brood, July to early September.
Lifecycle notes Eggs are round and cream colored; caterpillar is striped in shades of green; chrysalis is green brown.
Host plants Grasses.
Nectar sources Unknown.

1¾ to 2 inches

RIDING'S SATYR
NEOMINOIS RIDINGSII

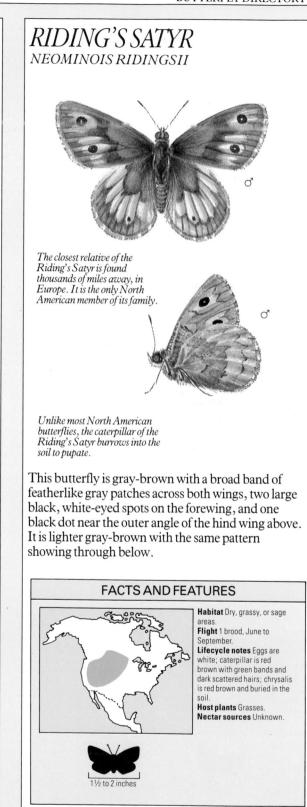

The closest relative of the Riding's Satyr is found thousands of miles away, in Europe. It is the only North American member of its family.

Unlike most North American butterflies, the caterpillar of the Riding's Satyr burrows into the soil to pupate.

This butterfly is gray-brown with a broad band of featherlike gray patches across both wings, two large black, white-eyed spots on the forewing, and one black dot near the outer angle of the hind wing above. It is lighter gray-brown with the same pattern showing through below.

FACTS AND FEATURES

Habitat Dry, grassy, or sage areas.
Flight 1 brood, June to September.
Lifecycle notes Eggs are white; caterpillar is red brown with green bands and dark scattered hairs; chrysalis is red brown and buried in the soil.
Host plants Grasses.
Nectar sources Unknown.

1½ to 2 inches

CANADA ARCTIC
OENEIS MACOUNII

The Canada Arctic is dull orange with a jagged border of dark brown above; there are heavy veins of dark brown and two black, white-eyed spots on the forewing and one smaller black spot on the hind wing. Below the orange center of the forewing is surrounded by a shimmering brown border; there is a shimmering brown hind wing and one black, white-eyed spot on the forewing.

Flights of the Canada Arctic occur only every other year in response to the short summers of the butterfly's far North range.

The caterpillar stage of each Canada Arctic exists for two years before pupating.

FACTS AND FEATURES

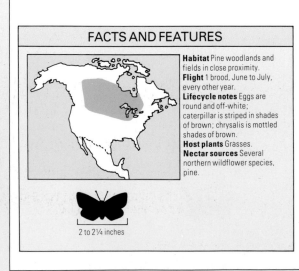

Habitat Pine woodlands and fields in close proximity.
Flight 1 brood, June to July, every other year.
Lifecycle notes Eggs are round and off-white; caterpillar is striped in shades of brown; chrysalis is mottled shades of brown.
Host plants Grasses.
Nectar sources Several northern wildflower species, pine.

2 to 2¼ inches

CHRYXUS ARCTIC
OENEIS CHRYXUS

This butterfly is brown with broad, submarginal bands of dull orange, much larger on the hind wing; there are two black spots in orange on the forewing and one on the hind wing above. There are shades of brown with a large area of orange crossed by black bands on the forewing and one black, white-eyed spot on each wing below.

The Chryxus Arctic is more widespread than most Arctic species.

The winter months, sometimes over a two-year period, are spent in the caterpillar stage.

FACTS AND FEATURES

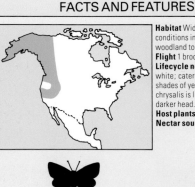

Habitat Wide range of conditions in the North, from woodland to prairie.
Flight 1 brood, May to August.
Lifecycle notes Egg is off-white; caterpillar is striped in shades of yellow and brown; chrysalis is light brown with a darker head.
Host plants Grasses.
Nectar sources Unknown.

1¾ to 2¼ inches

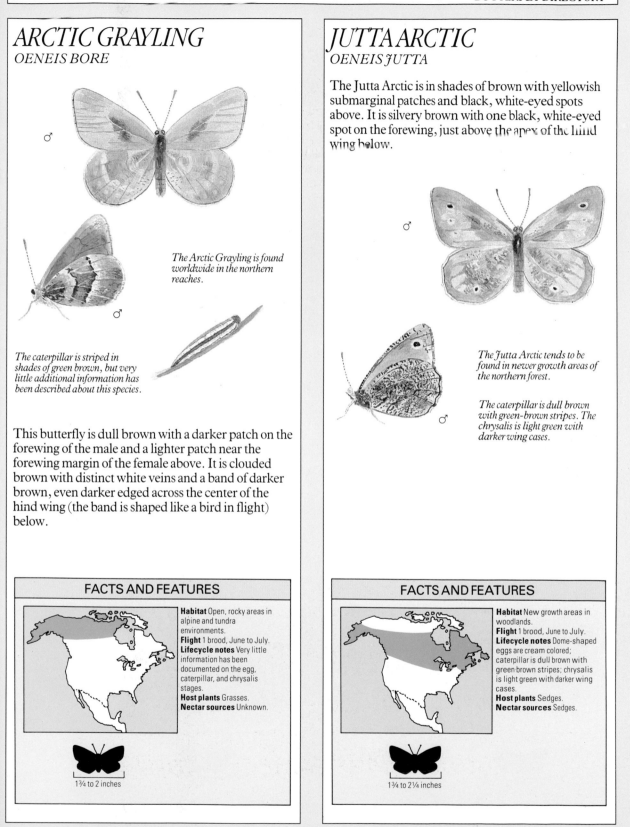

ARCTIC GRAYLING
OENEIS BORE

♂

The Arctic Grayling is found worldwide in the northern reaches.

♂

The caterpillar is striped in shades of green brown, but very little additional information has been described about this species.

This butterfly is dull brown with a darker patch on the forewing of the male and a lighter patch near the forewing margin of the female above. It is clouded brown with distinct white veins and a band of darker brown, even darker edged across the center of the hind wing (the band is shaped like a bird in flight) below.

FACTS AND FEATURES

Habitat Open, rocky areas in alpine and tundra environments.
Flight 1 brood, June to July.
Lifecycle notes Very little information has been documented on the egg, caterpillar, and chrysalis stages.
Host plants Grasses.
Nectar sources Unknown.

1¾ to 2 inches

JUTTA ARCTIC
OENEIS JUTTA

The Jutta Arctic is in shades of brown with yellowish submarginal patches and black, white-eyed spots above. It is silvery brown with one black, white-eyed spot on the forewing, just above the apex of the hind wing below.

♂

The Jutta Arctic tends to be found in newer growth areas of the northern forest.

The caterpillar is dull brown with green-brown stripes. The chrysalis is light green with darker wing cases.

♂

FACTS AND FEATURES

Habitat New growth areas in woodlands.
Flight 1 brood, June to July.
Lifecycle notes Dome-shaped eggs are cream colored; caterpillar is dull brown with green brown stripes; chrysalis is light green with darker wing cases.
Host plants Sedges.
Nectar sources Sedges.

1¾ to 2¼ inches

MELISSA ARCTIC
OENEIS MELISSA

Above, this butterfly is brown without markings. Below, it is a shimmering dark brown with indistinct white veins and a border of alternating white and brown bars.

♂

In New Hampshire, a population of this species is known commonly as the White Mountain Butterfly. It is a remnant population, isolated there thousands of years ago.

♂

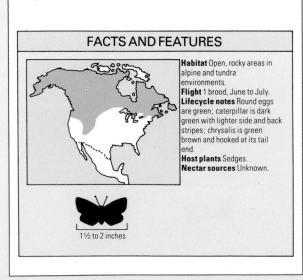

The winter months are spent in the caterpillar stage, buried in leaf litter.

FACTS AND FEATURES

Habitat Open, rocky areas in alpine and tundra environments.
Flight 1 brood, June to July.
Lifecycle notes Round eggs are green; caterpillar is dark green with lighter side and back stripes; chrysalis is green brown and hooked at its tail end.
Host plants Sedges.
Nectar sources Unknown.

1½ to 2 inches

POLIXENES ARCTIC
OENEIS POLIXENES

This butterfly is dull brown with lighter dots submarginally above. It is dull brown with a darker band across its hind wing and a submarginal area of yellow tinting on its hind wing below.

♂

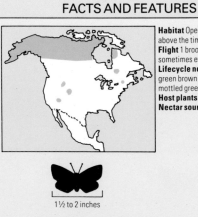

♂

A population of Polixenes Arctic, known commonly as the Katahdin Arctic, exists in Maine's Baxter State Park. It has a reddish hue to its brown coloring.

The winter months, sometimes over a two-year span, are spent in the caterpillar stage.

FACTS AND FEATURES

Habitat Open, rocky areas above the timberline.
Flight 1 brood, July to August, sometimes every other year.
Lifecycle notes Caterpillar is green brown; chrysalis is mottled green and brown tones.
Host plants Grasses.
Nectar sources Unknown.

1½ to 2 inches

MONARCH
DANAUS PLEXIPPUS

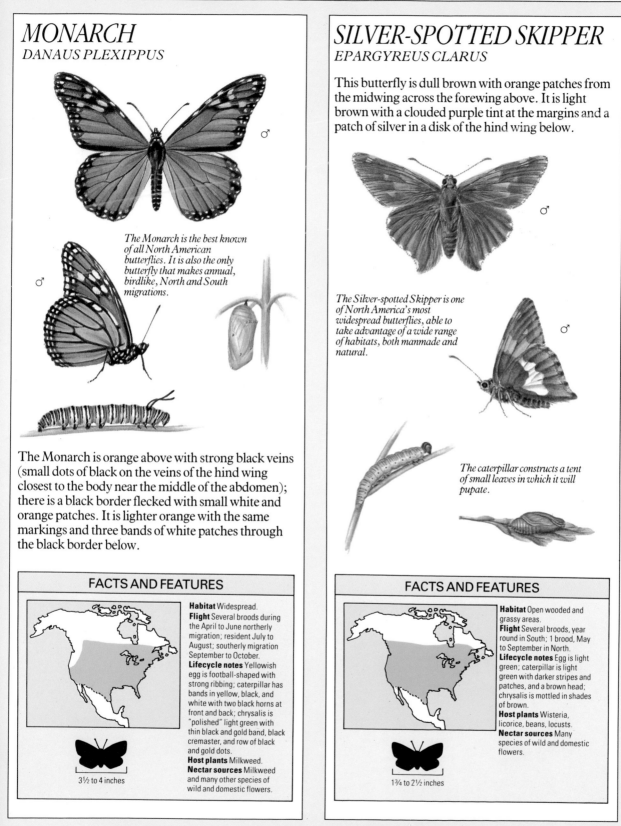

The Monarch is the best known of all North American butterflies. It is also the only butterfly that makes annual, birdlike, North and South migrations.

The Monarch is orange above with strong black veins (small dots of black on the veins of the hind wing closest to the body near the middle of the abdomen); there is a black border flecked with small white and orange patches. It is lighter orange with the same markings and three bands of white patches through the black border below.

FACTS AND FEATURES

Habitat Widespread.
Flight Several broods during the April to June northerly migration; resident July to August; southerly migration September to October.
Lifecycle notes Yellowish egg is football-shaped with strong ribbing; caterpillar has bands in yellow, black, and white with two black horns at front and back; chrysalis is "polished" light green with thin black and gold band, black cremaster, and row of black and gold dots.
Host plants Milkweed.
Nectar sources Milkweed and many other species of wild and domestic flowers.

3½ to 4 inches

SILVER-SPOTTED SKIPPER
EPARGYREUS CLARUS

This butterfly is dull brown with orange patches from the midwing across the forewing above. It is light brown with a clouded purple tint at the margins and a patch of silver in a disk of the hind wing below.

The Silver-spotted Skipper is one of North America's most widespread butterflies, able to take advantage of a wide range of habitats, both manmade and natural.

The caterpillar constructs a tent of small leaves in which it will pupate.

FACTS AND FEATURES

Habitat Open wooded and grassy areas.
Flight Several broods, year round in South; 1 brood, May to September in North.
Lifecycle notes Egg is light green; caterpillar is light green with darker stripes and patches, and a brown head; chrysalis is mottled in shades of brown.
Host plants Wisteria, licorice, beans, locusts.
Nectar sources Many species of wild and domestic flowers.

1¾ to 2½ inches

LONG-TAILED SKIPPER
URBANUS PROTEUS

A long tail protrudes behind the body of this butterfly. It is brown with patches of tan across the middle of the forewing; there is an irridescent green and blue tint at the base of the hind wing above. It is gray with bands of white and black patches across the middle of the wings and submarginally below.

The Long-tailed Skipper, which can be quite abundant, is a pest in agricultural areas, where it is nicknamed the Bean-leaf Roller.

The caterpillar makes host plants out of a large number of species, one reason for its abundance.

FACTS AND FEATURES

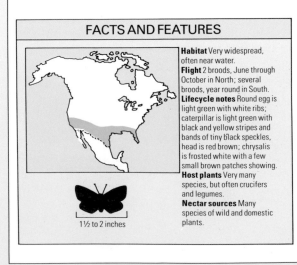

Habitat Very widespread, often near water.
Flight 2 broods, June through October in North; several broods, year round in South.
Lifecycle notes Round egg is light green with white ribs; caterpillar is light green with black and yellow stripes and bands of tiny black speckles, head is red brown; chrysalis is frosted white with a few small brown patches showing.
Host plants Very many species, but often crucifers and legumes.
Nectar sources Many species of wild and domestic plants.

1½ to 2 inches

GOLDEN-BANDED SKIPPER
AUTOCHTON CELLUS

The Golden-banded Skipper has one of the widest ranges of the large Skippers.

The caterpillar feeds only at night, spending the daylight hours in a tent made of leaves drawn together with silk.

This butterfly is very dark brown above with a broad yellow band running parallel to the body, across the middle of the forewing; there is a smaller yellow patch closer to the apex. Below, there is lighter coloring with the same pattern, but with an additional clouded gray area near the margin of the hind wing.

FACTS AND FEATURES

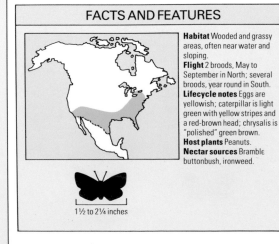

Habitat Wooded and grassy areas, often near water and sloping.
Flight 2 broods, May to September in North; several broods, year round in South.
Lifecycle notes Eggs are yellowish; caterpillar is light green with yellow stripes and a red-brown head; chrysalis is "polished" green brown.
Host plants Peanuts.
Nectar sources Bramble buttonbush, ironweed.

1½ to 2¼ inches

HOARY EDGE
ACHALARUS LYCIADES

The Hoary Edge is dark brown with several orange spots in a disk on the forewing above. It is mottled dark gray-brown next to the body, fading into lighter shades of brown on the forewing and white on the hind wing below.

Male Hoary Edges guard small woodland clearings, where they will eventually mate with passing females.

The winter months are spent in the mottled brown and dull yellow chrysalis stage.

FACTS AND FEATURES

Habitat Wooded areas with openings, often near new growth.
Flight 1 brood, May to July in North; several broods, year round in South.
Lifecycle notes Egg is cream colored and laid in strings of a half-dozen or so; caterpillar is green with blue-green stripes and scattered yellowish dots; chrysalis is mottled brown and dull yellow.
Host plants Trefoil, clover.
Nectar sources Unknown.

1½ to 1¾ inches

SOUTHERN CLOUDYWING
THORYBES BATHYLLUS

This butterfly is dull, dark brown with hourglass-shaped patches of gray near the middle of the forewing and a submarginal reddish tint above. It is brown with a broken band of white across the middle of the forewing and is clouded white approaching the margin of the hind wing below.

This well-camouflaged species is a rare sight to many, despite the fact that it is often common within its range.

The winter months are spent in the mottled brown chrysalis stage.

FACTS AND FEATURES

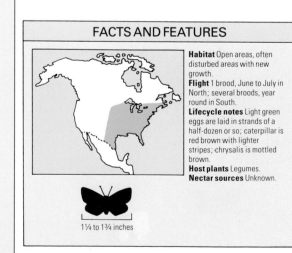

Habitat Open areas, often disturbed areas with new growth.
Flight 1 brood, June to July in North; several broods, year round in South.
Lifecycle notes Light green eggs are laid in strands of a half-dozen or so; caterpillar is red brown with lighter stripes; chrysalis is mottled brown.
Host plants Legumes.
Nectar sources Unknown.

1¼ to 1¾ inches

117

NORTHERN CLOUDYWING
THORYBES PYLADES

This butterfly's coloring is shades of brown with small, triangular patches of gray white at the costa of the forewing and submarginal speckling of gray white on the forewing above. There is similar coloration, with indistinct black spots across the center of the hind wing below.

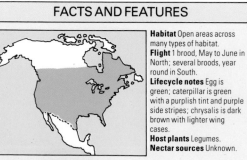

The Northern Cloudywing is a very widespread butterfly, including most of North America in its range.

The caterpillar builds a tent of silk in a leaf of a host plant, where it hides much of the time.

FACTS AND FEATURES

Habitat Open areas across many types of habitat.
Flight 1 brood, May to June in North; several broods, year round in South.
Lifecycle notes Egg is green; caterpillar is green with a purplish tint and purple side stripes; chrysalis is dark brown with lighter wing cases.
Host plants Legumes.
Nectar sources Unknown.

1¼ to 2 inches

EASTERN CLOUDYWING
THORYBES CONFUSIS

Above, this butterfly is dark brown with a dusting of white speckles and white-gray patches in a thin band at the costa of the forewing. It is colored in shades of brown, darker at the body and mottled, with indistinct black patches below.

The Eastern Cloudywing has a great deal of color variation across its subspecies.

The caterpillar builds a silken tent among the leaves of its legume host plants.

FACTS AND FEATURES

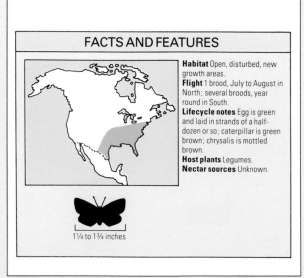

Habitat Open, disturbed, new growth areas.
Flight 1 brood, July to August in North; several broods, year round in South.
Lifecycle notes Egg is green and laid in strands of a half-dozen or so; caterpillar is green brown; chrysalis is mottled brown.
Host plants Legumes.
Nectar sources Unknown.

1¼ to 1¾ inches

SCALLOPED SOOTYWING
STAPHYLUS HAYHURSTII

The Scalloped Sootywing is widespread across many habitats, but is found particularly in moist and wooded spots.

The caterpillar is green with a red-brown head. The chrysalis is green-brown, frosted with white.

The outer margins of the hind wings are noticeably scalloped. It is dark brown, mottled with dark patches, and covered with white and cream speckles; there is a bluish tint near the body above. There is similar, although lighter, coloring below.

FACTS AND FEATURES

Habitat Moist, wooded spots across many habitat types.
Flight 2 broods, April to October in North; 3 broods, March to November in South.
Lifecycle notes Egg is pale orange; caterpillar is green with red-brown head; chrysalis is green brown, frosted with white.
Host plants Amaranth.
Nectar sources Unknown.

1 to 1¼ inches

DREAMY DUSKYWING
ERYNNIS ICELUS

There are multiple bands of brown, gray, and white spots across the forewings. The hind wings are plainer above. Below, it is similar to above, but with subtler markings

The Dreamy Duskywing uses numerous types of tree as host plants.

The caterpillar is light green and hairy with a red, orange, and yellow head; it hibernates during the winter.

FACTS AND FEATURES

Habitat Foothills and scrub oak flats.
Flight 1 brood, May.
Lifecycle notes Egg is green; caterpillar is light green and hairy with a red, orange, and yellow head, and hibernates during winters; chrysalis is brown to green.
Host plants Various types of oaks.
Nectar sources Unknown.

1 to 2 inches

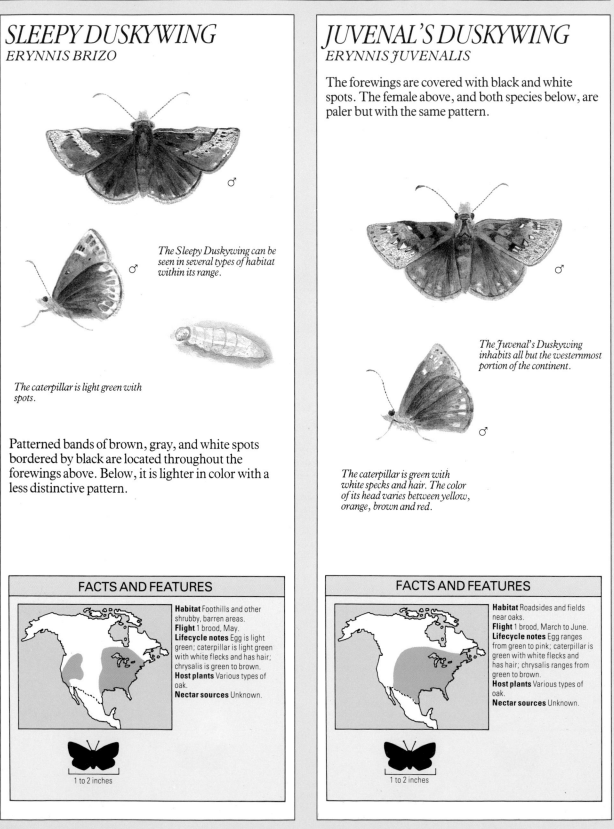

SLEEPY DUSKYWING
ERYNNIS BRIZO

The Sleepy Duskywing can be seen in several types of habitat within its range.

The caterpillar is light green with spots.

Patterned bands of brown, gray, and white spots bordered by black are located throughout the forewings above. Below, it is lighter in color with a less distinctive pattern.

FACTS AND FEATURES

Habitat Foothills and other shrubby, barren areas.
Flight 1 brood, May.
Lifecycle notes Egg is light green; caterpillar is light green with white flecks and has hair; chrysalis is green to brown.
Host plants Various types of oak.
Nectar sources Unknown.

1 to 2 inches

JUVENAL'S DUSKYWING
ERYNNIS JUVENALIS

The forewings are covered with black and white spots. The female above, and both species below, are paler but with the same pattern.

The Juvenal's Duskywing inhabits all but the westernmost portion of the continent.

The caterpillar is green with white specks and hair. The color of its head varies between yellow, orange, brown and red.

FACTS AND FEATURES

Habitat Roadsides and fields near oaks.
Flight 1 brood, March to June.
Lifecycle notes Egg ranges from green to pink; caterpillar is green with white flecks and has hair; chrysalis ranges from green to brown.
Host plants Various types of oak.
Nectar sources Unknown.

1 to 2 inches

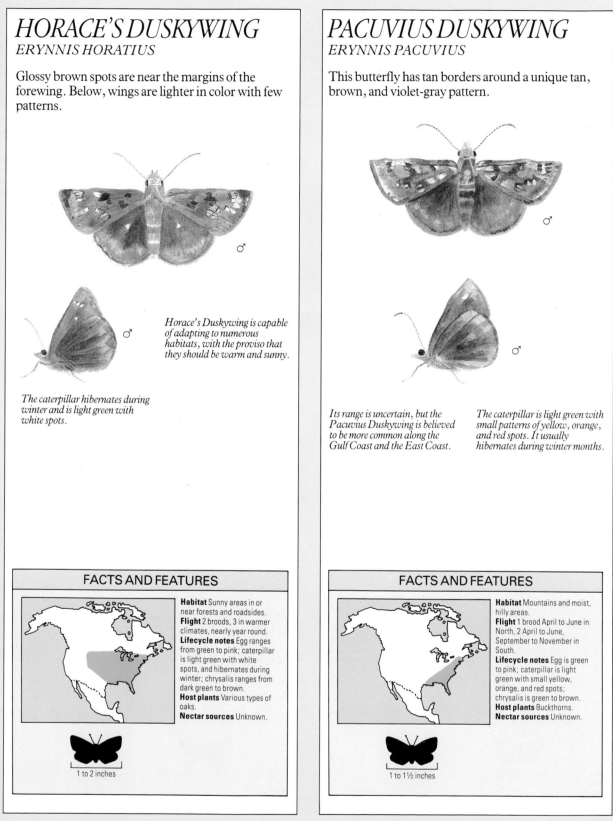

HORACE'S DUSKYWING
ERYNNIS HORATIUS

Glossy brown spots are near the margins of the forewing. Below, wings are lighter in color with few patterns.

♂

Horace's Duskywing is capable of adapting to numerous habitats, with the proviso that they should be warm and sunny.

♂

The caterpillar hibernates during winter and is light green with white spots.

PACUVIUS DUSKYWING
ERYNNIS PACUVIUS

This butterfly has tan borders around a unique tan, brown, and violet-gray pattern.

♂

♂

Its range is uncertain, but the Pacuvius Duskywing is believed to be more common along the Gulf Coast and the East Coast.

The caterpillar is light green with small patterns of yellow, orange, and red spots. It usually hibernates during winter months.

FACTS AND FEATURES

Habitat Sunny areas in or near forests and roadsides.
Flight 2 broods, 3 in warmer climates, nearly year round.
Lifecycle notes Egg ranges from green to pink; caterpillar is light green with white spots, and hibernates during winter; chrysalis ranges from dark green to brown.
Host plants Various types of oaks.
Nectar sources Unknown.

1 to 2 inches

FACTS AND FEATURES

Habitat Mountains and moist, hilly areas.
Flight 1 brood April to June in North, 2 April to June, September to November in South.
Lifecycle notes Egg is green to pink; caterpillar is light green with small yellow, orange, and red spots; chrysalis is green to brown.
Host plants Buckthorns.
Nectar sources Unknown.

1 to 1½ inches

ZARUCCO DUSKYWING
ERYNNIS ZARUCCO

There are puffs of light brown near the margins of the wings above.

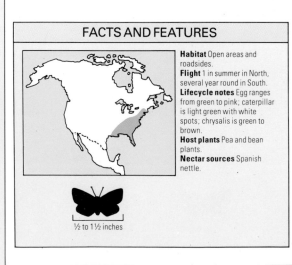

♂

The Zarucco Duskywing's range is mainly along the East Coast, with concentration in Florida.

The caterpillar is light green with white spots.

FACTS AND FEATURES

Habitat Open areas and roadsides.
Flight 1 in summer in North, several year round in South.
Lifecycle notes Egg ranges from green to pink; caterpillar is light green with white spots; chrysalis is green to brown.
Host plants Pea and bean plants.
Nectar sources Spanish nettle.

½ to 1½ inches

FUNEREAL DUSKYWING
ERYNNIS FUNERALIS

The dark brown forewings are interrupted by darker patches; the hind wings are broad with white edges above. The wings are lighter below.

♂

♂

The Funereal Duskywing is named after its dark, somber coloring. Able to use many species of legumes as host plants, the Funereal Duskywing is expanding its range.

The caterpillar is green with yellow spots and stripes.

FACTS AND FEATURES

Habitat Mountains, deserts, and moist areas.
Flight Continuous broods, nearly year round.
Lifecycle notes Caterpillar is green with yellow spots and stripes; chrysalis is green.
Host plants Woody plants.
Nectar sources Unknown.

½ to 1½ inches

WILD INDIGO DUSKYWING
ERYNNIS BAPTISIAE

Above, the dark brown wings have patches of large, light brown spots and some white spots near the tips. Below is similar to above except that the patches and spots are less prevalent.

This butterfly ranges over a wide area.

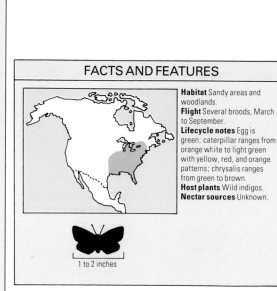

The caterpillar is orange white to green with yellow to red spots.

SMALL CHECKERED SKIPPER
PYRGUS SCRIPTURA

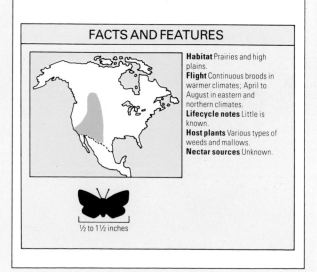

The small Checkered Skipper is known as one of the first butterflies seen in spring within its range.

This butterfly can be seen nearly year round in warmer climates.

A single row of white spots similar to a checkered pattern rims the borders of the hind wing. Additional white spots are scattered throughout the center of the wings above. Below, it is gray-olive with spots.

FACTS AND FEATURES

Habitat Sandy areas and woodlands.
Flight Several broods, March to September.
Lifecycle notes Egg is green; caterpillar ranges from orange white to light green with yellow, red, and orange patterns; chrysalis ranges from green to brown.
Host plants Wild indigos.
Nectar sources Unknown.

1 to 2 inches

FACTS AND FEATURES

Habitat Prairies and high plains.
Flight Continuous broods in warmer climates; April to August in eastern and northern climates.
Lifecycle notes Little is known.
Host plants Various types of weeds and mallows.
Nectar sources Unknown.

½ to 1½ inches

COMMON CHECKERED SKIPPER
PYRGUS COMMUNIS

The colors on wings vary, but they nearly always have a blue, powdery sheen in the center above. There are four bands of green to tan aligned along the wings below.

The Common Checkered Skipper is widespread.

The caterpillar is tan with dark lines. The winter months are spent in either the caterpillar or chrysalis stage.

FACTS AND FEATURES

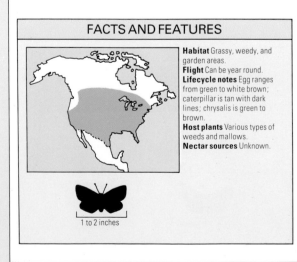

Habitat Grassy, weedy, and garden areas.
Flight Can be year round.
Lifecycle notes Egg ranges from green to white brown; caterpillar is tan with dark lines; chrysalis is green to brown.
Host plants Various types of weeds and mallows.
Nectar sources Unknown.

1 to 2 inches

COMMON SOOTYWING
PHOLISOR CATULLUS

Rows of white spots shaped like semicircles align the wings above. The edges of the hind wing are mostly brown below.

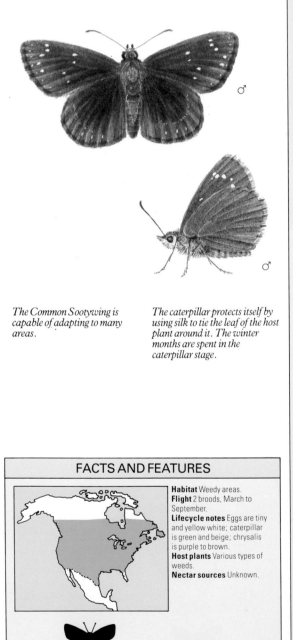

The Common Sootywing is capable of adapting to many areas.

The caterpillar protects itself by using silk to tie the leaf of the host plant around it. The winter months are spent in the caterpillar stage.

FACTS AND FEATURES

Habitat Weedy areas.
Flight 2 broods, March to September.
Lifecycle notes Eggs are tiny and yellow white; caterpillar is green and beige; chrysalis is purple to brown.
Host plants Various types of weeds.
Nectar sources Unknown.

1 to 2 inches

GREAT BASIN SOOTYWING
PHOLISORA LIBYA

The dark wings have small, white spots above. Below, rows of white spots cross the hind wings.

♂

The Great Basin Sootywing lives mostly in deserts and heartland regions.

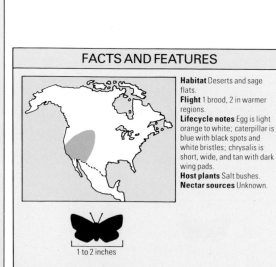

♂

The caterpillar is blue with black spots and white hairs.

FACTS AND FEATURES

Habitat Deserts and sage flats.
Flight 1 brood, 2 in warmer regions.
Lifecycle notes Egg is light orange to white; caterpillar is blue with black spots and white bristles; chrysalis is short, wide, and tan with dark wing pads.
Host plants Salt bushes.
Nectar sources Unknown.

1 to 2 inches

ARCTIC SKIPPER
CARTEROCEPHALUS PALAEMON

Large orange spots are located throughout the wings and smaller orange spots are aligned along the wing edges.

♂

The Arctic Skipper is common within its range.

♂

The caterpillar is green to white with dark back stripes and yellow side stripes above spots. It hibernates during the winter months.

FACTS AND FEATURES

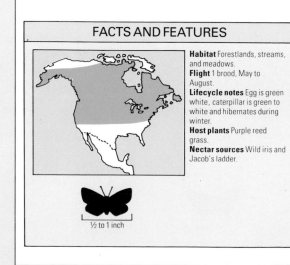

Habitat Forestlands, streams, and meadows.
Flight 1 brood, May to August.
Lifecycle notes Egg is green white, caterpillar is green to white and hibernates during winter.
Host plants Purple reed grass.
Nectar sources Wild iris and Jacob's ladder.

½ to 1 inch

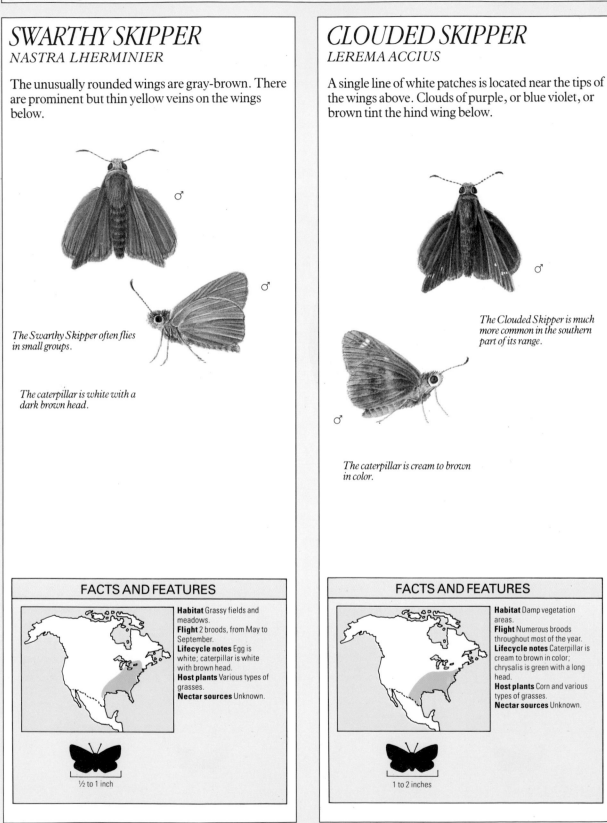

SWARTHY SKIPPER
NASTRA LHERMINIER

The unusually rounded wings are gray-brown. There are prominent but thin yellow veins on the wings below.

♂

♂

The Swarthy Skipper often flies in small groups.

The caterpillar is white with a dark brown head.

CLOUDED SKIPPER
LEREMA ACCIUS

A single line of white patches is located near the tips of the wings above. Clouds of purple, or blue violet, or brown tint the hind wing below.

♂

The Clouded Skipper is much more common in the southern part of its range.

♂

The caterpillar is cream to brown in color.

FACTS AND FEATURES

Habitat Grassy fields and meadows.
Flight 2 broods, from May to September.
Lifecycle notes Egg is white; caterpillar is white with brown head.
Host plants Various types of grasses.
Nectar sources Unknown.

½ to 1 inch

FACTS AND FEATURES

Habitat Damp vegetation areas.
Flight Numerous broods throughout most of the year.
Lifecycle notes Caterpillar is cream to brown in color; chrysalis is green with a long head.
Host plants Corn and various types of grasses.
Nectar sources Unknown.

1 to 2 inches

LEAST SKIPPERLING
ANCYLOXYPHA NUMITOR

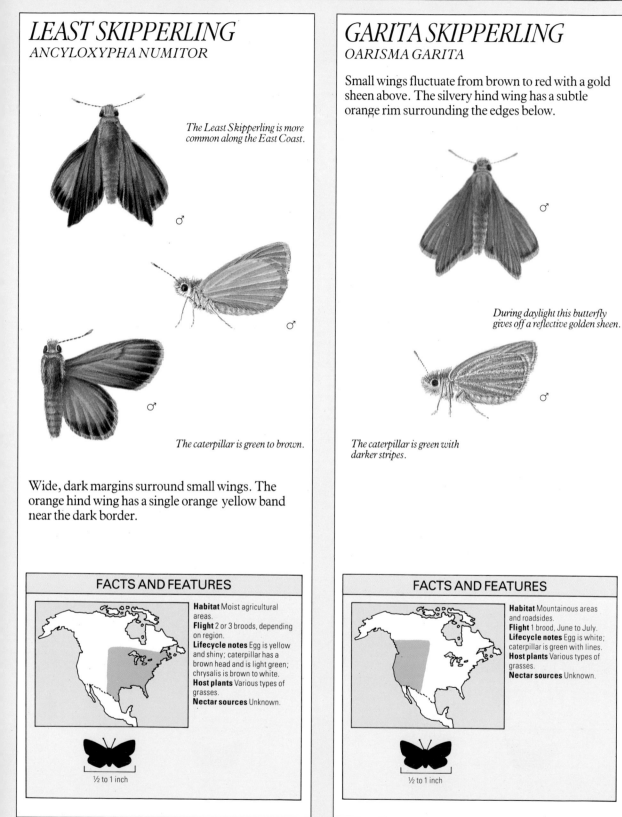

The Least Skipperling is more common along the East Coast.

♂

♂

♂

The caterpillar is green to brown.

Wide, dark margins surround small wings. The orange hind wing has a single orange yellow band near the dark border.

GARITA SKIPPERLING
OARISMA GARITA

Small wings fluctuate from brown to red with a gold sheen above. The silvery hind wing has a subtle orange rim surrounding the edges below.

♂

During daylight this butterfly gives off a reflective golden sheen.

♂

The caterpillar is green with darker stripes.

FACTS AND FEATURES

Habitat Moist agricultural areas.
Flight 2 or 3 broods, depending on region.
Lifecycle notes Egg is yellow and shiny; caterpillar has a brown head and is light green; chrysalis is brown to white.
Host plants Various types of grasses.
Nectar sources Unknown.

½ to 1 inch

FACTS AND FEATURES

Habitat Mountainous areas and roadsides.
Flight 1 brood, June to July.
Lifecycle notes Egg is white; caterpillar is green with lines.
Host plants Various types of grasses.
Nectar sources Unknown.

½ to 1 inch

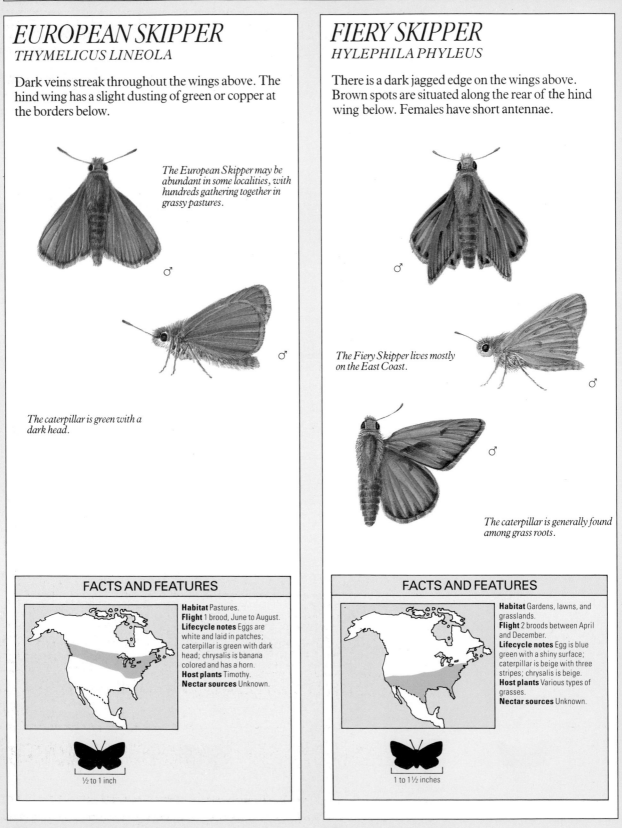

EUROPEAN SKIPPER
THYMELICUS LINEOLA

Dark veins streak throughout the wings above. The hind wing has a slight dusting of green or copper at the borders below.

The European Skipper may be abundant in some localities, with hundreds gathering together in grassy pastures.

The caterpillar is green with a dark head.

FACTS AND FEATURES

Habitat Pastures.
Flight 1 brood, June to August.
Lifecycle notes Eggs are white and laid in patches; caterpillar is green with dark head; chrysalis is banana colored and has a horn.
Host plants Timothy.
Nectar sources Unknown.

½ to 1 inch

FIERY SKIPPER
HYLEPHILA PHYLEUS

There is a dark jagged edge on the wings above. Brown spots are situated along the rear of the hind wing below. Females have short antennae.

The Fiery Skipper lives mostly on the East Coast.

The caterpillar is generally found among grass roots.

FACTS AND FEATURES

Habitat Gardens, lawns, and grasslands.
Flight 2 broods between April and December.
Lifecycle notes Egg is blue green with a shiny surface; caterpillar is beige with three stripes; chrysalis is beige.
Host plants Various types of grasses.
Nectar sources Unknown.

1 to 1½ inches

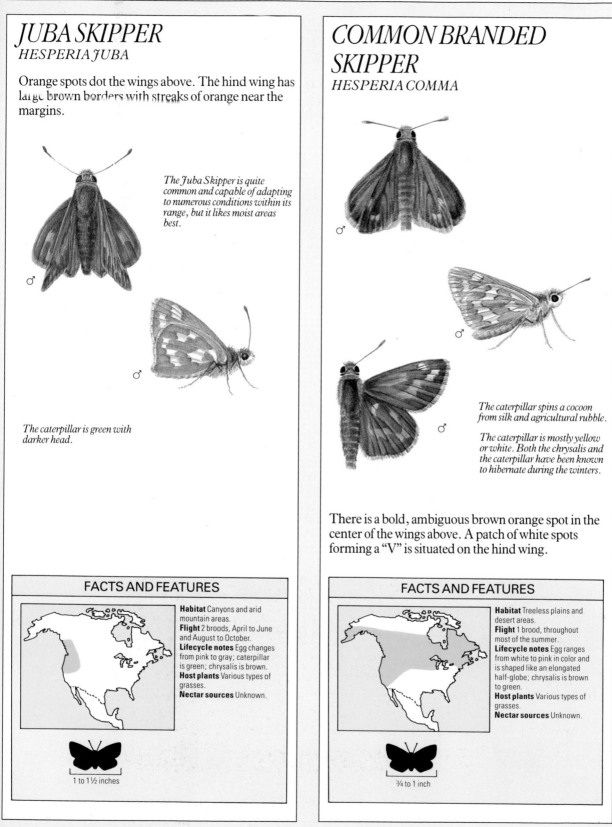

JUBA SKIPPER
HESPERIA JUBA

Orange spots dot the wings above. The hind wing has large brown borders with streaks of orange near the margins.

The Juba Skipper is quite common and capable of adapting to numerous conditions within its range, but it likes moist areas best.

The caterpillar is green with darker head.

COMMON BRANDED SKIPPER
HESPERIA COMMA

The caterpillar spins a cocoon from silk and agricultural rubble.

The caterpillar is mostly yellow or white. Both the chrysalis and the caterpillar have been known to hibernate during the winters.

There is a bold, ambiguous brown orange spot in the center of the wings above. A patch of white spots forming a "V" is situated on the hind wing.

FACTS AND FEATURES

Habitat Canyons and arid mountain areas.
Flight 2 broods, April to June and August to October.
Lifecycle notes Egg changes from pink to gray; caterpillar is green; chrysalis is brown.
Host plants Various types of grasses.
Nectar sources Unknown.

1 to 1½ inches

FACTS AND FEATURES

Habitat Treeless plains and desert areas.
Flight 1 brood, throughout most of the summer.
Lifecycle notes Egg ranges from white to pink in color and is shaped like an elongated half-globe; chrysalis is brown to green.
Host plants Various types of grasses.
Nectar sources Unknown.

¾ to 1 inch

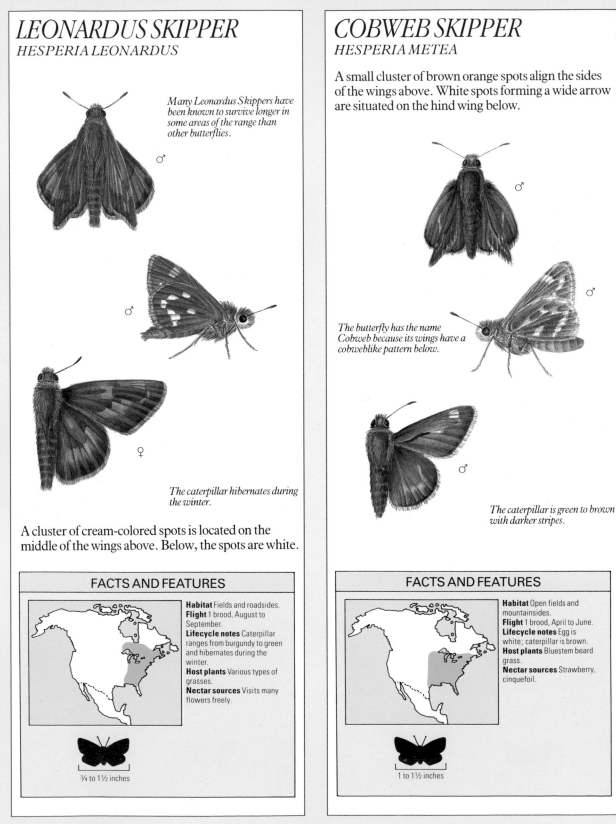

LEONARDUS SKIPPER
HESPERIA LEONARDUS

Many Leonardus Skippers have been known to survive longer in some areas of the range than other butterflies.

♂

♂

♀

The caterpillar hibernates during the winter.

A cluster of cream-colored spots is located on the middle of the wings above. Below, the spots are white.

FACTS AND FEATURES

Habitat Fields and roadsides.
Flight 1 brood, August to September.
Lifecycle notes Caterpillar ranges from burgundy to green and hibernates during the winter.
Host plants Various types of grasses.
Nectar sources Visits many flowers freely.

¾ to 1½ inches

COBWEB SKIPPER
HESPERIA METEA

A small cluster of brown orange spots align the sides of the wings above. White spots forming a wide arrow are situated on the hind wing below.

♂

♂

The butterfly has the name Cobweb because its wings have a cobweblike pattern below.

♂

The caterpillar is green to brown with darker stripes.

FACTS AND FEATURES

Habitat Open fields and mountainsides.
Flight 1 brood, April to June.
Lifecycle notes Egg is white; caterpillar is brown.
Host plants Bluestem beard grass.
Nectar sources Strawberry, cinquefoil.

1 to 1½ inches

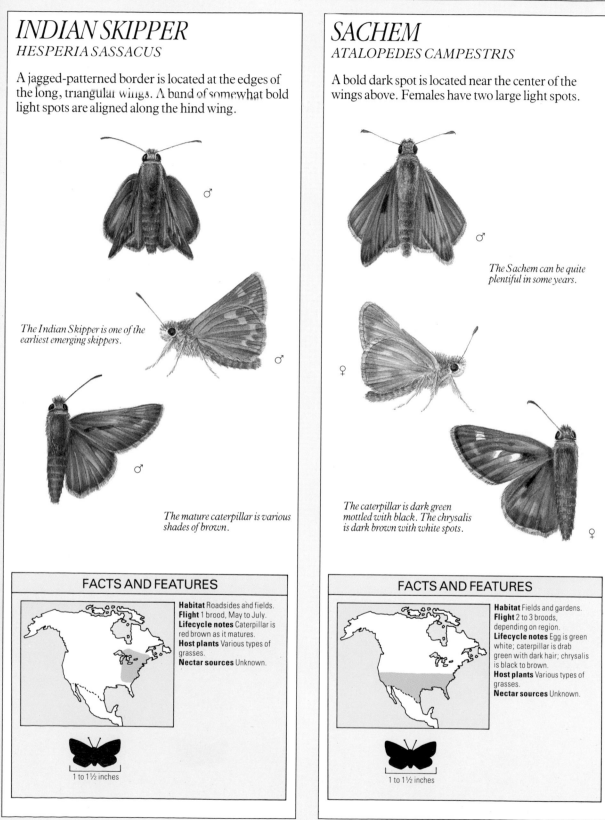

INDIAN SKIPPER
HESPERIA SASSACUS

A jagged-patterned border is located at the edges of the long, triangular wings. A band of somewhat bold light spots are aligned along the hind wing.

♂

The Indian Skipper is one of the earliest emerging skippers.

♂

♂

The mature caterpillar is various shades of brown.

FACTS AND FEATURES

Habitat Roadsides and fields.
Flight 1 brood, May to July.
Lifecycle notes Caterpillar is red brown as it matures.
Host plants Various types of grasses.
Nectar sources Unknown.

1 to 1½ inches

SACHEM
ATALOPEDES CAMPESTRIS

A bold dark spot is located near the center of the wings above. Females have two large light spots.

♂

The Sachem can be quite plentiful in some years.

♀

The caterpillar is dark green mottled with black. The chrysalis is dark brown with white spots.

♀

FACTS AND FEATURES

Habitat Fields and gardens.
Flight 2 to 3 broods, depending on region.
Lifecycle notes Egg is green white; caterpillar is drab green with dark hair; chrysalis is black to brown.
Host plants Various types of grasses.
Nectar sources Unknown.

1 to 1½ inches

YELLOWPATCH SKIPPER
POLITES CORAS

A patch of yellow spots runs across the wings above. A cluster of yellow arrowheads is on the hind wing below.

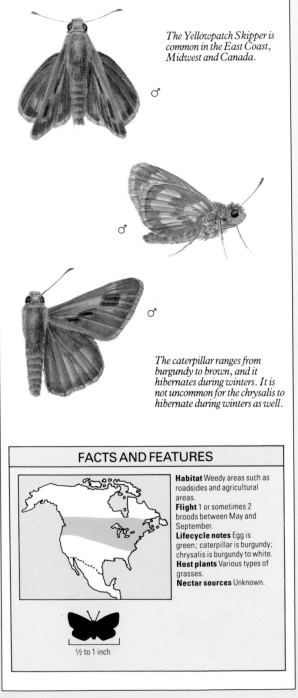

The Yellowpatch Skipper is common in the East Coast, Midwest and Canada.

♂

♂

♂

The caterpillar ranges from burgundy to brown, and it hibernates during winters. It is not uncommon for the chrysalis to hibernate during winters as well.

FACTS AND FEATURES

Habitat Weedy areas such as roadsides and agricultural areas.
Flight 1 or sometimes 2 broods between May and September.
Lifecycle notes Egg is green; caterpillar is burgundy; chrysalis is burgundy to white.
Host plants Various types of grasses.
Nectar sources Unknown.

½ to 1 inch

SANDHILL SKIPPER
POLITES SABULETI

There are wide, dark bands near the margins of the wings above. The outer rim is light orange to brown on the hind wing below. Females have yellow spots on the hind wing below.

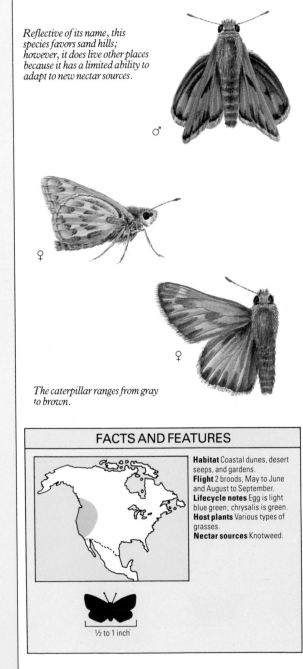

Reflective of its name, this species favors sand hills; however, it does live other places because it has a limited ability to adapt to new nectar sources.

♂

♀

♀

The caterpillar ranges from gray to brown.

FACTS AND FEATURES

Habitat Coastal dunes, desert seeps, and gardens.
Flight 2 broods, May to June and August to September.
Lifecycle notes Egg is light blue green; chrysalis is green.
Host plants Various types of grasses.
Nectar sources Knotweed.

½ to 1 inch

TAWNY-EDGED SKIPPER
POLITES THEMISTOCLES

It has short, pointed brown-green wings above. Below, there is a tawny orange area near the front of the wing, like the name suggests. Sometimes an indistinct cluster of light spots aligns the yellow orange hind wing.

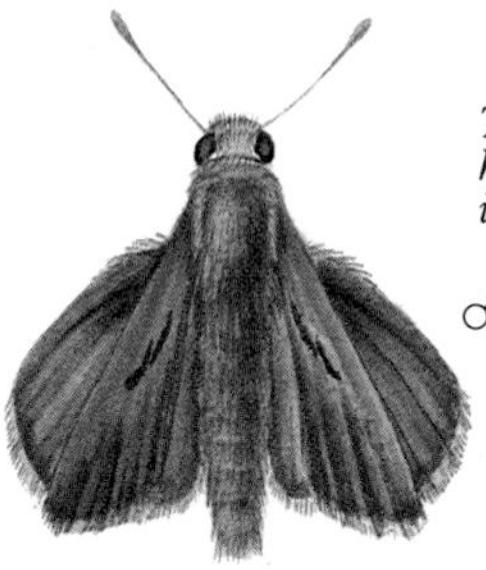

This species chooses varying habits in different regions within its normal range.

♂

♂

♂

The chrysalis ranges from a cream color to brown, and it hibernates during the winter.

FACTS AND FEATURES

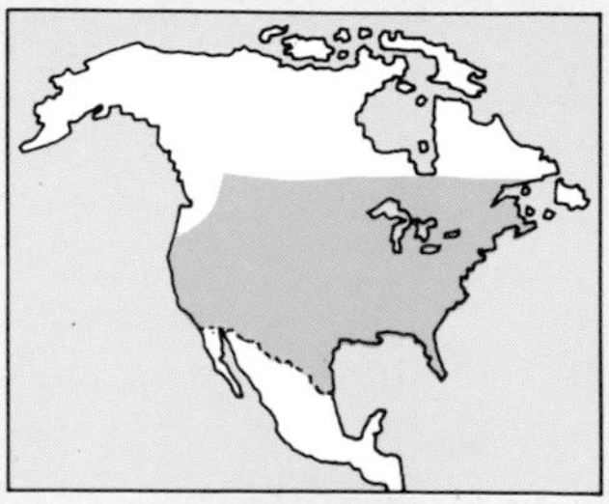

Habitat Grasslands.
Flight 1 to 2 broods, depending on warmth of climate.
Lifecycle notes Caterpillar ranges from tan to maroon; chrysalis ranges from cream to brown.
Host plants Various types of grasses.
Nectar sources Coneflower, dogbane, chickory, alfalfa.

½ to 1 inch

CROSSLINE SKIPPER
POLITES ORIGENES

The Crossline Skipper is abundant in areas providing a favorable climate and feeding conditions.

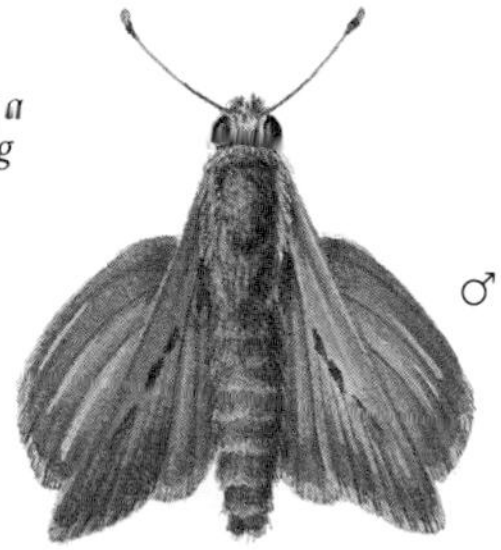

♂

♂

♀

The caterpillar is dark brown mottled with white. The winter months are spent in the caterpillar stage.

A single patch of gray-brown flakes aligns the streamlined forewing above. Females may not have brown-orange color. Both sexes are light green-brown to gold below.

FACTS AND FEATURES

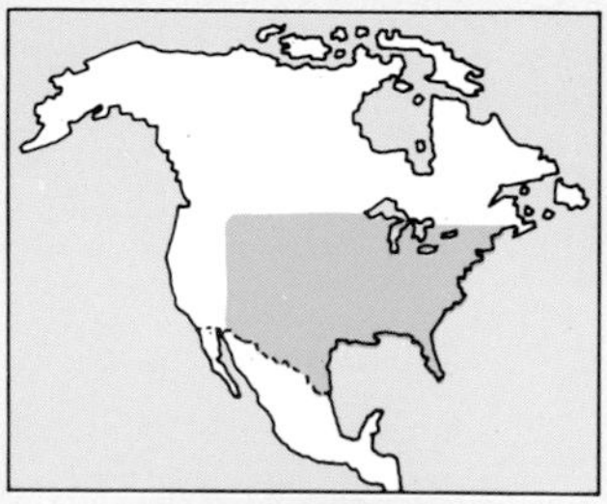

Habitat Grasslands.
Flight 1 brood, June to August.
Lifecycle notes Egg is light green; caterpillar is dark brown with black head.
Host plants Bunchgrass.
Nectar sources Unknown.

1 to 1½ inches

LONG DASH
POLITES MYSTIC

The Long Dash usually lives near areas with streams, waterways, or damp grassy meadows.

The caterpillar makes a shelter by using parts of leaves to build a shell around itself.

A single, wide black band on the border of the forewing accents the streaks of orange, brown, and yellow on the male above. Females have an overall browner color. Both are brown yellow below with rectangular yellow spots.

FACTS AND FEATURES

Habitat Streams and damp or wet agricultural areas.
Flight 1 to 2 broods, depending on warmth of climate.
Lifecycle notes Caterpillar is brown with short black hair, may shed skin several times, builds its own leaf shelter, and hibernates for the winter.
Host plants Various types of grasses.
Nectar sources Unknown.

1 to 1½ inches

WHIRLABOUT
POLITES VIBEX

The male is brown yellow with several dark spots located on the wings above. Two disjointed bands of brown align on the hind wing below. The female is less colorful – a gloomy brown above. A double rounded, violet-tan band surrounds the gray-yellow or gray-bronze hind wing below.

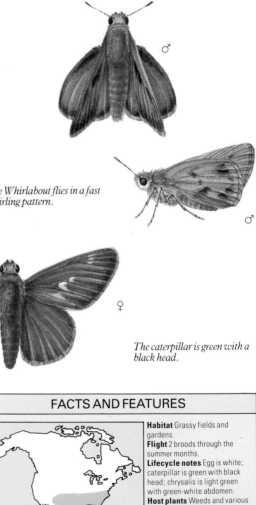

The Whirlabout flies in a fast whirling pattern.

The caterpillar is green with a black head.

FACTS AND FEATURES

Habitat Grassy fields and gardens.
Flight 2 broods through the summer months.
Lifecycle notes Egg is white; caterpillar is green with black head; chrysalis is light green with green-white abdomen.
Host plants Weeds and various lawn grasses.
Nectar sources Unknown.

1 to 1½ inches

BROKEN DASH
WALLENGRENIA OTHO

A dark, wide margin near the edges of the wings surrounds the large brown-orange spot in the center of each wing above. A band of indistinct red-beige spots are aligned along the rim of the hind wing below.

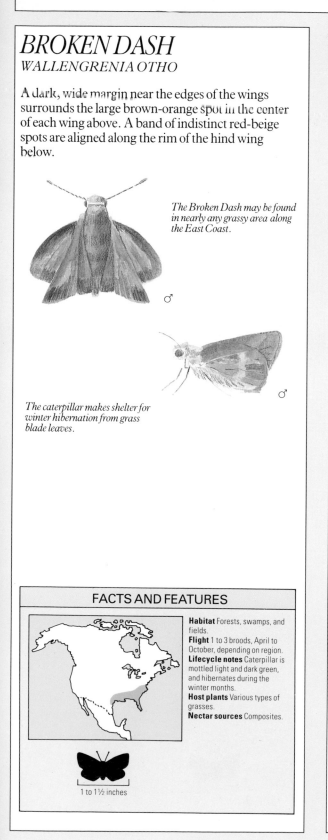

The Broken Dash may be found in nearly any grassy area along the East Coast.

The caterpillar makes shelter for winter hibernation from grass blade leaves.

FACTS AND FEATURES

Habitat Forests, swamps, and fields.
Flight 1 to 3 broods, April to October, depending on region.
Lifecycle notes Caterpillar is mottled light and dark green, and hibernates during the winter months.
Host plants Various types of grasses.
Nectar sources Composites.

1 to 1½ inches

NORTHERN BROKEN DASH
WALLENGRENIA EGEREMET

Light brown borders surround peach-colored patches in the center of the wings above. The hind wing has several tan spots.

Its range is from Canada to Florida.

The caterpillar is quite colorful, ranging from yellow green to brown. The winter months are spent in the caterpillar stage.

FACTS AND FEATURES

Habitat Shrubs and fields.
Flight Ranges from 1 to 2 broods, depending on region.
Lifecycle notes Egg is green yellow; caterpillar is yellow green; chrysalis is green.
Host plants Various types of grasses.
Nectar sources Unknown.

1 to 1½ inches

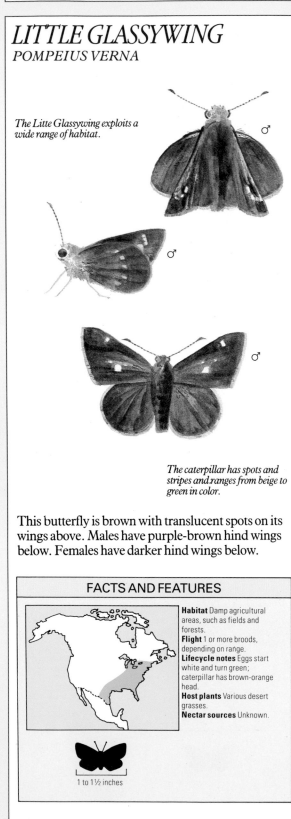

LITTLE GLASSYWING
POMPEIUS VERNA

The Litte Glassywing exploits a wide range of habitat.

♂

♂

♂

The caterpillar has spots and stripes and ranges from beige to green in color.

This butterfly is brown with translucent spots on its wings above. Males have purple-brown hind wings below. Females have darker hind wings below.

FACTS AND FEATURES

Habitat Damp agricultural areas, such as fields and forests.
Flight 1 or more broods, depending on range.
Lifecycle notes Eggs start white and turn green; caterpillar has brown-orange head.
Host plants Various desert grasses.
Nectar sources Unknown.

1 to 1½ inches

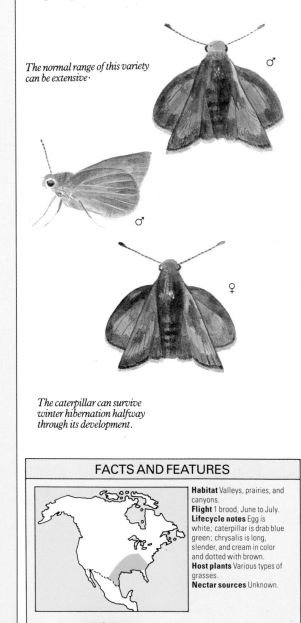

BUNCHGRASS SKIPPER
PROBLEMA BYSSUS

Dark brown surrounds orange brown wings with thin, black streaks and dark veins above. The hind wing ranges from yellow to brown-red below.

The normal range of this variety can be extensive·

♂

♂

♀

The caterpillar can survive winter hibernation halfway through its development.

FACTS AND FEATURES

Habitat Valleys, prairies, and canyons.
Flight 1 brood, June to July.
Lifecycle notes Egg is white; caterpillar is drab blue green; chrysalis is long, slender, and cream in color and dotted with brown.
Host plants Various types of grasses.
Nectar sources Unknown.

1 to 1½ inches

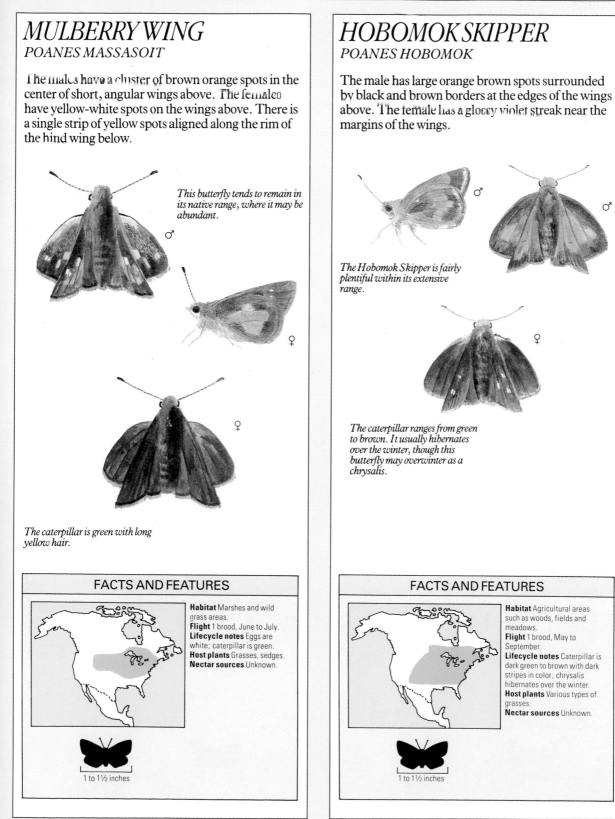

MULBERRY WING
POANES MASSASOIT

The males have a cluster of brown orange spots in the center of short, angular wings above. The females have yellow-white spots on the wings above. There is a single strip of yellow spots aligned along the rim of the hind wing below.

This butterfly tends to remain in its native range, where it may be abundant.

♂

♀

♀

The caterpillar is green with long yellow hair.

FACTS AND FEATURES

Habitat Marshes and wild grass areas.
Flight 1 brood, June to July.
Lifecycle notes Eggs are white; caterpillar is green.
Host plants Grasses, sedges.
Nectar sources Unknown.

1 to 1½ inches

HOBOMOK SKIPPER
POANES HOBOMOK

The male has large orange brown spots surrounded by black and brown borders at the edges of the wings above. The female has a glossy violet streak near the margins of the wings.

♂

♂

The Hobomok Skipper is fairly plentiful within its extensive range.

♀

The caterpillar ranges from green to brown. It usually hibernates over the winter, though this butterfly may overwinter as a chrysalis.

FACTS AND FEATURES

Habitat Agricultural areas such as woods, fields and meadows.
Flight 1 brood, May to September.
Lifecycle notes Caterpillar is dark green to brown with dark stripes in color; chrysalis hibernates over the winter.
Host plants Various types of grasses.
Nectar sources Unknown.

1 to 1½ inches

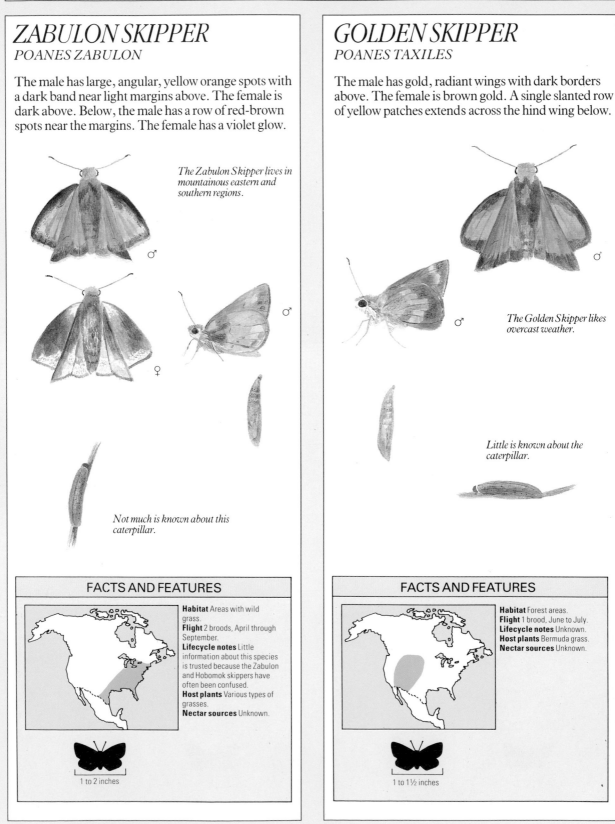

ZABULON SKIPPER
POANES ZABULON

The male has large, angular, yellow orange spots with a dark band near light margins above. The female is dark above. Below, the male has a row of red-brown spots near the margins. The female has a violet glow.

The Zabulon Skipper lives in mountainous eastern and southern regions.

♂

♀

♂

Not much is known about this caterpillar.

FACTS AND FEATURES

Habitat Areas with wild grass.
Flight 2 broods, April through September.
Lifecycle notes Little information about this species is trusted because the Zabulon and Hobomok skippers have often been confused.
Host plants Various types of grasses.
Nectar sources Unknown.

1 to 2 inches

GOLDEN SKIPPER
POANES TAXILES

The male has gold, radiant wings with dark borders above. The female is brown gold. A single slanted row of yellow patches extends across the hind wing below.

♂

The Golden Skipper likes overcast weather.

♂

Little is known about the caterpillar.

FACTS AND FEATURES

Habitat Forest areas.
Flight 1 brood, June to July.
Lifecycle notes Unknown.
Host plants Bermuda grass.
Nectar sources Unknown.

1 to 1½ inches

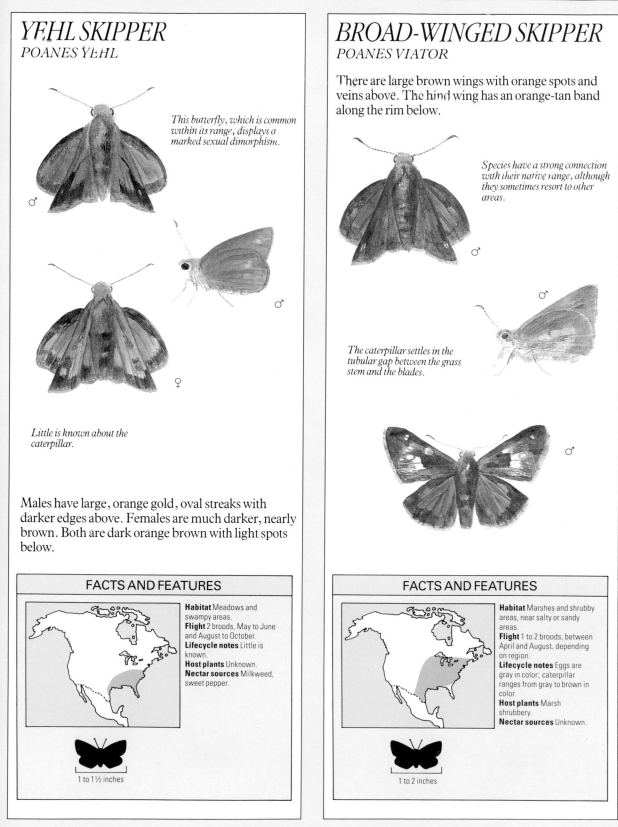

YEHL SKIPPER
POANES YEHL

This butterfly, which is common within its range, displays a marked sexual dimorphism.

♂

♂

♀

Little is known about the caterpillar.

Males have large, orange gold, oval streaks with darker edges above. Females are much darker, nearly brown. Both are dark orange brown with light spots below.

FACTS AND FEATURES

Habitat Meadows and swampy areas.
Flight 2 broods, May to June and August to October.
Lifecycle notes Little is known.
Host plants Unknown.
Nectar sources Milkweed, sweet pepper.

1 to 1½ inches

BROAD-WINGED SKIPPER
POANES VIATOR

There are large brown wings with orange spots and veins above. The hind wing has an orange-tan band along the rim below.

Species have a strong connection with their native range, although they sometimes resort to other areas.

♂

♂

The caterpillar settles in the tubular gap between the grass stem and the blades.

♂

FACTS AND FEATURES

Habitat Marshes and shrubby areas, near salty or sandy areas.
Flight 1 to 2 broods, between April and August, depending on region.
Lifecycle notes Eggs are gray in color; caterpillar ranges from gray to brown in color.
Host plants Marsh shrubbery.
Nectar sources Unknown.

1 to 2 inches

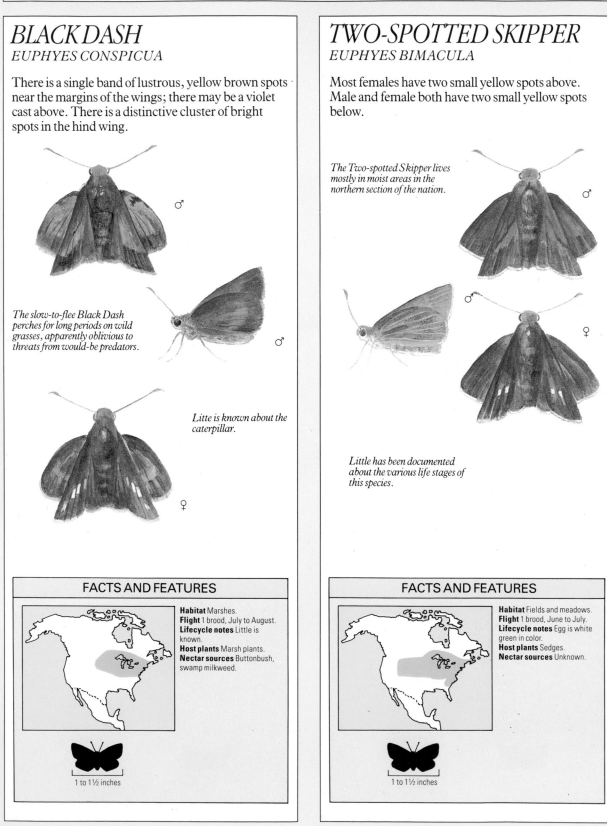

BLACK DASH
EUPHYES CONSPICUA

There is a single band of lustrous, yellow brown spots near the margins of the wings; there may be a violet cast above. There is a distinctive cluster of bright spots in the hind wing.

The slow-to-flee Black Dash perches for long periods on wild grasses, apparently oblivious to threats from would-be predators.

♂

♂

Litte is known about the caterpillar.

♀

FACTS AND FEATURES

Habitat Marshes.
Flight 1 brood, July to August.
Lifecycle notes Little is known.
Host plants Marsh plants.
Nectar sources Buttonbush, swamp milkweed.

1 to 1½ inches

TWO-SPOTTED SKIPPER
EUPHYES BIMACULA

Most females have two small yellow spots above. Male and female both have two small yellow spots below.

The Two-spotted Skipper lives mostly in moist areas in the northern section of the nation.

♂

♂

♀

Little has been documented about the various life stages of this species.

FACTS AND FEATURES

Habitat Fields and meadows.
Flight 1 brood, June to July.
Lifecycle notes Egg is white green in color.
Host plants Sedges.
Nectar sources Unknown.

1 to 1½ inches

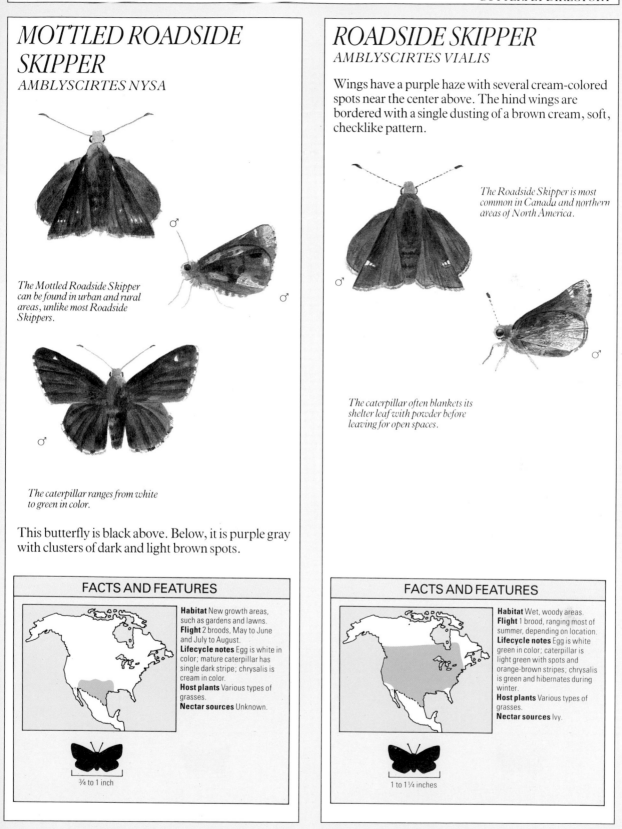

MOTTLED ROADSIDE SKIPPER
AMBLYSCIRTES NYSA

The Mottled Roadside Skipper can be found in urban and rural areas, unlike most Roadside Skippers.

The caterpillar ranges from white to green in color.

This butterfly is black above. Below, it is purple gray with clusters of dark and light brown spots.

FACTS AND FEATURES

Habitat New growth areas, such as gardens and lawns.
Flight 2 broods, May to June and July to August.
Lifecycle notes Egg is white in color; mature caterpillar has single dark stripe; chrysalis is cream in color.
Host plants Various types of grasses.
Nectar sources Unknown.

¾ to 1 inch

ROADSIDE SKIPPER
AMBLYSCIRTES VIALIS

Wings have a purple haze with several cream-colored spots near the center above. The hind wings are bordered with a single dusting of a brown cream, soft, checklike pattern.

The Roadside Skipper is most common in Canada and northern areas of North America.

The caterpillar often blankets its shelter leaf with powder before leaving for open spaces.

FACTS AND FEATURES

Habitat Wet, woody areas.
Flight 1 brood, ranging most of summer, depending on location.
Lifecycle notes Egg is white green in color; caterpillar is light green with spots and orange-brown stripes; chrysalis is green and hibernates during winter.
Host plants Various types of grasses.
Nectar sources Ivy.

1 to 1¼ inches

143

BELL'S ROADSIDE SKIPPER
AMBLYSCIRTES BELLI

Charcoal in color with multiple, prominent, white spots on the wings above, this butterfly is dark gray below.

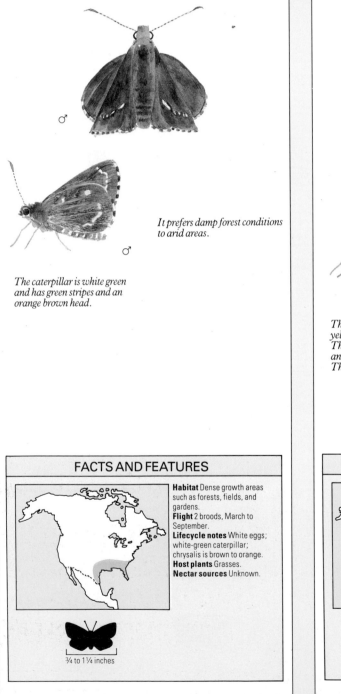

It prefers damp forest conditions to arid areas.

The caterpillar is white green and has green stripes and an orange brown head.

FACTS AND FEATURES

Habitat Dense growth areas such as forests, fields, and gardens.
Flight 2 broods, March to September.
Lifecycle notes White eggs; white-green caterpillar; chrysalis is brown to orange.
Host plants Grasses.
Nectar sources Unknown.

¾ to 1¼ inches

EUFALA SKIPPER
LERODEA EUFALA

There are white dots usually on the middle of the wings above. There are white or gray margins around the borders of the hind wing.

This is one of the most adaptable members of this family, both in its range of habitats and in the flowers and plants it eats.

The caterpillar is lime green with yellow and darker green spots. The chrysalis is long, slender, and has green and yellow stripes. The head has a horn.

FACTS AND FEATURES

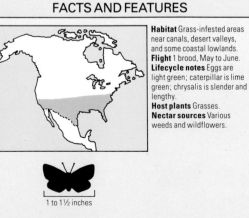

Habitat Grass-infested areas near canals, desert valleys, and some coastal lowlands.
Flight 1 brood, May to June.
Lifecycle notes Eggs are light green; caterpillar is lime green; chrysalis is slender and lengthy.
Host plants Grasses.
Nectar sources Various weeds and wildflowers.

1 to 1½ inches

BRAZILIAN SKIPPER
CALPODES ETHLIUS

Large groups are able to travel long distances quickly. Droves are often transitory and able to lay eggs in new areas and completely disappear within a day.

♂

♂

♂

The chrysalis is slim, light green in color, and is elongated at both the head and tail.

Discolored, nearly see-through dots are closely scattered around the center of the wings above and below. There are brown-red margins on the hind wing.

FACTS AND FEATURES

Habitat Gardens.
Flight 3 broods, throughout most of the year.
Lifecycle notes Caterpillar is faded green with brown spots and a black and orange head.
Host plants Cannas.
Nectar sources Unknown.

1½ to 2 inches

SALT MARSH SKIPPER
PANOQUINA PANOQUIN

The butterfly is tan above, and has short, white lines scattered on the hind wing below.

The Salt Marsh Skipper is abundant and can be found along much of the East Coast and in southern states.

♂

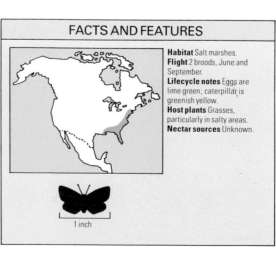

♂

Caterpillars thrive in ocean-lined areas and range in color from yellowish white to yellowish green.

FACTS AND FEATURES

Habitat Salt marshes.
Flight 2 broods, June and September.
Lifecycle notes Eggs are lime green; caterpillar is greenish yellow.
Host plants Grasses, particularly in salty areas.
Nectar sources Unknown.

1 inch

LONG-WINGED SKIPPER
PANOQUINA OCOLA

Streamlined in shape, the Long-winged Skipper is
dark yellow-brown in color above and below.

♂

♂

*The Long-winged Skipper
occasionally makes mass
migrations in search of new food
sources.*

*The caterpillar changes color
several times during its
development from yellow to
green.*

FACTS AND FEATURES

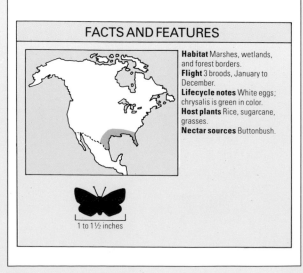

Habitat Marshes, wetlands,
and forest borders.
Flight 3 broods, January to
December.
Lifecycle notes White eggs;
chrysalis is green in color.
Host plants Rice, sugarcane,
grasses.
Nectar sources Buttonbush.

1 to 1½ inches

YUCCA GIANT SKIPPER
MEGATHYMUS YUCCAE

There is a bright yellow, circular spot on the forewing
above and a band of darker yellow spots near the
margins of the hind wing below.

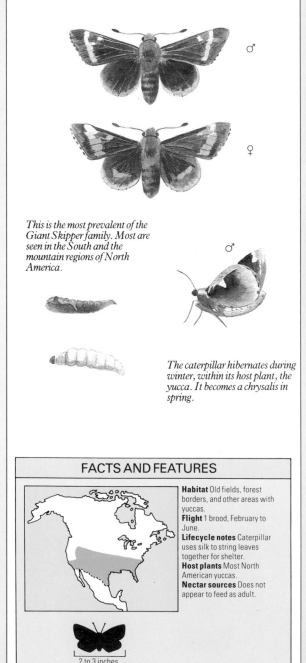

♂

♀

*This is the most prevalent of the
Giant Skipper family. Most are
seen in the South and the
mountain regions of North
America.*

♂

*The caterpillar hibernates during
winter, within its host plant, the
yucca. It becomes a chrysalis in
spring.*

FACTS AND FEATURES

Habitat Old fields, forest
borders, and other areas with
yuccas.
Flight 1 brood, February to
June.
Lifecycle notes Caterpillar
uses silk to string leaves
together for shelter.
Host plants Most North
American yuccas.
Nectar sources Does not
appear to feed as adult.

2 to 3 inches

COFAQUI GIANT SKIPPER
MEGATHYMUS COFAQUI

A band of yellow spots is located near the outer margins of the short, wide wings.

The Cofaqui Giant Skipper is located mostly in southern regions.

The caterpillar likes to attach itself into the root of the host plant.

GREAT PURPLE HAIRSTREAK
ATLIDES HALESUS

The male is a shimmering blue bordered in black above. The female is less brilliant. Both are pink-gray with blue and green patches below.

The Great Purple Hairstreak is a strong flier that covers large areas in its daily meanderings.

The caterpillar is green with a dark stripe along its back and a yellow stripe on each side. Winter months are spent in the brown and black chrysalis stage.

FACTS AND FEATURES

Habitat Wooded areas near marshes and swamps.
Flight 2 broods, February to May and August to November.
Lifecycle notes Chrysalis can be on found host plant.
Host plants Yuccas.
Nectar sources Unknown.

2 to 2½ inches

FACTS AND FEATURES

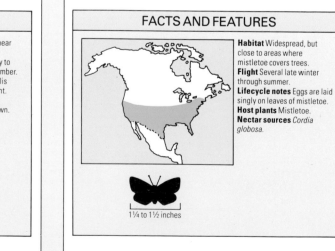

Habitat Widespread, but close to areas where mistletoe covers trees.
Flight Several late winter through summer.
Lifecycle notes Eggs are laid singly on leaves of mistletoe.
Host plants Mistletoe.
Nectar sources *Cordia globosa.*

1¼ to 1½ inches

147

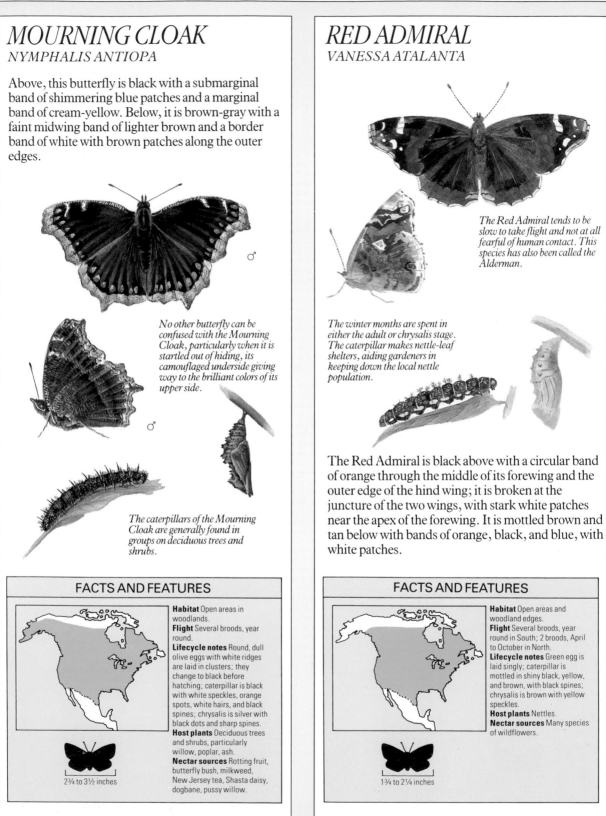

MOURNING CLOAK
NYMPHALIS ANTIOPA

Above, this butterfly is black with a submarginal band of shimmering blue patches and a marginal band of cream-yellow. Below, it is brown-gray with a faint midwing band of lighter brown and a border band of white with brown patches along the outer edges.

♂

No other butterfly can be confused with the Mourning Cloak, particularly when it is startled out of hiding, its camouflaged underside giving way to the brilliant colors of its upper side.

♂

The caterpillars of the Mourning Cloak are generally found in groups on deciduous trees and shrubs.

FACTS AND FEATURES

Habitat Open areas in woodlands.
Flight Several broods, year round.
Lifecycle notes Round, dull olive eggs with white ridges are laid in clusters; they change to black before hatching; caterpillar is black with white speckles, orange spots, white hairs, and black spines; chrysalis is silver with black dots and sharp spines.
Host plants Deciduous trees and shrubs, particularly willow, poplar, ash.
Nectar sources Rotting fruit, butterfly bush, milkweed, New Jersey tea, Shasta daisy, dogbane, pussy willow.

2¾ to 3½ inches

RED ADMIRAL
VANESSA ATALANTA

The Red Admiral tends to be slow to take flight and not at all fearful of human contact. This species has also been called the Alderman.

The winter months are spent in either the adult or chrysalis stage. The caterpillar makes nettle-leaf shelters, aiding gardeners in keeping down the local nettle population.

The Red Admiral is black above with a circular band of orange through the middle of its forewing and the outer edge of the hind wing; it is broken at the juncture of the two wings, with stark white patches near the apex of the forewing. It is mottled brown and tan below with bands of orange, black, and blue, with white patches.

FACTS AND FEATURES

Habitat Open areas and woodland edges.
Flight Several broods, year round in South; 2 broods, April to October in North.
Lifecycle notes Green egg is laid singly; caterpillar is mottled in shiny black, yellow, and brown, with black spines; chrysalis is brown with yellow speckles.
Host plants Nettles.
Nectar sources Many species of wildflowers.

1¾ to 2¼ inches

WHITE ADMIRAL
BASILARCHIA ARTHEMIS

Above, this butterfly is black with a V-shaped band of stark white patches on both wings, a band of orange spots outside the white patches, and a submarginal double band of metallic blue crescents outside the orange band on the hind wing. Below, it is tan with white, orange, and blue bands from above showing through.

This butterfly is sometimes called the Banded Purple. Male White Admirals readily attack any moving object that "invades" their chosen territory.

In fall the caterpillar wraps leaves about itself in a protective casing, in which it will spend the winter months.

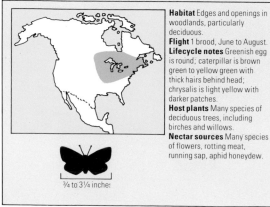

FACTS AND FEATURES

Habitat Edges and openings in woodlands, particularly deciduous.
Flight 1 brood, June to August.
Lifecycle notes Greenish egg is round; caterpillar is brown green to yellow green with thick hairs behind head; chrysalis is light yellow with darker patches.
Host plants Many species of deciduous trees, including birches and willows.
Nectar sources Many species of flowers, rotting meat, running sap, aphid honeydew.

¾ to 3¼ inches

RED-SPOTTED PURPLE
BASILARCHIA ASTYANAX

This butterfly is black with a shading of purple and irridescent blue; there are submarginal double bands of irridescent blue bars and a few small white patches at the apex of the forewing above. It is black-brown with orange patches near the body; there is a band of orange patches and submarginal double bands of blue below.

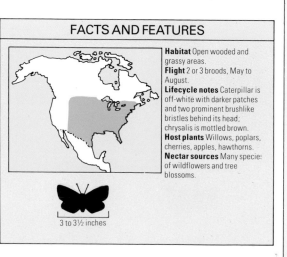

The Red-spotted Purple is one of the species that mimics the coloring of the Pipevine Swallowtail, gaining some safety from predators through the latter's foul taste.

The caterpillar is off-white with darker patches. The chrysalis is mottled shades of brown.

FACTS AND FEATURES

Habitat Open wooded and grassy areas.
Flight 2 or 3 broods, May to August.
Lifecycle notes Caterpillar is off-white with darker patches and two prominent brushlike bristles behind its head; chrysalis is mottled brown.
Host plants Willows, poplars, cherries, apples, hawthorns.
Nectar sources Many species of wildflowers and tree blossoms.

3 to 3½ inches

WEIDEMEYER'S ADMIRAL
BASILARCHIA WEIDEMEYERII

There is a large, bat-shaped section of dull black around the body, followed by a broad band of elongated white patches and a submarginal band of small white bars, above. It is very partitioned in pale white and black with a band of clouded orange and an overall bluish tint to the hind wing below.

While the various Admirals are generally distinct in their ranges, they may hybridize where those ranges overlap.

The caterpillar is gray with white patches. The chrysalis is mottled brown and off-white.

FACTS AND FEATURES

Habitat Wooded waterways.
Flight 1 brood, June to August
Lifecycle notes Egg is greenish brown, caterpillar is gray with white patches; chrysalis is mottled brown and off-white.
Host plants Willows, cottonwoods.
Nectar sources Unknown.

2¾ to 3½ inches

LORQUIN'S ADMIRAL
BASILARCHIA LORQUINI

This butterfly is black, with a midwing band of white patches and golden orange at the forewing apex above. It is orange with the same band of white patches and a sharply zigzagging thin band of black on the hind wing below.

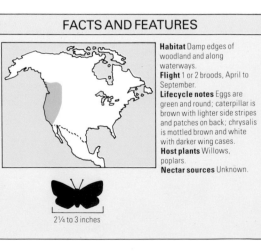

The Lorquin's Admiral, named for a 19th century lepidopterist, is fiercely defensive of its territory, including the air space to some height. Birds are often driven off by the butterfly's harassment.

The caterpillar is various shades of brown with lighter side stripes and patches on the back. The chrysalis is mottled brown and white with darker wing cases.

FACTS AND FEATURES

Habitat Damp edges of woodland and along waterways.
Flight 1 or 2 broods, April to September.
Lifecycle notes Eggs are green and round; caterpillar is brown with lighter side stripes and patches on back; chrysalis is mottled brown and white with darker wing cases.
Host plants Willows, poplars.
Nectar sources Unknown.

2¼ to 3 inches

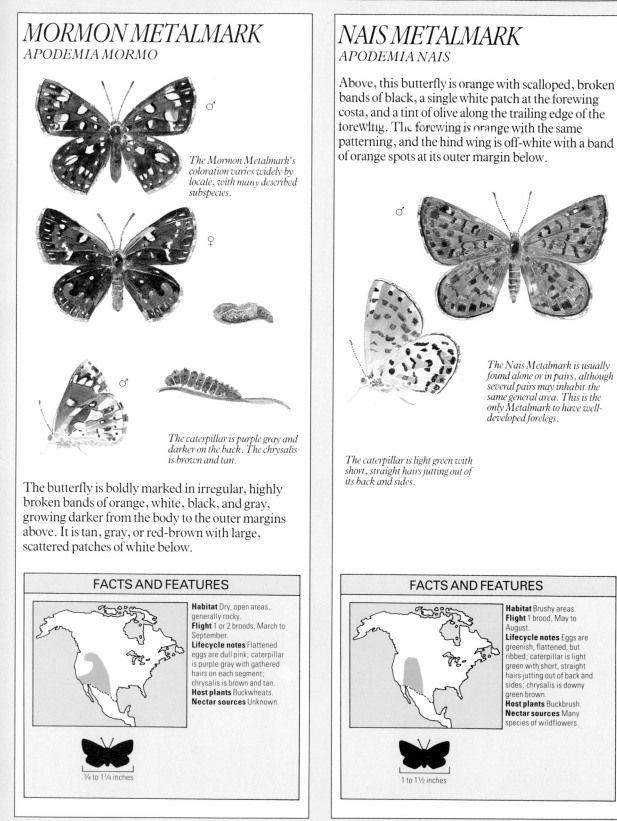

MORMON METALMARK
APODEMIA MORMO

♂

The Mormon Metalmark's coloration varies widely by locale, with many described subspecies.

♀

♂

The caterpillar is purple gray and darker on the back. The chrysalis is brown and tan.

The butterfly is boldly marked in irregular, highly broken bands of orange, white, black, and gray, growing darker from the body to the outer margins above. It is tan, gray, or red-brown with large, scattered patches of white below.

FACTS AND FEATURES

Habitat Dry, open areas, generally rocky.
Flight 1 or 2 broods, March to September.
Lifecycle notes Flattened eggs are dull pink; caterpillar is purple gray with gathered hairs on each segment; chrysalis is brown and tan.
Host plants Buckwheats.
Nectar sources Unknown.

¾ to 1¼ inches

NAIS METALMARK
APODEMIA NAIS

Above, this butterfly is orange with scalloped, broken bands of black, a single white patch at the forewing costa, and a tint of olive along the trailing edge of the forewing. The forewing is orange with the same patterning, and the hind wing is off-white with a band of orange spots at its outer margin below.

♂

The Nais Metalmark is usually found alone or in pairs, although several pairs may inhabit the same general area. This is the only Metalmark to have well-developed forelegs.

The caterpillar is light green with short, straight hairs jutting out of its back and sides.

FACTS AND FEATURES

Habitat Brushy areas.
Flight 1 brood, May to August.
Lifecycle notes Eggs are greenish, flattened, but ribbed; caterpillar is light green with short, straight hairs jutting out of back and sides; chrysalis is downy green brown.
Host plants Buckbrush.
Nectar sources Many species of wildflowers.

1 to 1½ inches

PEARLY CRESCENTSPOT
PHYCIODES THAROS

The male is orange above, with a band of black-outline circular patches near the body and a heavy black mottling at the apex of the forewing; there is a band of black-outline patches with black dots inside followed by a heavy black border on the hind wing. The female's black markings are more delicate above. Both are yellow orange with thin zigzagging bands of red-brown and a brown patch on the margin below.

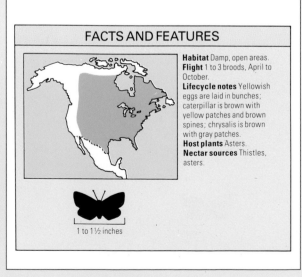

The Pearly Crescentspot is one of the most common butterflies in open, grassy areas across the North American continent.

The winter months are spent in the brown and yellow caterpillar stage. The chrysalis is brown with gray patches.

FACTS AND FEATURES

Habitat Damp, open areas.
Flight 1 to 3 broods, April to October.
Lifecycle notes Yellowish eggs are laid in bunches; caterpillar is brown with yellow patches and brown spines; chrysalis is brown with gray patches.
Host plants Asters.
Nectar sources Thistles, asters.

1 to 1½ inches

FIELD CRESCENTSPOT
PHYCIODES CAMPESTRIS

This butterfly is gray-brown with checkered bands of cream, orange, and brown above. Below, it is tan to orange with broken bands of cream, edged with red-brown, and a band of small brown dots near the center of the hind wing.

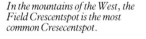

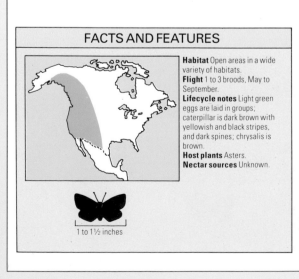

In the mountains of the West, the Field Crescentspot is the most common Cresecentspot.

The dark brown caterpillar is generally found in groups before spending the winter months alone.

FACTS AND FEATURES

Habitat Open areas in a wide variety of habitats.
Flight 1 to 3 broods, May to September.
Lifecycle notes Light green eggs are laid in groups; caterpillar is dark brown with yellowish and black stripes, and dark spines; chrysalis is brown.
Host plants Asters.
Nectar sources Unknown.

1 to 1½ inches

MYLITTA CRESCENTSPOT
PHYCIODES MYLITTA

Above, the Mylitta Crescentspot is orange with thin zigzagging bands of black curving around the front of the body and a submarginal band of scalloped orange patches with black dots in them on the hind wing. It is tan with black markings similar to above on the forewing, with large silver patches in bands across the hind wing below.

GORGONE CRESCENTSPOT
CHARIDRYAS GORGONE

The Gorgone Crescentspot is widespread throughout the central part of the continent and utilizes many different species of weeds.

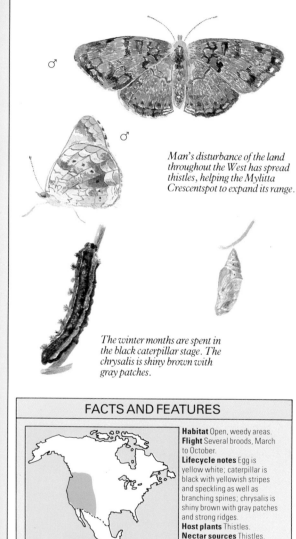

Man's disturbance of the land throughout the West has spread thistles, helping the Mylitta Crescentspot to expand its range.

After spending the first half of the caterpillar stage together in groups, the caterpillars then spend the winter months buried in leaf litter.

Above, the Gorgone Crescentspot is orange with a border and bands of black; there are thin white patches along the outer edges and thin orange crescents near the outer margin of the hind wing above. It is orange with black and bands of cream patches on the forewing, and tan with bands of cream and thick, cream-colored crescents on the hind wing below.

The winter months are spent in the black caterpillar stage. The chrysalis is shiny brown with gray patches.

FACTS AND FEATURES

Habitat Open, weedy areas.
Flight Several broods, March to October.
Lifecycle notes Egg is yellow white; caterpillar is black with yellowish stripes and speckling as well as branching spines; chrysalis is shiny brown with gray patches and strong ridges.
Host plants Thistles.
Nectar sources Thistles.

1 to 1½ inches

FACTS AND FEATURES

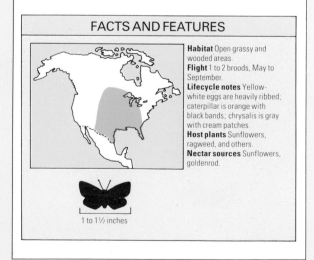

Habitat Open grassy and wooded areas.
Flight 1 to 2 broods, May to September.
Lifecycle notes Yellow-white eggs are heavily ribbed; caterpillar is orange with black bands; chrysalis is gray with cream patches.
Host plants Sunflowers, ragweed, and others.
Nectar sources Sunflowers, goldenrod.

1 to 1½ inches

SILVERY CRESCENTSPOT
CHARIDRYAS NYCTEIS

This butterfly is orange above with zigzagging black bands at the cells, and there are black borders with a band of black patches with white centers near the outer edge of the hind wing. Below, it has an orange forewing with zigzagging black bands and a few cream patches at the apex; the hind wing is tan with the same band of patches from above showing through.

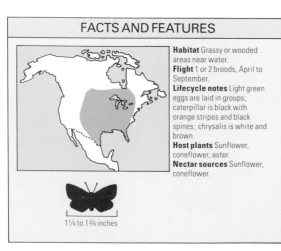

The preferred nectar flowers of the adult vary with locale, but include coneflowers whenever they are available.

Brown spots on sunflower or coneflower leaves often reveal that the caterpillar of the Silvery Crescentspot has been there.

CHALCEDON CHECKERSPOT
OCCIDRYAS CHALCEDONA

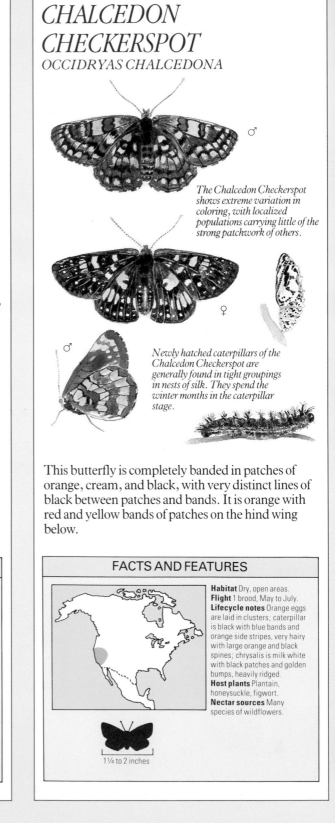

The Chalcedon Checkerspot shows extreme variation in coloring, with localized populations carrying little of the strong patchwork of others.

Newly hatched caterpillars of the Chalcedon Checkerspot are generally found in tight groupings in nests of silk. They spend the winter months in the caterpillar stage.

This butterfly is completely banded in patches of orange, cream, and black, with very distinct lines of black between patches and bands. It is orange with red and yellow bands of patches on the hind wing below.

FACTS AND FEATURES

Habitat Grassy or wooded areas near water.
Flight 1 or 2 broods, April to September.
Lifecycle notes Light green eggs are laid in groups; caterpillar is black with orange stripes and black spines; chrysalis is white and brown.
Host plants Sunflower, coneflower, aster.
Nectar sources Sunflower, coneflower.

1¼ to 1¾ inches

FACTS AND FEATURES

Habitat Dry, open areas.
Flight 1 brood, May to July.
Lifecycle notes Orange eggs are laid in clusters; caterpillar is black with blue bands and orange side stripes, very hairy with large orange and black spines; chrysalis is milk white with black patches and golden bumps, heavily ridged.
Host plants Plantain, honeysuckle, figwort.
Nectar sources Many species of wildflowers.

1¼ to 2 inches

NORTHERN CHECKERSPOT
CHARIDRYAS PALLA

The male is covered with orange patches divided by black lines; there is a particularly noticeable black zigzagging band across the center of the wings above. The female is clouded black with irregular bands of cream patches and a submarginal band of pale orange bars above. Both are orange with broad bands of cream patches, divided by black lines on the hind wing below.

During summer, the Northern Checkerspot is a common sight at puddles.

The winter months are spent in the caterpillar stage. The chrysalis is tan with patches of gray.

DESERT CHECKERSPOT
CHARIDRYAS NEUMOEGENI

The Desert Checkerspot is orange above, with a few thin, zigzagging black bands and a scalloped black line near the outer margins. It is orange with a few cream patches near the apex of the forewing, and orange with broad bands of white, black-edged patches on the hind wing below.

Wet years will produce a much more abundant flight than dry years.

The winter months are spent in the black caterpillar stage. The chrysalis is gray with black patches.

FACTS AND FEATURES

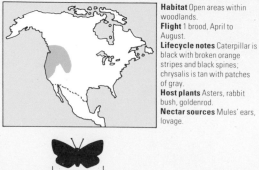

Habitat Open areas within woodlands.
Flight 1 brood, April to August.
Lifecycle notes Caterpillar is black with broken orange stripes and black spines; chrysalis is tan with patches of gray.
Host plants Asters, rabbit bush, goldenrod.
Nectar sources Mules' ears, lovage.

1½ to 1¾ inches

FACTS AND FEATURES

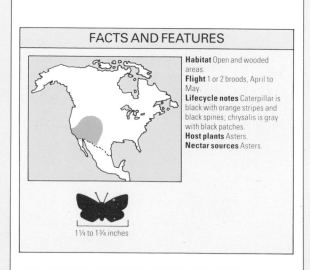

Habitat Open and wooded areas.
Flight 1 or 2 broods, April to May.
Lifecycle notes Caterpillar is black with orange stripes and black spines; chrysalis is gray with black patches.
Host plants Asters.
Nectar sources Asters.

1¼ to 1¾ inches

HARRIS' CHECKERSPOT
CHARIDRYAS HARRISII

This butterfly is black with a band of rectangular orange patches followed by a band of crescent-shaped orange patches; there is a wide black border with thin white bars along the outer margins above. Below, it is pale orange with white, black-edged patches at the body, followed by bands of white, orange, and black patches.

The female Harris' Checkerspots lay large numbers of eggs, although most of their offspring will not reach maturity.

When first hatched, caterpillars stay together in a silken nest. The winter months are spent in the caterpillar stage.

FACTS AND FEATURES

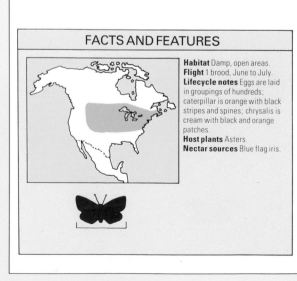

Habitat Damp, open areas.
Flight 1 brood, June to July.
Lifecycle notes Eggs are laid in groupings of hundreds; caterpillar is orange with black stripes and spines; chrysalis is cream with black and orange patches.
Host plants Asters.
Nectar sources Blue flag iris.

BORDERED PATCH
CHLOSYNE LACINIA

This butterfly is black with white bars along the margins; there is a submarginal band of white patches and a band of orange to white patches across the middle of the wings above. Below, the hind wing is black with yellow to cream bands and orange patches near the head and the corner of the trailing edge.

The Bordered Patch shows an immense amount of diversity in its coloration.

The winter months are spent in the caterpillar stage, after the young caterpillars scatter from communal feeding areas.

FACTS AND FEATURES

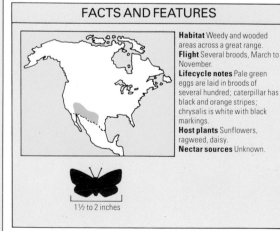

1½ to 2 inches

Habitat Weedy and wooded areas across a great range.
Flight Several broods, March to November.
Lifecycle notes Pale green eggs are laid in broods of several hundred; caterpillar has black and orange stripes; chrysalis is white with black markings.
Host plants Sunflowers, ragweed, daisy.
Nectar sources Unknown.

BALTIMORE
EUPHYDRYAS PHAETON

Above, the Baltimore is black, with red orange patches at the wing cells followed by four broken bands of white or cream patches and a wide, scalloped band of orange patches with a black border. It is black with very even, curving bands of orange around a curving band of black, with even rows of white or cream patches below.

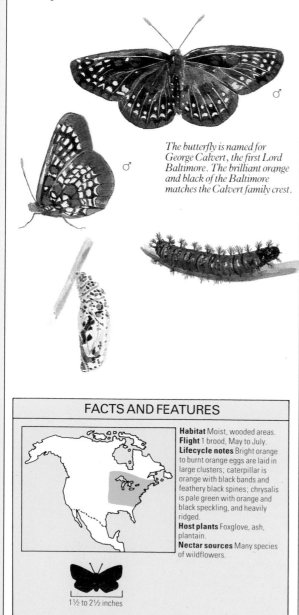

The butterfly is named for George Calvert, the first Lord Baltimore. The brilliant orange and black of the Baltimore matches the Calvert family crest.

ANICIA CHECKERSPOT
OCCIDRYAS ANICIA

The appearance of this butterfly is highly variable, from orange with bands of white patches and clouded black, to clouded black with bands of white and orange patches above. Bands of orange and cream patches, heavily scalloped as they approach the outer edge, are on the hind wing below.

Very few other butterflies are as highly variable in coloring as the Anicia Checkerspot. It is also commonly called the Paintbrush Checkerspot.

The winter months are spent in the caterpillar stage, when it is about half grown.

FACTS AND FEATURES

Habitat Moist, wooded areas.
Flight 1 brood, May to July.
Lifecycle notes Bright orange to burnt orange eggs are laid in large clusters; caterpillar is orange with black bands and feathery black spines; chrysalis is pale green with orange and black speckling, and heavily ridged.
Host plants Foxglove, ash, plantain.
Nectar sources Many species of wildflowers.

1½ to 2½ inches

FACTS AND FEATURES

Habitat Grassy areas in meadows and forests.
Flight 1 brood, April to August.
Lifecycle notes Orange eggs are laid in clusters; caterpillar is white with black stripes and black spines; chrysalis is white with black patches.
Host plants Plantain, figwort, borage.
Nectar sources Unknown.

1 to 2 inches

INDEX

Page numbers in italic indicate photographs in the introduction.

Acadian Hairstreak 84
Achalarus lyciades 117
Acmon Blue 90
Admirals 148-50
Aglais milberti 27, 71
Agraulis vanillae 58
Alderman 148
Alpines 109-11
Amblyscirtes aesculapius 142
Amblyscirtes belli 144
Amblyscirtes hegon 142
Amblyscirtes nysa 143
Amblyscirtes vialis 143
American Copper 19, 75
American Painted Lady 17, 20, 72
Anaea andria 73
Ancyloxypha numitor 127
Anglewings 20, 69-70
Anicia Checkerspot 157
Anise Swallowtail 36
Anthocharis midea 48
Anthocharis sara 47
Antillean Blue 85
Aphrodite 60
Apodemia mormo 151
Apodemia nais 151
Appalachian Brown 104
Arctic Alpine 109
Arctic Grayling 113
Arctic Skipper 125
Arctics 112-14
Artogeia napi 43
Artogeia virginiensis 44
Ascia monuste 45
Asterocampa celtis 27, 74
Atalopedes campestris 131
Atlantis Fritillary 63
Atlides halesus 147
Atrytonopsis hianna 141
Autochton cellus 116

Baltimore 10, 11, 12, 157
Banded Alpine 109
Banded Hairstreak 99
Banded Purple 149
Barred Sulphur 56
Basilarchia archippus 17, 20, 27, 73
Basilarchia arthemis 20, 27, 149
Basilarchia astyanax 20, 27, 28, 149
Basilarchia lorquini 22, 150
Basilarchia weidemeyerii 150
Battus philenor 11, 12, 16, 33
Battus polydamus 33
Becker's White 41

Bell's Roadside Skipper 144
Black Dash 140
Black Swallowtail *13*
Blue Copper 77
Blue Swallowtail 33
Blueberry Sulphur 52
Blues 10, 84-91
Bog Fritillary 64
Bordered Patch 156
boxes for butterflies 27
Bramble Green Hairstreak 82
Brazilian Skipper 145
breeding butterflies 29
Brephidium exilis 84
Broad-winged Skipper 139
Broken Dash 135
Bronze Copper 78
Brown Elfin 95
Browns 103-4
Buckeye 19, 20, 28, *28*, 94
Bunchgrass Skipper 136
butterflies
    adults 13
    caterpillars 10-12, 20
        chrysalis *11*, 12, 21, *21*
        eggs 10
        evolution 8
        mating 13
        "puddling" 18, 19
        threats to 21
        wings 14, *15*
        wintering 19
butterfly boxes 27
butterfly breeding 29
butterfly farms 21
butterfly gardens 20-1, *20*, 22-8
Butterfly Worlds 20

Cabbage White 28, 44
Calephelis borealis 94
Calephelis muticum 57
Calephelis virginiensis 57
California Dogface 53
California Hairstreak 92
California Ringlet 107
California White 42
Callippe Fritillary 62
Callophrys comstocki 82
Callophrys dumetorum 82
Callophrys sheridanii 83
Calpodes ethlius 145
Calycopis cecrops 93
Canada Arctic 112
Carolina Satyr 104
Carterocephalus palaemon 125
caterpillars 10-12, 20
Celastrina ladon 87
Cercyonis pegala 27, 108
Cercyonis sthenele 108
Chalcedon Checkerspot 154

Chalceria heteronea 77
Chalceria rubidus 76
Charidryas gorgone 153
Charidryas harrisii 9, 156
Charidryas neumoegeni 155
Charidryas nycteis 154
Charidryas palla 155
Checkered White 42
Checkerspots 10, 155-7
Chlosyne lacinia 156
chrysalis *11*, 12, 21, *21*
Chryxus Arctic 112
Clodius Parnassian 48
Clossiana bellona 65
Clossiana epithore 66
Clossiana freija 67
Clossiana frigga 65
Clossiana improba 66
Clossiana selene 11, 64
Clossiana titania 67
Clouded Skipper 126
Clouded Sulphur 49
Cloudless Giant Sulphur 20, 53
Cloudywings 117-18
Cobweb Skipper 130
Coenonympha california 107
Coenonympha haydenii 106
Coenonympha inornata 107
Cofaqui Giant Skipper 147
Colias alexandra 8, 50
Colias eurytheme 8, 49
Colias gigantea 52
Colias hecla 50
Colias interior 51
Colias nastes 51
Colias pelidne 52
Colias philodice 49
Colorado Hairstreak 91
Comma 18, 68
Common Alpine 111
Common Blue 8, 90
Common Branded Skipper 129
Common Checkered Skipper 124
Common Hairstreak 93
Common Sootywing 124
Common Sulphur 49
Common White 42
Compton Tortoiseshell 71
Coppers 75-80
Coral Hairstreak 102
Cotton Borer 93
Creamy Marblewing 45
Crescentspots 152-4
Crossline Skipper 133
Cyllopsis gemma 106

Danaus plexippus 10, *12*, 17, 18, *19*, 29, 115
    caterpillars *11*

eggs *11*
    wintering 19-20
Desert Checkerspot 155
Desert Green Hairstreak 82
Diana 59
Dingy Arctic Fritillary 66
Dogface Butterfly 53
Dorcas Copper 80
Dotted Blue 87
Dreamy Duskywing 119
Dun Skipper 141
Duskywings 119-23
Dusted Skipper 141
Dwarf Yellow 56

Early Elfin 66
Eastern Black Swallowtail 17, 34
Eastern Cloudywing 118
Eastern Pine Elfin 97
Eastern Tailed Blue 86
Edith's Copper 78
Edwards' Fritillary 61
Edwards' Hairstreak 9, 99
Elfins 95-8
Emerald-studded Blue 90
Enodia anthedon 103
Enodia portlandia 102
Epargyreus clarus 19, 115
Epidemia dorcas 80
Epidemia helloides 80
Epidemia mariposa 79
Epidemia nivalis 79
Erebia discoidalis 110
Erebia epipsodea 111
Erebia fasciata 109
Erebia rossii 109
Erebia youngi 110
Erynnis baptisiae 123
Erynnis brizo 120
Erynnis funeralis 122
Erynnis horatius 121
Erynnis icelus 119
Erynnis juvenalis 120
Erynnis pacuvius 121
Erynnis zarucco 122
Euchloe ausonides 45
Euchloe creusa 46
Euchloe hyantis 47
Euchloe olympia 46
Eufala Skipper 144
Euphilotes enoptes 87
Euphyes bimacula 140
Euphyes conspicua 140
Euphydryas phaeton 10, *11*, 157
Euphyes ruricola 141
Euptoieta claudia 59
Eurema daira 56
Eurema lisa 55
Eurema nicippe 55
Euristrymon favonius 101

Euristrymon ontario 92
European Skipper 128
Eurytides marcellus 40
Everes amyntula 86
Everes comyntas 86
Eyed Brown 17, 103

Fairy Yellow 56
Falcate Orangetip 10, *11*, 48
farming butterflies 21
Faunus Anglewing 69
Feniseca tarquinius 17, 74
Field Crescentspot 152
Fiery Skipper 128
food plants 22, 24-6
Freya's Fritillary 67
Frigga's Fritillary 65
Fritillaries 58-67
Frosted Elfin 97
Funereal Duskywing 122

Gaeides editha 78
Gaeides xanthoides 77
gardens for butterflies 20-1, *20*, 22-8
Garita Skipperling 127
Gemmed Satyr 106
Georgia Satyr 105
Giant Swallowtail 37
Glaucopsyche lygdamus 88
Goatweed Butterfly 73
Gold Rim Swallowtail 33
Golden Skipper 138
Golden-banded Skipper 116
Gorgone Crescentspot 153
Gray Comma 70
Gray Hairstreak 93
Great Basin Sootywing 125
Great Basin Wood Nymph 108
Great Gray Copper 77
Great Northern Sulphur 52
Great Purple Hairstreak 147
Great Southern White 45
Great Spangled Fritillary 60
Green-clouded Swallowtail 39
Greenish Blue 89
Greenland Sulphur 50
Gulf Fritillary 58
Hackberry Butterfly 27, 74
Hairstreaks 20, 81-4, 91-5, 98-102, 147
Harkenclenus titus 102
Harris' Checkerspot 9, 156
Harvester 17, 74
Hayden's Ringlet 106
Hedgerow Hairstreak 101
Hemiargus ceraunus 85
Hemiargus isola 91
Heraclides cresphontes 37
Hermeuptychia sosybius 104
Hesperia comma 129

Hesperia juba 129
Hesperia leonardus 130
Hesperia metea 130
Hesperia sassacus 131
Hickery Hairstreak 100
Hoary Edge 117
Hoary Elfin 96
Hobomok Skipper 137
Hop Merchant 68
Horace's Duskywing 121
host plants 10
Hylephila phyleus 128
Hyllolycaena hyllus 78
Hypaurotis crysalus 91

Icaricia acmon 90
Icaricia icarioides 90
Incisalia augustinus 95
Incisalia eryphon 98
Incisalia fotis 96
Incisalia irus 97
Incisalia niphon 97
Incisalis polios 96
Indian Skipper 131

Juba Skipper 129
Juniper Hairstreak 81
Jutta Arctic 113
Junonia coenia 19, 20, 28, *28*, 94
Juvenal's Duskywing 120

Karner Blue 89
King's Hairstreak 100
Kricogonia lyside 54

Labrador Sulphur 51
Lace-winged Roadside Skipper 142
Large Wood Nymph 27, 108
Least Skipperling 127
Leonardus Skipper 130
Lepidoptera 8-9
Leptotes marina 85
Lerema accius 126
Lerodea eufala 144
Libytheana bachmanii 58
Lilac-bordered Copper 79
Little Glassywing 136
Little Metalmark 57
Little Wood Satyr 105
Little Yellow 55
Long Dash 134
Long-tailed Skipper 116
Long-winged Skipper 146
Lorquin's Admiral 22, 150
Lustrous Copper 76
Lycaeides argyrognomon 88
Lycaeides melissa 89
Lycaena cupreus 76
Lycaena phlaeas 19, 75

Lyside 54

Marblewings 45-7
Marine Blue 85
Mariposa Copper 79
Meadow Fritillary 65
Megathymus cofaqui 147
Megathymus yuccae 146
Megisto cymela 105
Melissa Arctic 114
Metalmarks 57, 94, 151
Milbert's Tortoiseshell 27, 71
Mitoura gryneus 81
Mitoura siva 81
Mitoura spinetorum 98
Monarch 10, *12*, 17, 18, *19*, 29, 115
    caterpillars *11*
    eggs *11*
    wintering 19-20
Mormon Fritillary 63
Mormon Metalmark 151
Mottled Roadside Skipper 143
Mountain Swallowtail 36
Mourning Cloak 12, 19, 20, 27, 28, *29*, 148
Mulberry Wing 137
Mustard White 43
Mylitta Crescentspot 153

Nais Metalmark 151
Nastra lherminier 126
Nathalis iole 56
nectar source 23, 24-7
Neominois ridingsii 111
Neonympha areolatus 105
Nivalis Copper 79
Northern Blue 88
Northern Broken Dash 135
Northern Checkerspot 155
Northern Cloudywing 118
Northern Hairstreak 92, 101
Northern Marblewing 46
Northern Metalmark 94
Northern Pearly Eye 103
Nymphalis antiopa 12, 19, 20, 27, 28, *29*, 148
Nymphalis vau-album 71

Oarisma garita 127
Occidryas anicia 157
Occidryas chalcedona 154
Oeneis bore 113
Oeneis chryxus 112
Oeneis jutta 113
Oeneis macounii 112
Oeneis melissa 114
Oeneis polixenes 114
Old World Swallowtail 35
Olive Hairstreak 81

Olympia Marblewing 46
Orange Giant Sulphur 54
Orange Sulphur *8*, 49
Orange-bordered Blue 89
Orangetips 47-8

Pacuvius Duskywing 121
Paintbrush Checkerspot 157
Painted Lady 20, 72
Palamedes Swallowtail 40
Pale Tiger Swallowtail 39
Panoquina ocola 146
Panoquina panoquin 145
Papilio bairdii 35
Papilio brevicauda 34
Papilio indra 36
Papilio machaon 35
Papilio polyxenes 17, 34
Papilio zelicaon 36
Parnassius clodius 48
Parrhasius m-album 95
Pearly Crescentspot 19, 152
Pearly Eye 102
Pearly Marblewing 47
Pepper-and-salt Skipper 142
Phoebis agarithe 54
Phoebis sennae 20, 53
Pholisoria catullus 124
Pholisora libya 125
photographing butterflies 30-1
Phyciodes campestris 152
Phyciodes mylitta 153
Phyciodes tharos 19, 152
Pieris rapae 28, 44
Pine White 40
Pink-Edged Sulphur 51
Pipevine Swallowtail *11*, 12, *16*, 33
plants for butterflies 24-6
    food 22, 24-6
    host plants 10
    in gardens 22
    nectar source 23, 24-7
Plebejus saepiolus 89
Poanes hobomok 137
Poanes massasoit 137
Poanes taxiles 138
Poanes viator 139
Poanes yehl 139
Poanes zabulon 138
Polites coras 132
Polites mystic 134
Polites origenes 133
Polites sabuleti 132
Polites themistocles 133
Polites vibex 134
Polixes Arctic 114
Polydamas Swallowtail 33
Polygonia comma 18, 27, 68
Polygonia faunus 69

Polygonia interrogationis 10, *11*, 27, 68
Polygonia progne 70
Polygonia satyrus 27, 69
Polygonia zephyrus 70
Pompeius verna 136
Pontia beckerii 41
Pontia occidentalis 43
Pontia protodice 42
Pontia sisymbrii 42
Prairie Ringlet 107
Problema byssus 136
Proclossiana eunomia 64
Pterourus eurymedon 39
Pterourus glaucus 10, *11*, 17, 19, 23, 37
Pterourus multicaudatus 38
Pterourus palamedes 40
Pterourus rutulus 38
Pterourus troilus 39
Purple Lesser Fritillary 67
Purplish Copper 80
Pyrgus communis 124
Pyrgus scriptura 123

Queen 10
Queen Alexandra's Sulphur 50
Questionmark 10, *11*, 27, 68

Reakirt's Blue 91
Red Admiral 20, 27, *27*, 148
Red-banded Hairstreak 93
Red-disked Alpine 110
Red-spotted Purple 20, 27, 28, 149
Regal Fritillary 61
Riding's Satyr 111
Ringlets 106-7
Roadside Skipper 143
Ruddy Copper 76

Sachem 131
Sagebrush White 41
Salt Marsh Skipper 145
Sandhill Skipper 132
Sara Orangetip 47
Satyr Anglewing 27, 69
Satyrium acadica 84
Satyrium calanus 99
Satyrium californica 92
Satyrium caryaevorus 100
Satyrium edwardsii 9, 99
Satyrium fuliginosum 83
Satyrium kingi 100
Satyrium saepium 101
Satyrodes appalachia 104
Satyrodes eurydice 17, 103
Satyrs, 28, 104-6, 111
Scalloped Sootywing 119
Short-tailed Black Swallowtail 36
Short-tailed Swallowtail 34
Silver-bordered Fritillary *11*, 64
Silver-spotted Skipper 19, 115
Silvery Blue 88
Silvery Crescentspot 154
Skippers 8, 115-16, 123-33, 136-47
Sleepy Duskywing 120
Sleepy Orange 55
Small Checkered Skipper 123
Snout Butterfly 58
Solitary Blue 91
Sooty Hairstreak 83
Sootywings 119, 124-5
Southern Cloudywing 117
Southern Hairstreak 101
Southern Snout 58
Speyeria aphrodite 60
Speyeria atlantis 63

Speyeria callippe 62
Speyeria cybele 60
Speyeria diana 59
Speyeria edwardsii 61
Speyeria idalia 61
Speyeria mormonia 63
Speyeria zerene 62
Spicebush Swallowtail 39
Spring Azure 87
Spring White 42
Staphylus hayhurstii 119
Strymon melinus 93
Sulphurs 10, 17, 19, 49-54
Swallowtails 18, 20, 33-40
Swamp Metalmark 57
Swarthy Skipper 126

Tailed Copper 75
Tawny-edged Skipper 133
Tawny Emperor 10
Tharsalea arota 75
Thicket Hairstreak 98
Thorybes bathyllus 117
Thorybes confusis 118
Thorybes pylades 118
Thymelicus lineola 128
Tiger Swallowtail 10, *11*, 17, 19, *23*, 37
Titania's Fritillary 67
Tortoiseshells 20
Two-spotted Skipper 140
Two-tailed Tiger Swallowtail 38

Urbanus proteus 116

Vanessa atalanta 20, 27 148
Vanessa cardui 20, 72
Vanessa virginiensis 17, 20, 72
Variegated Fritillary 59

Veined White 43
Viceroy 17, 27, 73

Wallengrenia egeremet 135
Wallengrenia otho 135
Weidemeyer's Admiral 150
West Virginia White 44
Western Black Swallowtail 35
Western Meadow Fritillary 66
Western Pine Elfin 98
Western Pygmy Blue 84
Western Tailed Blue 86
Western Tiger Swallowtail 38
Western White 43
Whirlabout 134
White Admiral 20, 27, *27*, 149
White M Hairstreak 95
White Mountain Butterfly 114
White-lined Green Hairstreak 83
Whites 10, 41-5
Wild Indigo Duskywing 123
wood nymphs 108
Wyoming Ringlet 106

Xerces Society 21

Yehl Skipper 139
Yellowpatch Skipper 132
Yellows 55-6
Yucca Giant Skipper 146
Yukon Duskywing 122

Zabulon Skipper 138
Zarucco Duskywing 122
Zebra Swallowtail *8*, 19, 40
Zephyr Anglewing 70
Zephyr Longwing 18
Zerene cesonia 53
Zerene Fritillary 62

ACKNOWLEDGMENTS

The publishers would like to thank the following for providing photographs and for permission to reproduce copyright material.

Key: a = above; b = below; l = left; r = right; c = center; USP = Unicorn Stock Photos.

page 7 Dede Gilman, USP; p. 8 br Judy Hile, USP, bl Richard B. Dippold, USP, tr Dede Gilman, USP; p. 9 t Charles E. Schmidt, USP, b Macdonald Photography, USP; p. 11 t Gregory R. Scott, b Jānis Miglavs; p. 12 Les Van, USP; p. 13 R. Mars; p. 14 Jānis Miglavs; p. 15 Jānis Miglavs; p. 16 Jānis Miglavs; p. 17 t Gregory K. Scott, b Doug Adams, USP; p. 18 t Kimberly Burnham, USP, b Charles E. Young; p. 19 t Richard B. Dippold, USP, b Marcus Schneck; p20 John W. Mayo, USP; p. 21 Gregory K. Scott; p. 22 t Charles E. Young, b Jānis Miglavs; p. 23 t Michael A. Skeens, USP, b Betty Jo Stockton; p. 27 t Richard B. Dippold, USP, b Gregory K. Scott; p. 28 Charles Young; p. 29 Gregory K. Scott; p. 30 Jānis Miglavs; p. 31 Jānis Miglavs.